Graphic Classics:
H.P. Lovecraft

Volume Four
2002

©2002 SAVERIO TENUTA

EUREKA PRODUCTIONS
8778 Oak Grove Road, Mount Horeb, Wisconsin 53572

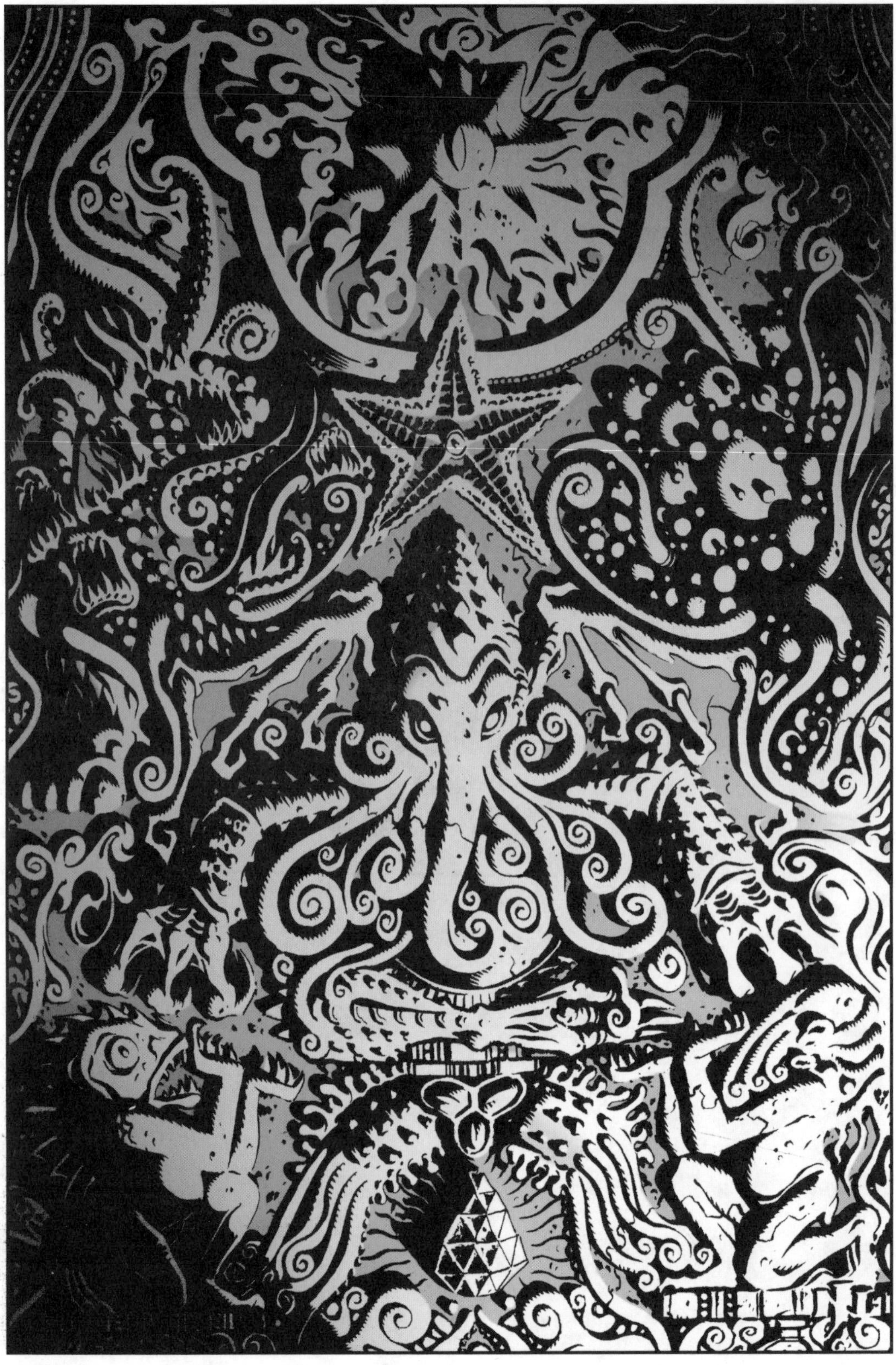

©2002 JIM NELSON

CONTENTS

*Cover illustration by Todd Schorr / Back cover illustration by Jeff Remmer
Additional illustrations by Saverio Tenuta, Jim Nelson, Paul Carrick, Giorgio Comolo*

This book is dedicated to the memory of Tom Sutton (1937–2002), Lovecraftian Supreme.

Graphic Classics: H.P. Lovecraft is published by Eureka Productions. ISBN #0-9712464-4-0. Price US $9.95, Canada $15.95. Available through The Rosebud Store, Eureka Productions, 8778 Oak Grove Road, Mount Horeb, WI 53572. The Graphic Classics website is at http://www.graphicclassics.com. Tom Pomplun, designer and publisher, tom@graphicclassics.com. Eileen Fitzgerald, editorial assistant. This compilation and all original works ©2002 Eureka Productions. All rights revert to creators after publication. Graphic Classics is a trademark of Eureka Productions. Printed in Canada.

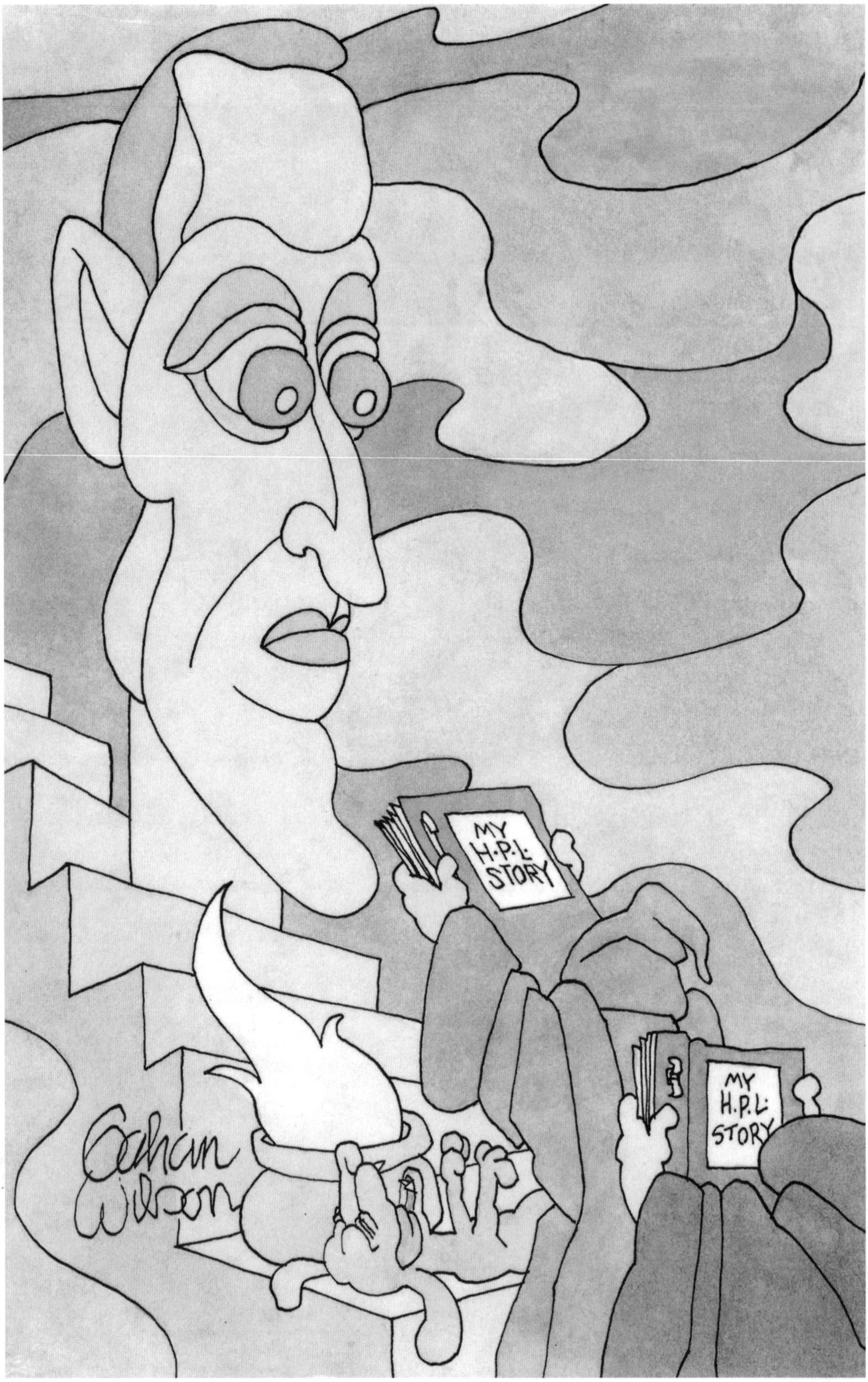
MY H.P.L. STORY
MY H.P.L. STORY
Gahan Wilson

Illustrating H.P.L.

by **Gahan Wilson**

Among his many other excellent qualities, Howard Phillips Lovecraft is one of the most illustrator-friendly authors in all of fantastic fiction.

This is no small accomplishment in a literary genre which — with its dragons and ghosts and demon-invoking wizards — is so remarkably kindly to the graphically-inclined.

Mind, I'm not saying that other specialized areas don't offer the visual artist interesting challenges. I suppose detective mysteries would be the runner-up with their lurid crime scenes and their determined detectives ranging from remarkably durable cops to colorfully eccentric private eyes bravely battling their richly varied villains. Action adventures likely come in as a strong third, though the heroes and heroines tend to be rather visually predictable with their hard bodies and steely eyes, and one violent battle pretty much looks like another even if the dashing major character is swinging from an ornate crystal chandelier in one story and a knotty jungle vine in the next. Of course it is very easy to see why mainstream novels, with their tremendous emphasis on their characters' interior agonies, have never made much use of visual expansions: the reader would soon tend to tire of yet another presentation —

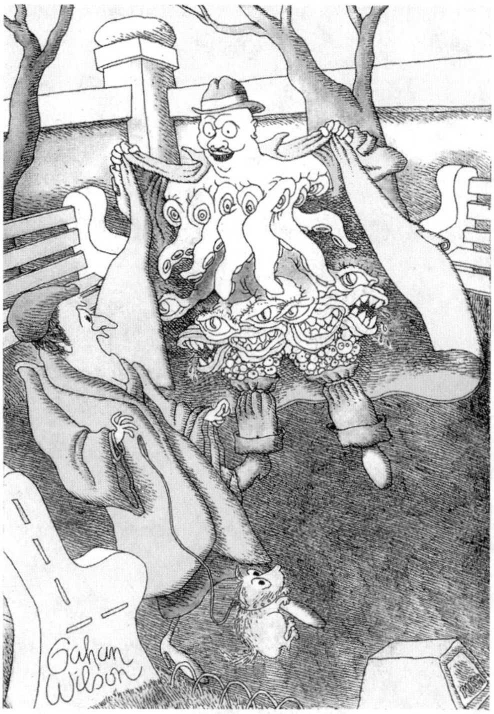
Gahan Wilson

no matter how imaginatively rendered — of the main protagonist's agonized grimaces and hand clenchings.

It is interesting to note that Lovecraft not uncommonly worked charming and often extremely humorous — you can bet that, as a budding cartoonist, I picked up on that! — little sketches into his letters. They are somewhat primitive, to be sure, but they are very intelligently rendered and have many astutely selected little touches.

A drawing of his I remember being particularly delighted to come across in one of those Arkham House collections of his letters shows an excellent Pickmanesque ghoul meditatively gnawing a little snack next to an antique, angel-head tombstone. The lower jaw is particularly worthy of your attention.

I have not yet seen what is going to go into the collection in this book, but I look forward to doing so because it's my bet that the various artists, confronted with the multitude of inspirations which Lovecraft always so generously offers, will find themselves swept up by the reliably astounding vortex of his imagination and find that they have excelled themselves.

In criticisms of his writings various commentators on the works of Lovecraft have put him down for his lavish use of un-specific adjectives (which accusation even the most profound admirer of H.P.L. must admit is not entirely inaccurate) but then they have used this as a springboard to imply that—unlike, say, Hemingway—he eschews the specific and precise for the vague and general and nothing could be further from the truth!

Take, as one truly spectacular and memorable example, his description of the dying Wilbur Whateley's body in *The Dunwich Horror*, revealed at last to the outside world by the watchdog's savaging of his clothes—has there ever been any-thing in the whole of literature more anatomically specific, even in the raciest (a term I suspect Lovecraft might have employed) of modern novels?

It goes on for two huge paragraphs and is further minutely elaborated upon during the richly detailed description of the body's swift but well-observed collapse into sludge which follows. I speak as one who has studied these passages with reverent care during the execution of a color car-toon for *Playboy* depicting a flasher in the park terrifying a little old lady and her small dog by opening his (its) raincoat to reveal him (it)self as none other than the monster Wilbur Whateley!

The secret of Lovecraft's superb illus-tratability (so I made the word up; so sue me) is that dear old H.P.L. hides nothing from the artist, bless his heart.

And it only begins with his villains and his monsters; if you want to really and truly draw a picture of witch-haunted Arkham with its tottering gambrel roofs you need only take a notebook along with you as you go lovingly through the stories con-cerning it, and H.P.L. will provide you with mountains of stimulating details to play with and dream on and draw.

So, as I say, I am eagerly looking for-ward to seeing what will be in this book as a result of the interaction of a group of extremely talented artists and the grand-fatherly guidance of Howard Phillips Lovecraft. I am sure they all had fun and I expect to do the same!

Opposite:
Whateley's demise, from *The Dunwich Horror*, illustrated by John Coulthart

ILLUSTRATION ©1996 GAHAN WILSON

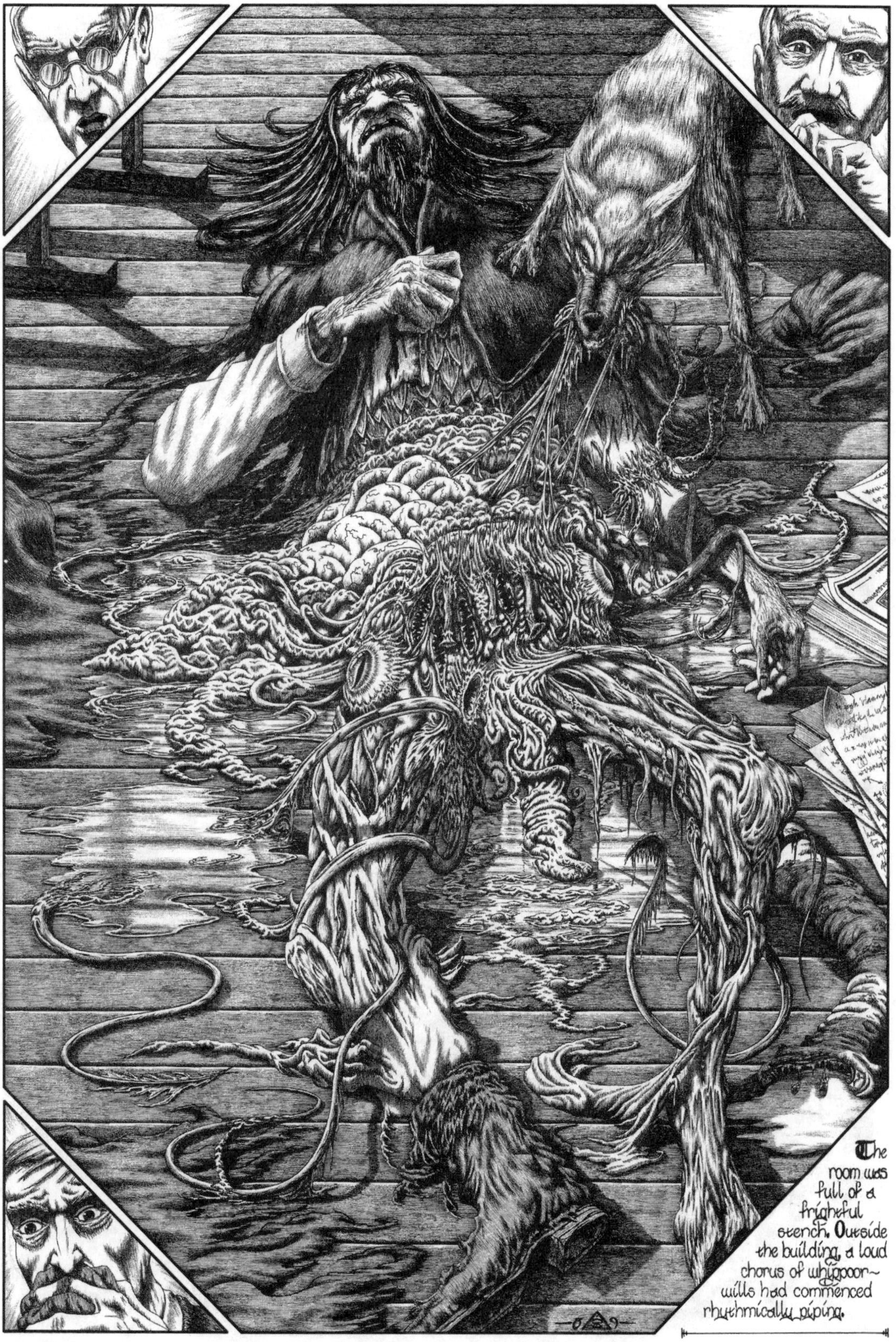
The room was full of a frightful stench. Outside the building, a loud chorus of whippoorwills had commenced rhythmically piping.

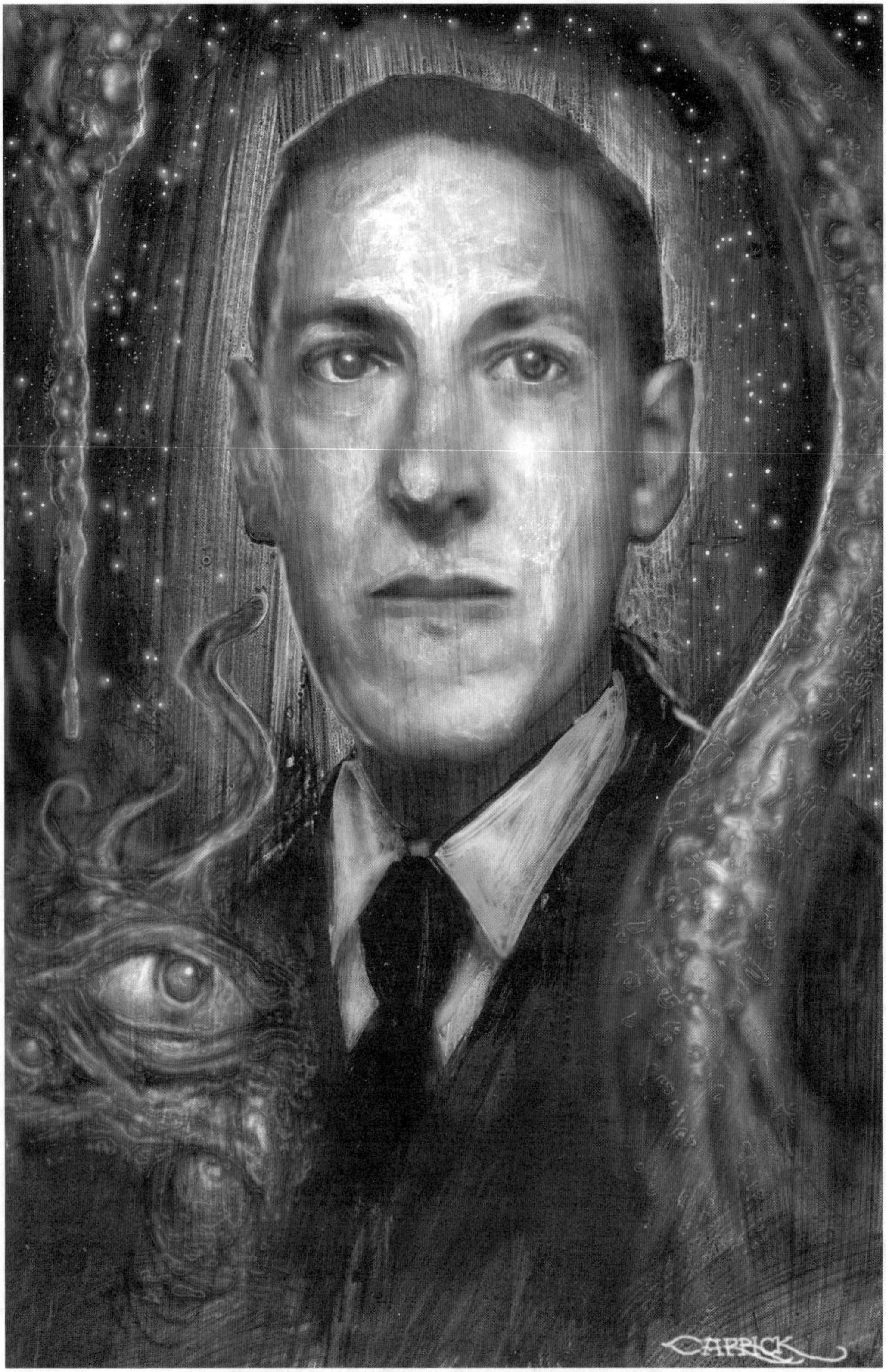
CARRICK

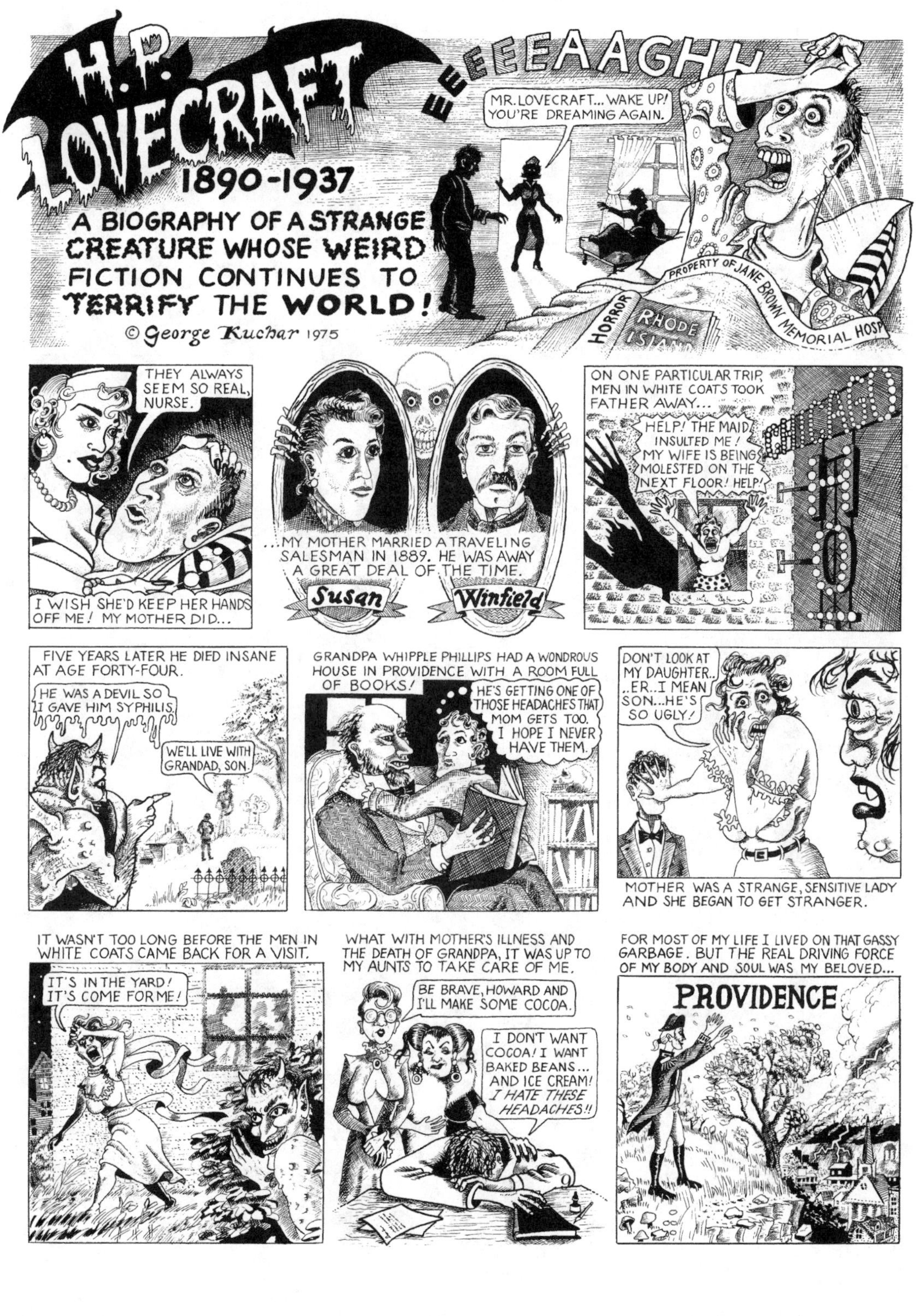
H.P. LOVECRAFT
1890-1937
A BIOGRAPHY OF A STRANGE CREATURE WHOSE WEIRD FICTION CONTINUES TO TERRIFY THE WORLD!
© George Kuchar 1975
EEEEEAAGHH
MR. LOVECRAFT... WAKE UP! YOU'RE DREAMING AGAIN.
PROPERTY OF JANE BROWN MEMORIAL HOSP
HORROR
RHODE ISLAND
THEY ALWAYS SEEM SO REAL, NURSE.
I WISH SHE'D KEEP HER HANDS OFF ME! MY MOTHER DID...
...MY MOTHER MARRIED A TRAVELING SALESMAN IN 1889. HE WAS AWAY A GREAT DEAL OF THE TIME.
Susan
Winfield
ON ONE PARTICULAR TRIP, MEN IN WHITE COATS TOOK FATHER AWAY...
HELP! THE MAID INSULTED ME! MY WIFE IS BEING MOLESTED ON THE NEXT FLOOR! HELP!
FIVE YEARS LATER HE DIED INSANE AT AGE FORTY-FOUR.
HE WAS A DEVIL SO I GAVE HIM SYPHILIS.
WE'LL LIVE WITH GRANDAD, SON.
GRANDPA WHIPPLE PHILLIPS HAD A WONDROUS HOUSE IN PROVIDENCE WITH A ROOM FULL OF BOOKS!
HE'S GETTING ONE OF THOSE HEADACHES THAT MOM GETS TOO. I HOPE I NEVER HAVE THEM.
DON'T LOOK AT MY DAUGHTER.. ..ER..I MEAN SON...HE'S SO UGLY!
MOTHER WAS A STRANGE, SENSITIVE LADY AND SHE BEGAN TO GET STRANGER.
IT WASN'T TOO LONG BEFORE THE MEN IN WHITE COATS CAME BACK FOR A VISIT.
IT'S IN THE YARD! IT'S COME FOR ME!
WHAT WITH MOTHER'S ILLNESS AND THE DEATH OF GRANDPA, IT WAS UP TO MY AUNTS TO TAKE CARE OF ME.
BE BRAVE, HOWARD AND I'LL MAKE SOME COCOA.
I DON'T WANT COCOA! I WANT BAKED BEANS... AND ICE CREAM! I HATE THESE HEADACHES!!
FOR MOST OF MY LIFE I LIVED ON THAT GASSY GARBAGE. BUT THE REAL DRIVING FORCE OF MY BODY AND SOUL WAS MY BELOVED...
PROVIDENCE

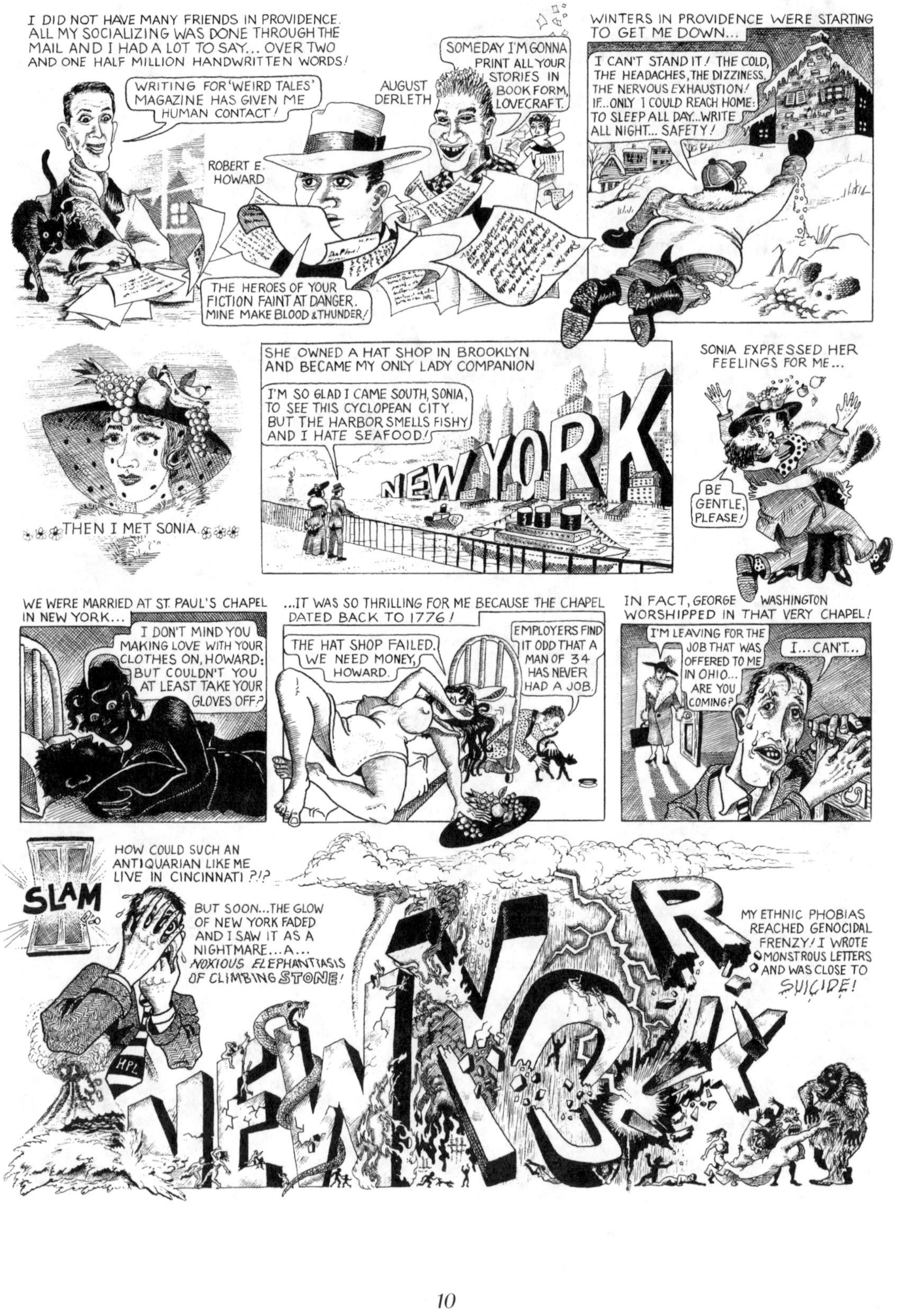
I DID NOT HAVE MANY FRIENDS IN PROVIDENCE. ALL MY SOCIALIZING WAS DONE THROUGH THE MAIL AND I HAD A LOT TO SAY... OVER TWO AND ONE HALF MILLION HANDWRITTEN WORDS!
WRITING FOR 'WEIRD TALES' MAGAZINE HAS GIVEN ME HUMAN CONTACT!
ROBERT E. HOWARD
THE HEROES OF YOUR FICTION FAINT AT DANGER. MINE MAKE BLOOD & THUNDER!
AUGUST DERLETH
SOMEDAY I'M GONNA PRINT ALL YOUR STORIES IN BOOK FORM, LOVECRAFT.
WINTERS IN PROVIDENCE WERE STARTING TO GET ME DOWN...
I CAN'T STAND IT! THE COLD, THE HEADACHES, THE DIZZINESS, THE NERVOUS EXHAUSTION! IF...ONLY I COULD REACH HOME: TO SLEEP ALL DAY...WRITE ALL NIGHT... SAFETY!
THEN I MET SONIA.
SHE OWNED A HAT SHOP IN BROOKLYN AND BECAME MY ONLY LADY COMPANION
I'M SO GLAD I CAME SOUTH, SONIA, TO SEE THIS CYCLOPEAN CITY. BUT THE HARBOR SMELLS FISHY AND I HATE SEAFOOD!
NEW YORK
SONIA EXPRESSED HER FEELINGS FOR ME...
BE GENTLE, PLEASE!
WE WERE MARRIED AT ST. PAUL'S CHAPEL IN NEW YORK...
I DON'T MIND YOU MAKING LOVE WITH YOUR CLOTHES ON, HOWARD: BUT COULDN'T YOU AT LEAST TAKE YOUR GLOVES OFF?
...IT WAS SO THRILLING FOR ME BECAUSE THE CHAPEL DATED BACK TO 1776!
THE HAT SHOP FAILED. WE NEED MONEY, HOWARD.
EMPLOYERS FIND IT ODD THAT A MAN OF 34 HAS NEVER HAD A JOB.
IN FACT, GEORGE WASHINGTON WORSHIPPED IN THAT VERY CHAPEL!
I'M LEAVING FOR THE JOB THAT WAS OFFERED TO ME IN OHIO... ARE YOU COMING?
I...CAN'T...
SLAM
HOW COULD SUCH AN ANTIQUARIAN LIKE ME LIVE IN CINCINNATI ?!?
BUT SOON...THE GLOW OF NEW YORK FADED AND I SAW IT AS A NIGHTMARE...A... NOXIOUS ELEPHANTIASIS OF CLIMBING STONE!
MY ETHNIC PHOBIAS REACHED GENOCIDAL FRENZY! I WROTE MONSTROUS LETTERS AND WAS CLOSE TO SUICIDE!
HPL

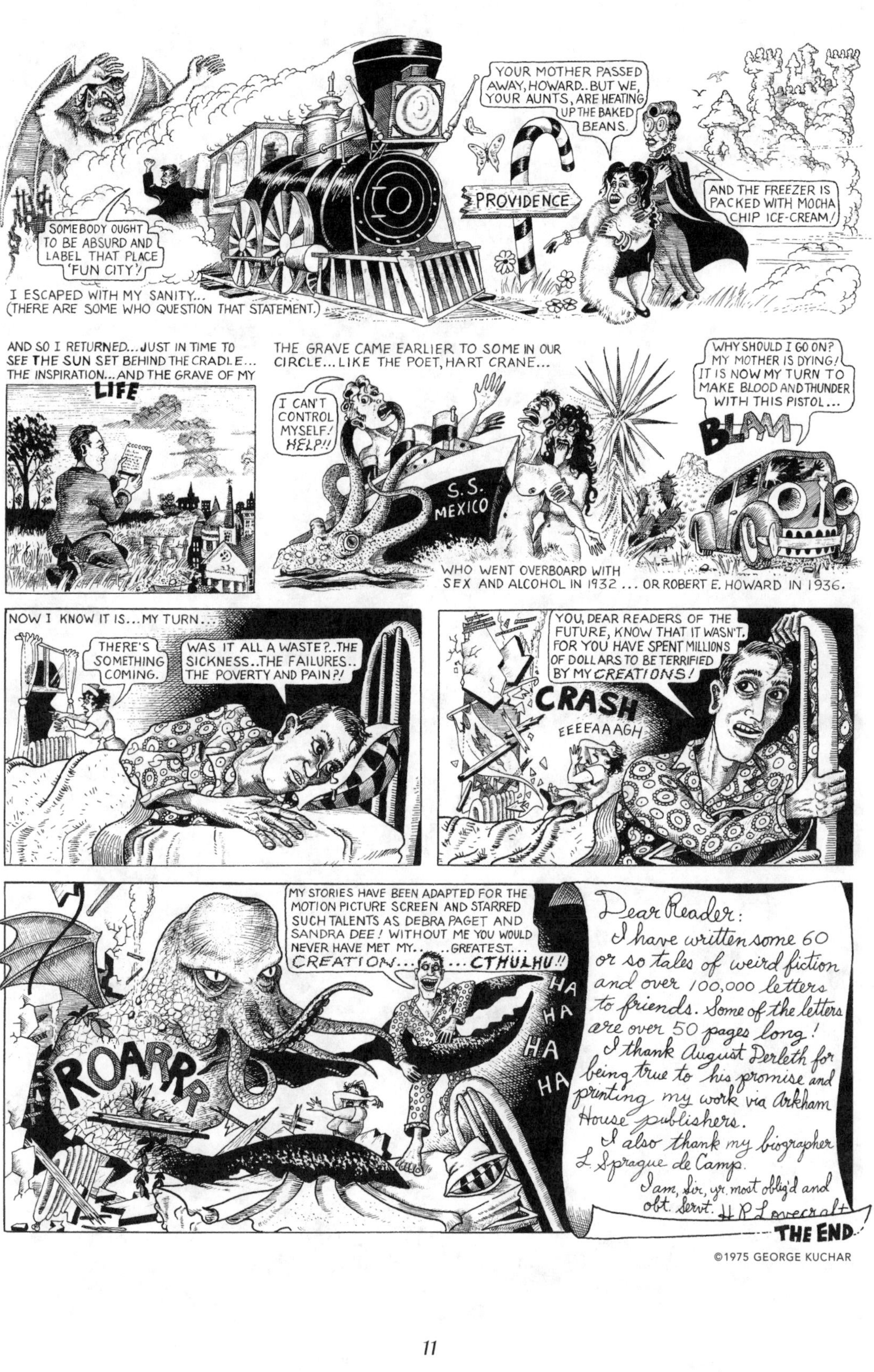

SOMEBODY OUGHT TO BE ABSURD AND LABEL THAT PLACE 'FUN CITY'!
I ESCAPED WITH MY SANITY... (THERE ARE SOME WHO QUESTION THAT STATEMENT.)
PROVIDENCE
YOUR MOTHER PASSED AWAY, HOWARD.. BUT WE, YOUR AUNTS, ARE HEATING UP THE BAKED BEANS.
AND THE FREEZER IS PACKED WITH MOCHA CHIP ICE-CREAM!
AND SO I RETURNED... JUST IN TIME TO SEE THE SUN SET BEHIND THE CRADLE... THE INSPIRATION... AND THE GRAVE OF MY LIFE
THE GRAVE CAME EARLIER TO SOME IN OUR CIRCLE... LIKE THE POET, HART CRANE...
I CAN'T CONTROL MYSELF! HELP!!
S.S. MEXICO
WHO WENT OVERBOARD WITH SEX AND ALCOHOL IN 1932 ... OR ROBERT E. HOWARD IN 1936.
WHY SHOULD I GO ON? MY MOTHER IS DYING! IT IS NOW MY TURN TO MAKE BLOOD AND THUNDER WITH THIS PISTOL...
BLAM
NOW I KNOW IT IS... MY TURN...
THERE'S SOMETHING COMING.
WAS IT ALL A WASTE?.. THE SICKNESS.. THE FAILURES.. THE POVERTY AND PAIN?!
YOU, DEAR READERS OF THE FUTURE, KNOW THAT IT WASN'T. FOR YOU HAVE SPENT MILLIONS OF DOLLARS TO BE TERRIFIED BY MY CREATIONS!
CRASH
EEEEAAAGH
MY STORIES HAVE BEEN ADAPTED FOR THE MOTION PICTURE SCREEN AND STARRED SUCH TALENTS AS DEBRA PAGET AND SANDRA DEE! WITHOUT ME YOU WOULD NEVER HAVE MET MY... ...GREATEST... CREATION... ...CTHULHU!!
HA HA HA HA
ROARRR
Dear Reader:
I have written some 60 or so tales of weird fiction and over 100,000 letters to friends. Some of the letters are over 50 pages long!
I thank August Derleth for being true to his promise and printing my work via Arkham House publishers.
I also thank my biographer L. Sprague de Camp.
I am, Sir, yr. most oblig'd and obt. Servt. H P Lovecraft
THE END

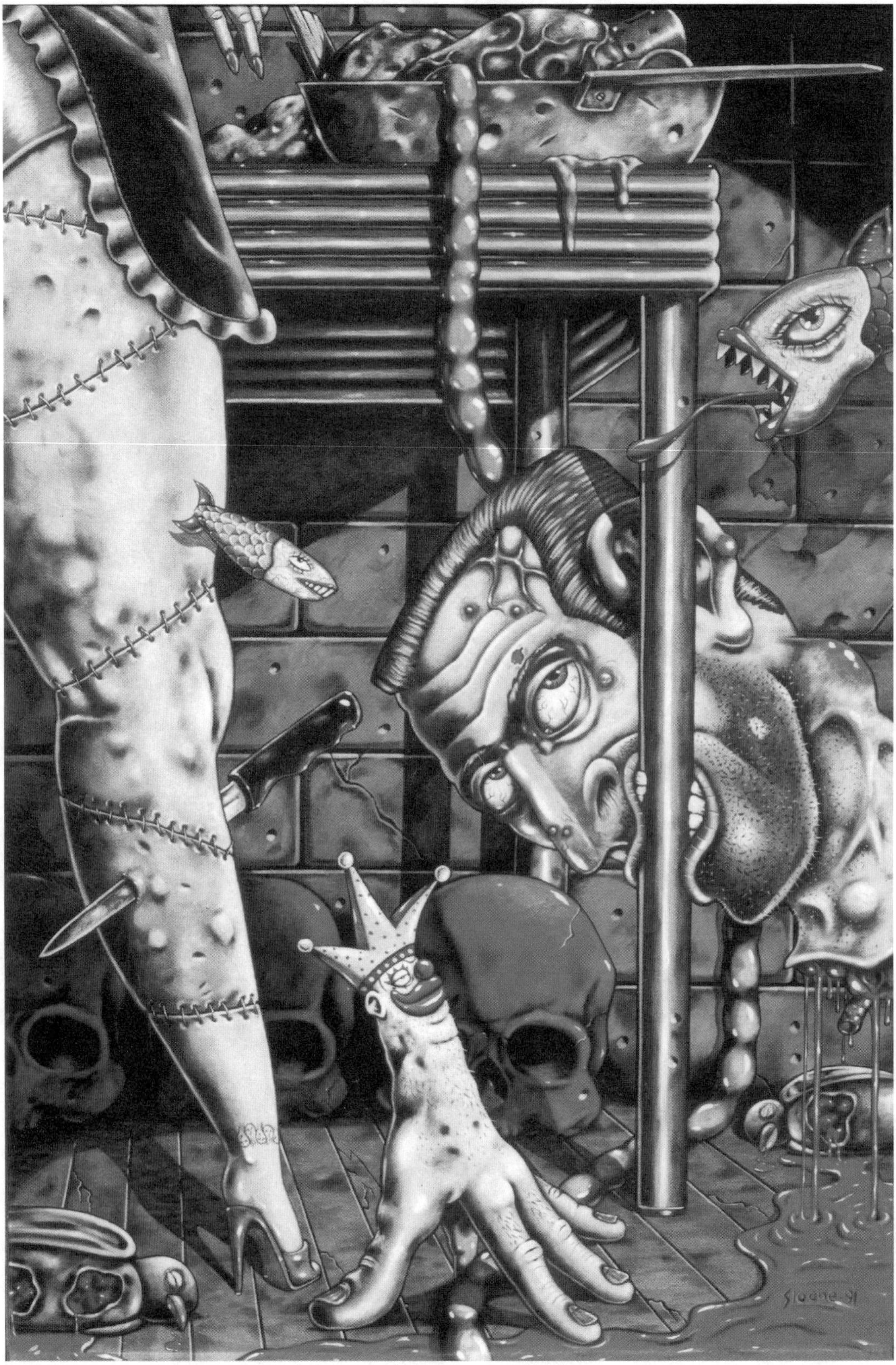
sloane 91

Herbert West: Reanimator

illustrated by

PART ONE: FROM THE DARK

RICHARD CORBEN

PART TWO: THE PLAGUE-DEMON

RICK GEARY

PART THREE: THE HORROR FROM THE SHADOWS

J.B. BONIVERT

PART FOUR: THE TOMB-LEGIONS

MARK A. NELSON

frontispiece by

R.K. SLOANE

story by

H.P. LOVECRAFT

edited and abridged by Tom Pomplun

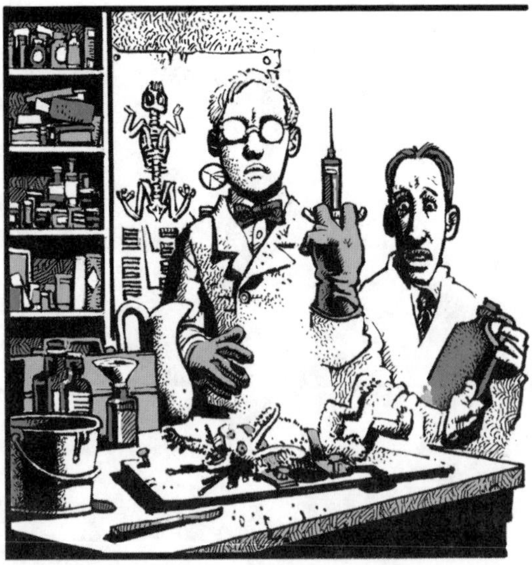

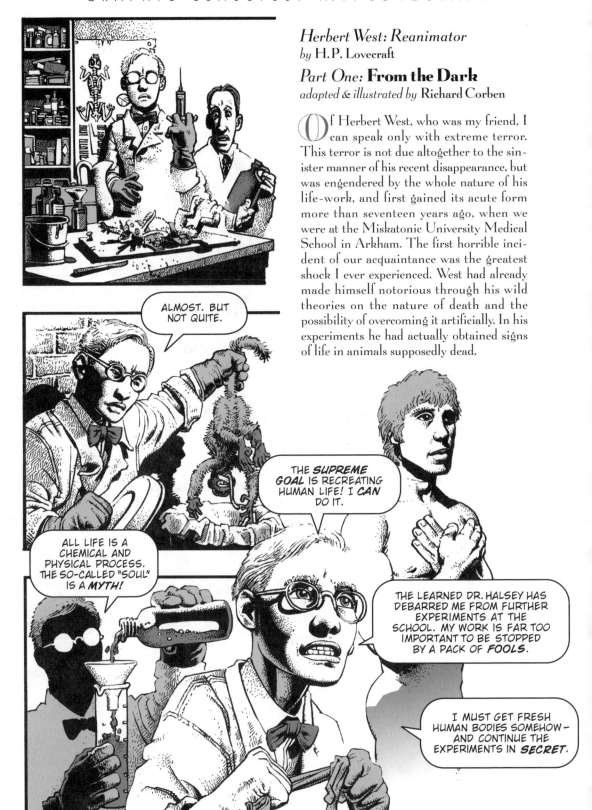

Herbert West: Reanimator
by H.P. Lovecraft

Part One: **From the Dark**

adapted & illustrated by Richard Corben

Of Herbert West, who was my friend, I can speak only with extreme terror. This terror is not due altogether to the sinister manner of his recent disappearance, but was engendered by the whole nature of his life-work, and first gained its acute form more than seventeen years ago, when we were at the Miskatonic University Medical School in Arkham. The first horrible incident of our acquaintance was the greatest shock I ever experienced. West had already made himself notorious through his wild theories on the nature of death and the possibility of overcoming it artificially. In his experiments he had actually obtained signs of life in animals supposedly dead.

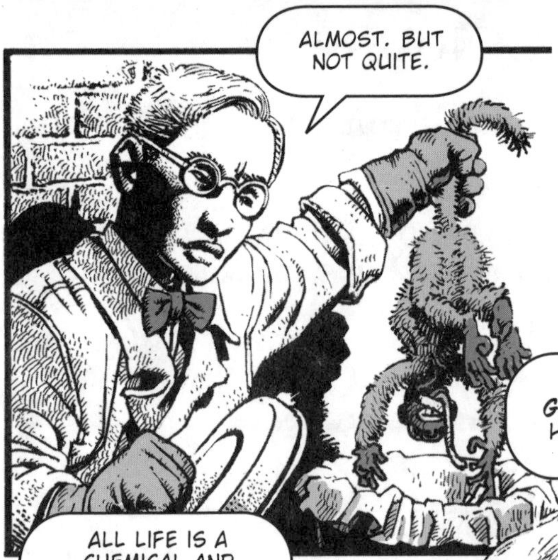
ALMOST. BUT NOT QUITE.

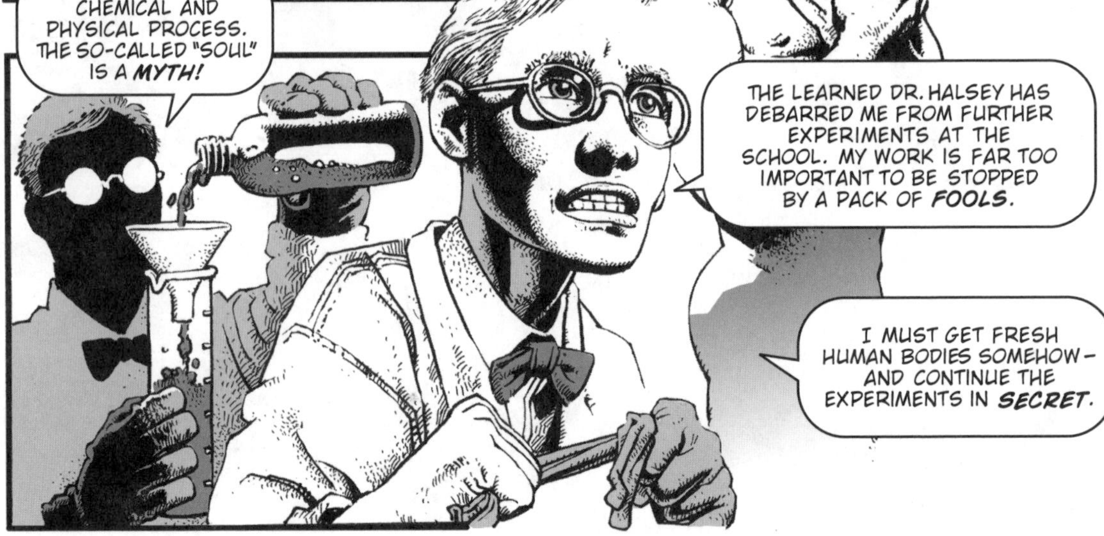
THE SUPREME GOAL IS RECREATING HUMAN LIFE! I CAN DO IT.
ALL LIFE IS A CHEMICAL AND PHYSICAL PROCESS. THE SO-CALLED "SOUL" IS A MYTH!
THE LEARNED DR. HALSEY HAS DEBARRED ME FROM FURTHER EXPERIMENTS AT THE SCHOOL. MY WORK IS FAR TOO IMPORTANT TO BE STOPPED BY A PACK OF FOOLS.
I MUST GET FRESH HUMAN BODIES SOMEHOW— AND CONTINUE THE EXPERIMENTS IN SECRET.

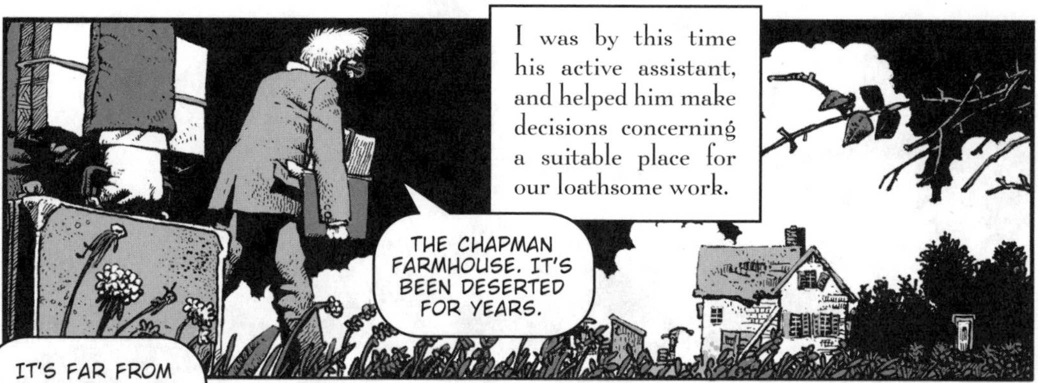
I was by this time his active assistant, and helped him make decisions concerning a suitable place for our loathsome work.
THE CHAPMAN FARMHOUSE. IT'S BEEN DESERTED FOR YEARS.

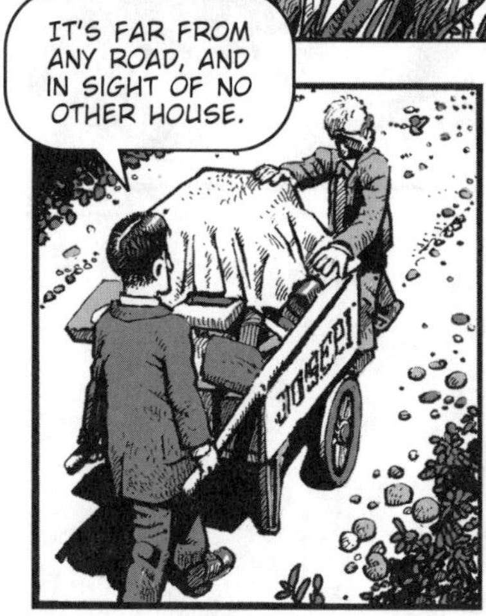
IT'S FAR FROM ANY ROAD, AND IN SIGHT OF NO OTHER HOUSE.

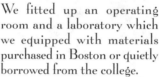

We fitted up an operating room and a laboratory which we equipped with materials purchased in Boston or quietly borrowed from the college.

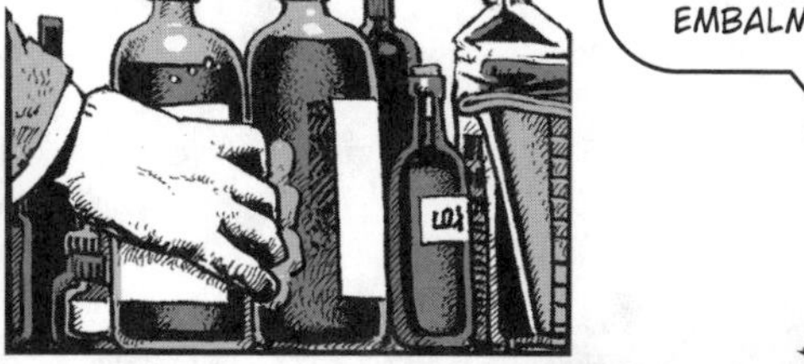

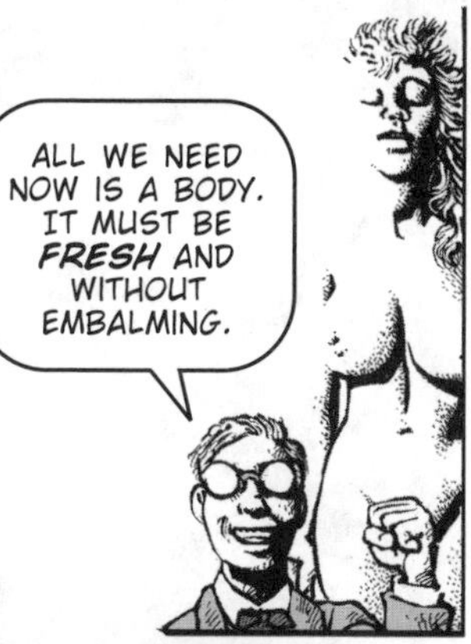
ALL WE NEED NOW IS A BODY. IT MUST BE *FRESH* AND WITHOUT EMBALMING.

Precautions were necessary, since rumours of strange lights and midnight activities would soon bring disaster on our enterprise. We provided spades and picks for the many burials we should have to make in the cellar.

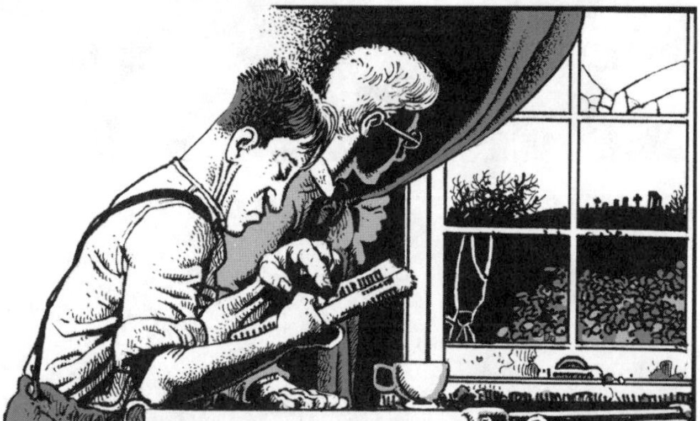

We followed the local death-notices like ghouls. Not for many weeks did we hear of anything suitable; though we talked with morgue and hospital authorities as often as we could without exciting suspicion. In the end, though, luck favoured us; for one day we heard of an almost ideal case in the potter's field.

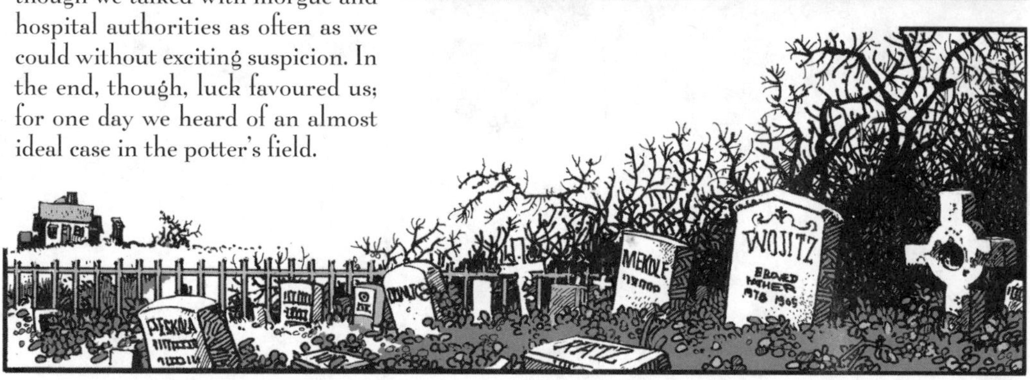

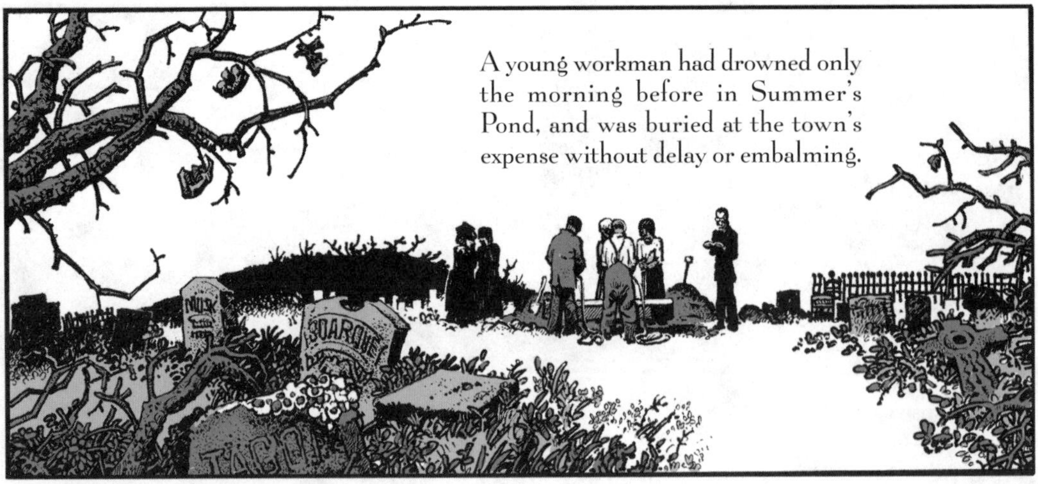
A young workman had drowned only the morning before in Summer's Pond, and was buried at the town's expense without delay or embalming.

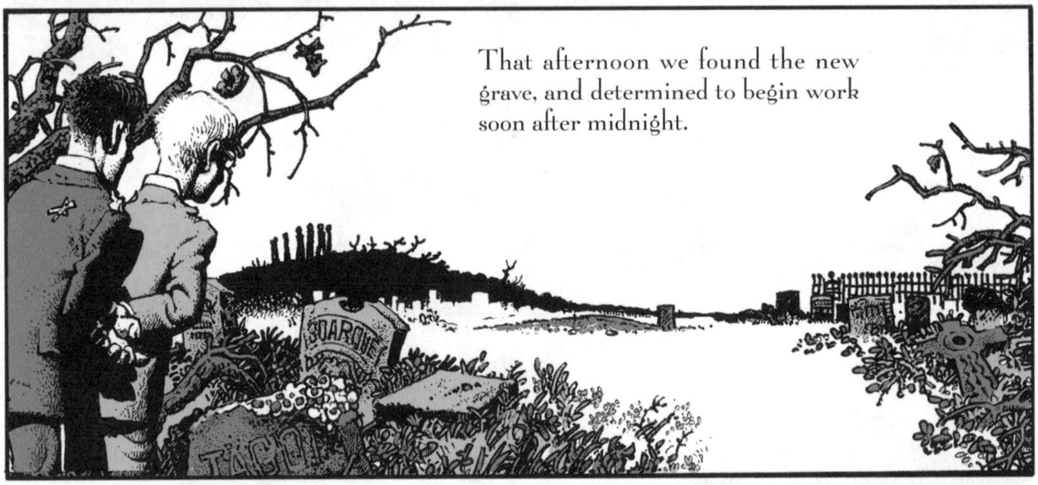
That afternoon we found the new grave, and determined to begin work soon after midnight.

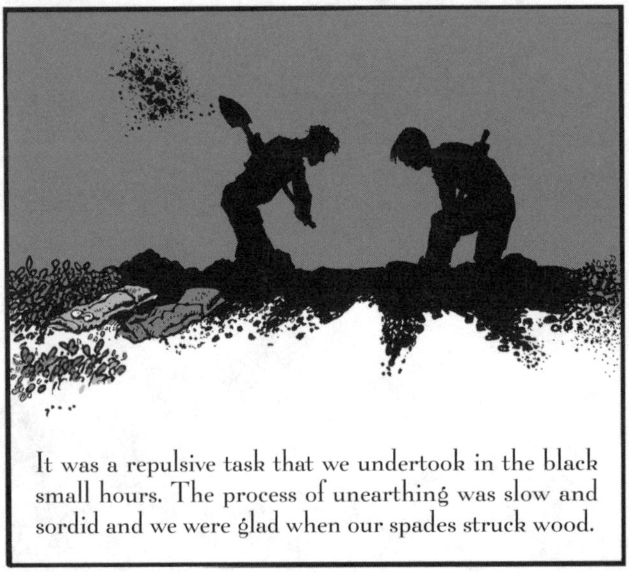
It was a repulsive task that we undertook in the black small hours. The process of unearthing was slow and sordid and we were glad when our spades struck wood.

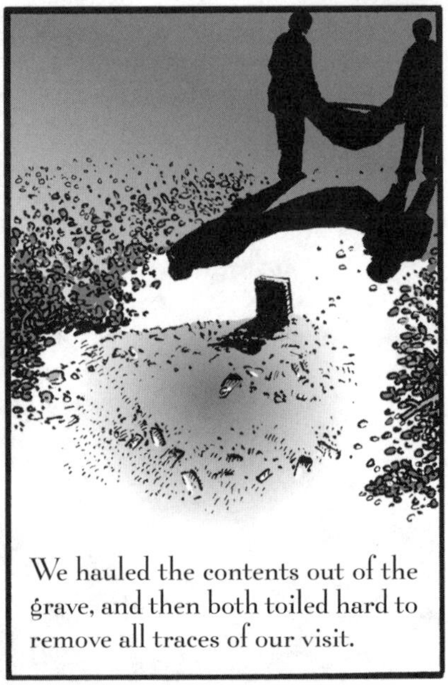
We hauled the contents out of the grave, and then both toiled hard to remove all traces of our visit.

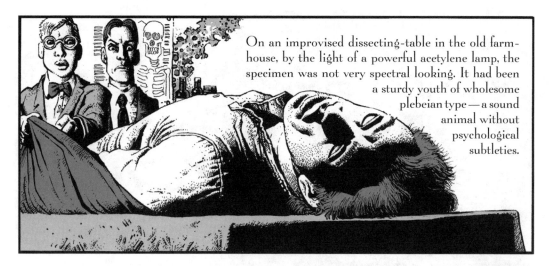

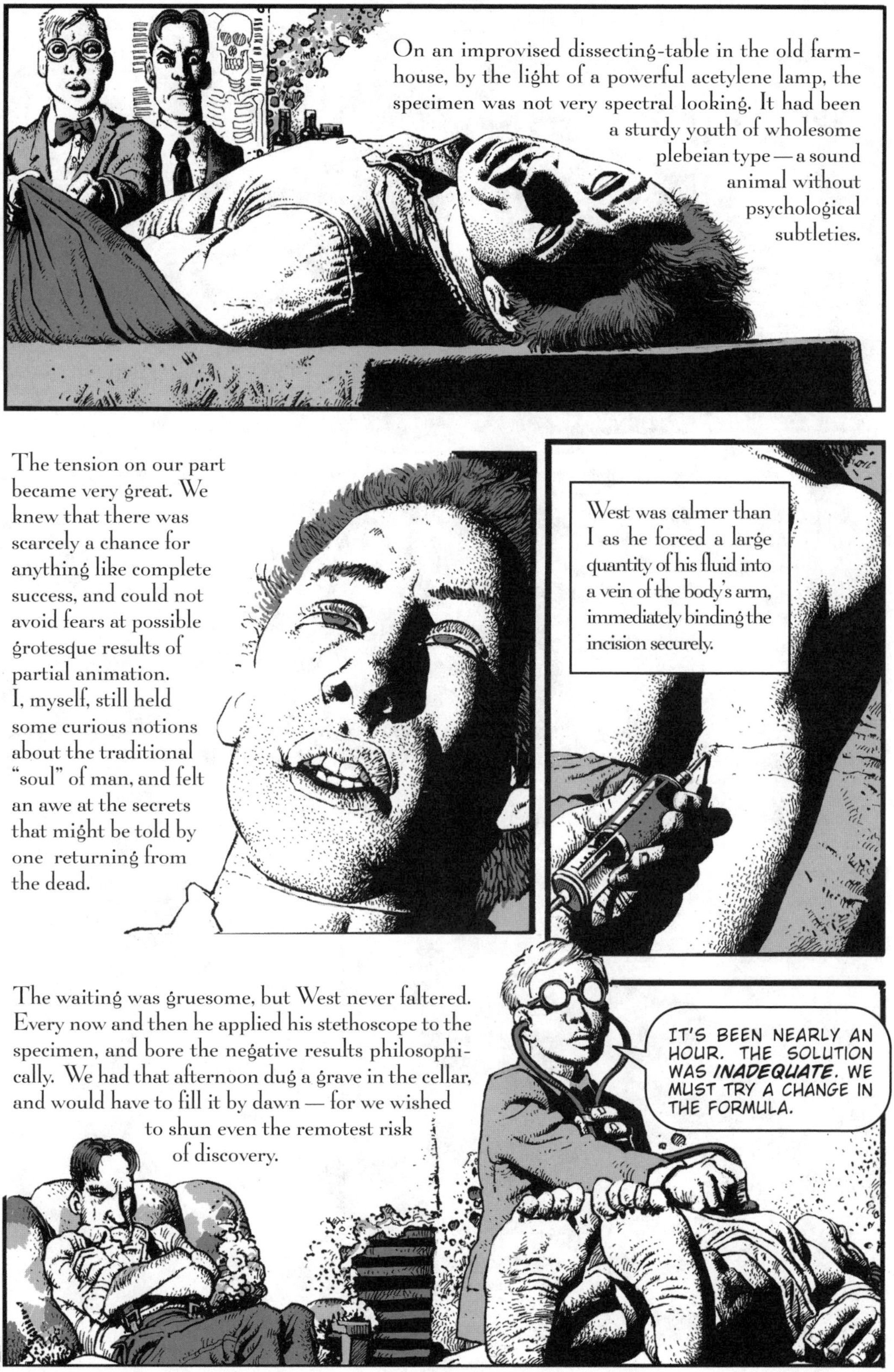

On an improvised dissecting-table in the old farm-house, by the light of a powerful acetylene lamp, the specimen was not very spectral looking. It had been a sturdy youth of wholesome plebeian type — a sound animal without psychological subtleties.

The tension on our part became very great. We knew that there was scarcely a chance for anything like complete success, and could not avoid fears at possible grotesque results of partial animation. I, myself, still held some curious notions about the traditional "soul" of man, and felt an awe at the secrets that might be told by one returning from the dead.

West was calmer than I as he forced a large quantity of his fluid into a vein of the body's arm, immediately binding the incision securely.

The waiting was gruesome, but West never faltered. Every now and then he applied his stethoscope to the specimen, and bore the negative results philosophically. We had that afternoon dug a grave in the cellar, and would have to fill it by dawn — for we wished to shun even the remotest risk of discovery.

IT'S BEEN NEARLY AN HOUR. THE SOLUTION WAS *INADEQUATE*. WE MUST TRY A CHANGE IN THE FORMULA.

Taking the solitary lamp into the adjacent laboratory, we left our silent guest on the slab in the dark. The awful event was very sudden, and wholly unexpected...

Not more unutterable could have been the chaos of hellish sound if the pit itself had opened to release the agony of the damned. I think we screamed ourselves as we stumbled frantically toward the town.

That evening two items in the paper, wholly unrelated, made it impossible for us to sleep. The old Chapman house had been burned to a heap of ashes; that we could understand because of the upset lamp.

Also, an attempt had been made to disturb a new grave in the potter's field, as if by futile and spadeless clawing at the earth.

That we could *not* understand, for we had patted down the mould very carefully.

And for years West would look frequently over his shoulder, and complain of fancied footsteps behind him.

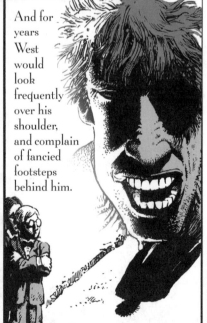

Part Two:
The Plague-Demon
adapted & illustrated by
Rick Geary

After the experience at the old farmhouse, West dropped his researches for a time. But the zeal of the born scientist returned, and he became importunate with the faculty.

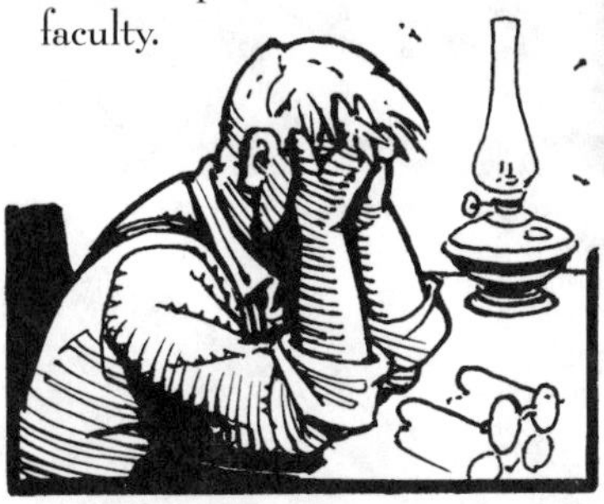

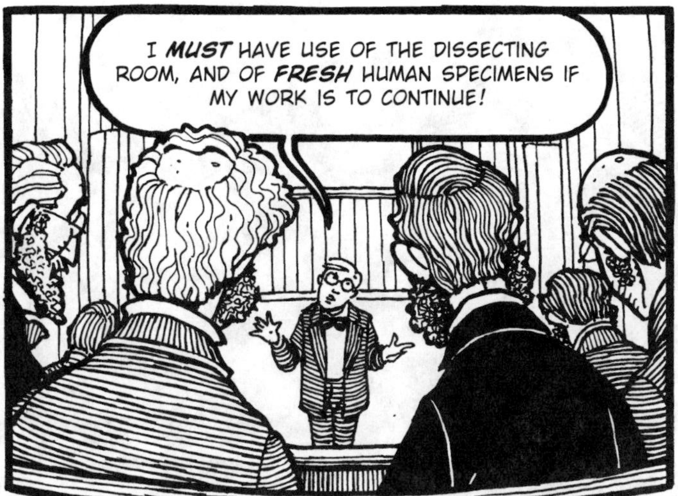
I MUST HAVE USE OF THE DISSECTING ROOM, AND OF FRESH HUMAN SPECIMENS IF MY WORK IS TO CONTINUE!

His pleas, however, were wholly in vain; for the decision of our sceptical dean, Dr. Allan Halsey, was inflexible, and the other professors all endorsed the verdict of their leader.

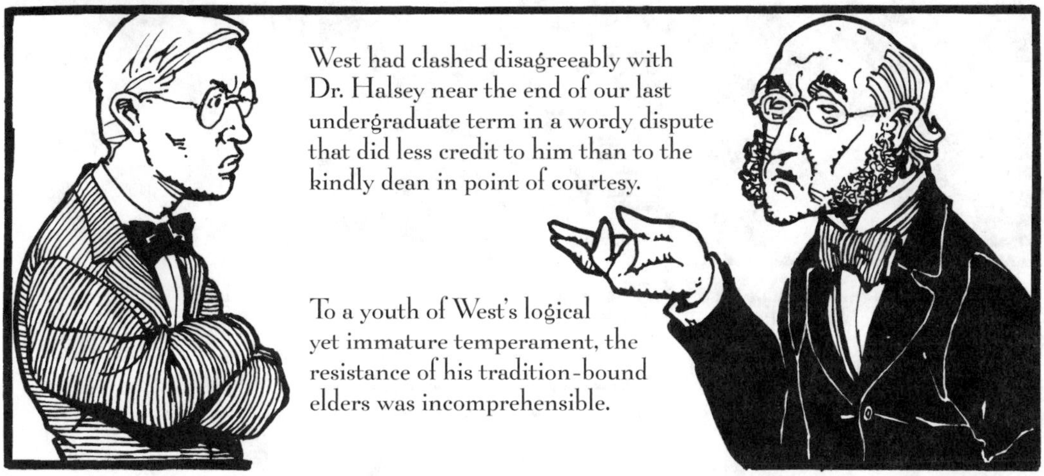
West had clashed disagreeably with Dr. Halsey near the end of our last undergraduate term in a wordy dispute that did less credit to him than to the kindly dean in point of courtesy.
To a youth of West's logical yet immature temperament, the resistance of his tradition-bound elders was incomprehensible.

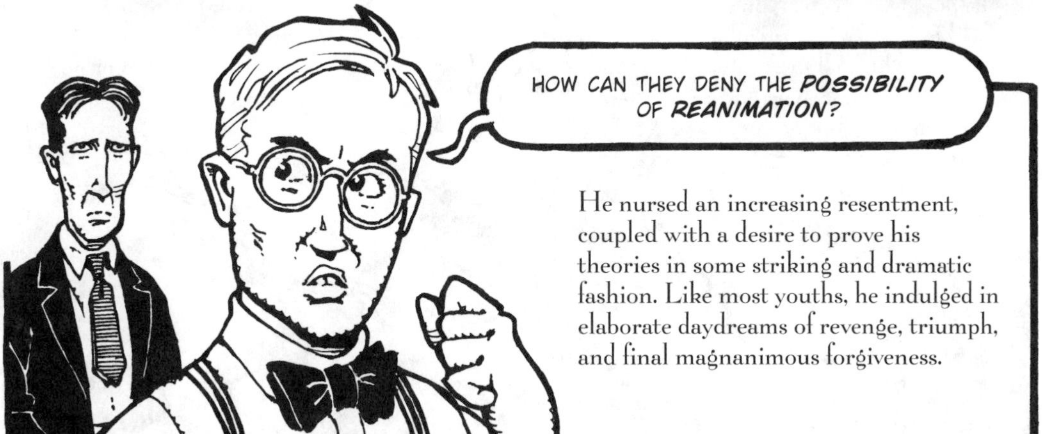
HOW CAN THEY DENY THE POSSIBILITY OF REANIMATION?
He nursed an increasing resentment, coupled with a desire to prove his theories in some striking and dramatic fashion. Like most youths, he indulged in elaborate daydreams of revenge, triumph, and final magnanimous forgiveness.

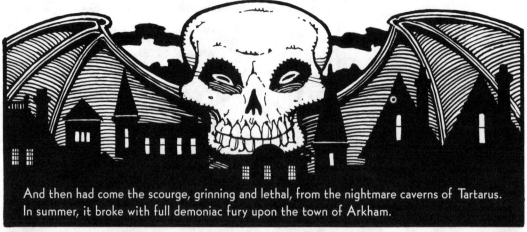

And then had come the scourge, grinning and lethal, from the nightmare caverns of Tartarus. In summer, it broke with full demoniac fury upon the town of Arkham.

West and I now had our degrees and, though not as yet licensed physicians, we were frantically pressed into public service.

The deaths ensued too frequently for the local undertakers fully to handle.

The irony was not lost on West — so many fresh specimens, yet none for his persecuted researches!

Every doctor of the medical faculty was helping to fight the typhoid plague. Dr. Halsey in particular had distinguished himself in sacrificing service. Before a month was over the fearless dean had become a popular hero.

West could not withhold admiration for his foe, but because of this was even more determined to prove to him the truth of his amazing doctrines.

Taking advantage of the disorganization, we managed to smuggle a recently deceased body into the university dissecting-room one night.

In my presence, West injected a new modification of his solution.

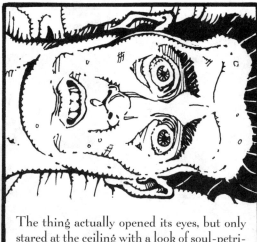

The thing actually opened its eyes, but only stared at the ceiling with a look of soul-petrifying horror before collapsing into inertness.

NOT *FRESH* ENOUGH! THE HOT SUMMER AIR DOES NOT FAVOUR CORPSES!

The peak of the epidemic was reached in August, and Dr. Halsey died on the 14th. The students all attended the hasty funeral on the 15th.

It was a popular affair, for the dean had been a public benefactor.

After the entombment we were feeling depressed, and we all spent the afternoon at the bar of the Commercial House.

As the evening advanced, and the others had gone home, or to various duties, West persuaded me to aid him in ...

"... making a night of it."

West's landlady saw us arrive at about two in the morning, with a third man between us.

She said that we had evidently dined and wined rather well.

At about 3 a.m. the whole house was aroused by the cries coming from West's room.

They found the two of us unconscious on the blood-stained carpet — scratched, and mauled.

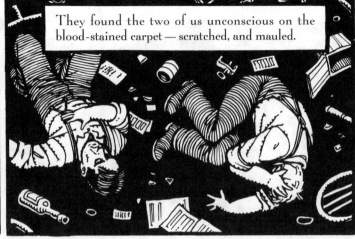

Only an open window told what had become of our assailant.

He was, West nervously said, a stranger whom we had met at a bar. We did not wish to have him hunted down.

That night saw the beginning of a second Arkham horror, eclipsing the plague itself.

At Christchurch Cemetery a watchman was clawed to death in a manner too hideous for description.

The next night, eight houses were entered by a thing which strewed Red Death in its wake.

A few persons who had glimpsed it said it was all white and like an ape or some anthropomorphic malformed fiend.

In all, seventeen mangled bodies were left behind by the sadistic monster that crept abroad.

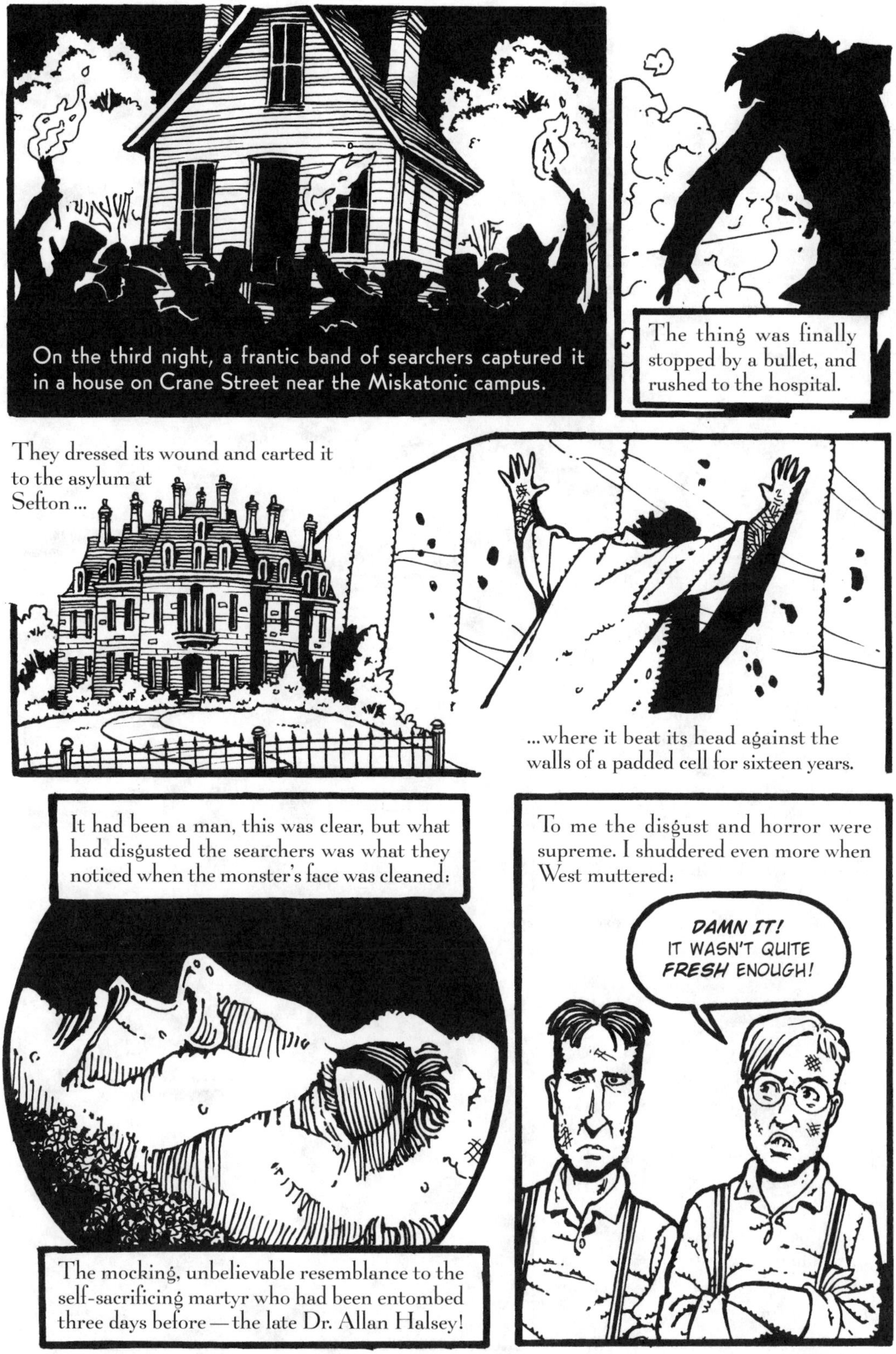
On the third night, a frantic band of searchers captured it in a house on Crane Street near the Miskatonic campus.
The thing was finally stopped by a bullet, and rushed to the hospital.
They dressed its wound and carted it to the asylum at Sefton...
...where it beat its head against the walls of a padded cell for sixteen years.
It had been a man, this was clear, but what had disgusted the searchers was what they noticed when the monster's face was cleaned:
The mocking, unbelievable resemblance to the self-sacrificing martyr who had been entombed three days before—the late Dr. Allan Halsey!
To me the disgust and horror were supreme. I shuddered even more when West muttered:
DAMN IT! IT WASN'T QUITE FRESH ENOUGH!

Part Three: **The Horror from the Shadows**

adapted & illustrated by J.B. Bonivert

Many men have related hideous things, not mentioned in print, which happened on the battlefields of the Great War. Yet despite the worst of them I believe I can myself relate the most hideous thing of all.

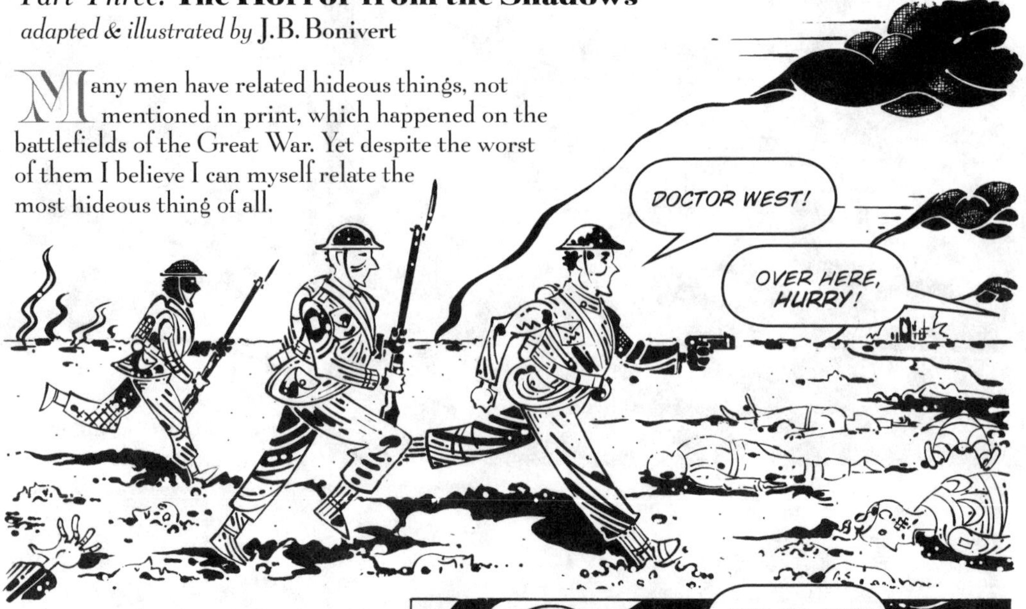
DOCTOR WEST!
OVER HERE, *HURRY!*

In 1915 I was a physician in a Canadian regiment in Flanders, and an assistant to the celebrated Boston surgical specialist, Dr. Herbert West. Dr. West had been avid to serve as surgeon in a great war, and when the chance had come, he carried me with him almost against my will. There were reasons why I could have been glad to let the war separate us, but I could not resist the imperious persuasion of West that I should accompany him in my usual capacity.

When I say that Dr. West was avid to serve in battle, I do not mean to imply that he was either naturally warlike or anxious for the safety of civilisation. There was, however, something he wanted in embattled Flanders; and in order to secure it had had to assume a military exterior. What he wanted was something connected with the peculiar branch of medical science which he had chosen quite clandestinely to follow, and in which he had achieved amazing and occasionally hideous results. It was, in fact, nothing more or less than an abundant supply of freshly killed men in every stage of dismemberment.

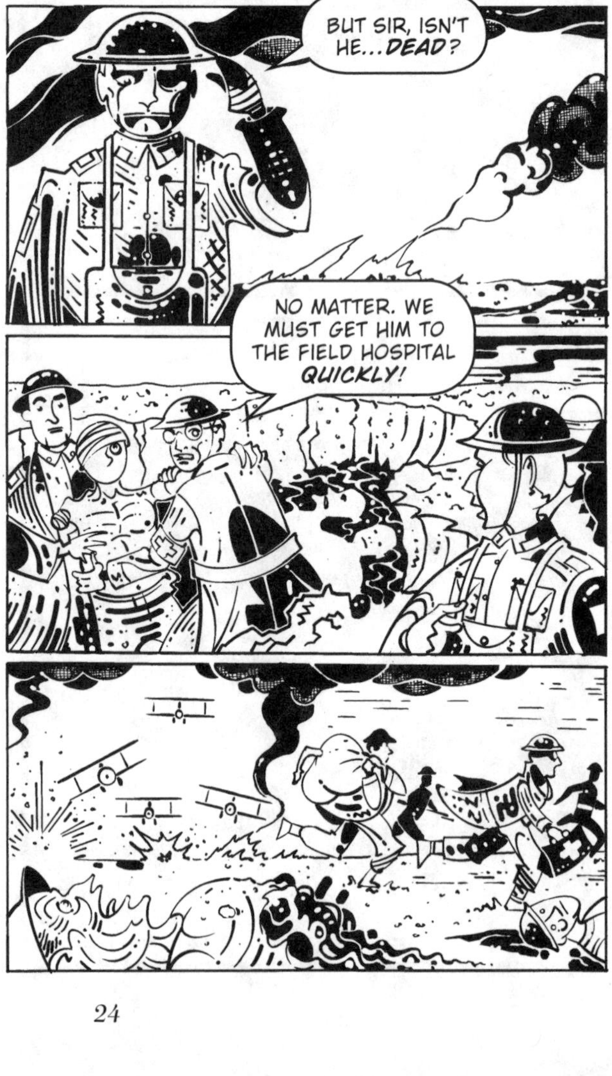
BUT SIR, ISN'T HE... *DEAD?*
NO MATTER. WE MUST GET HIM TO THE FIELD HOSPITAL *QUICKLY!*

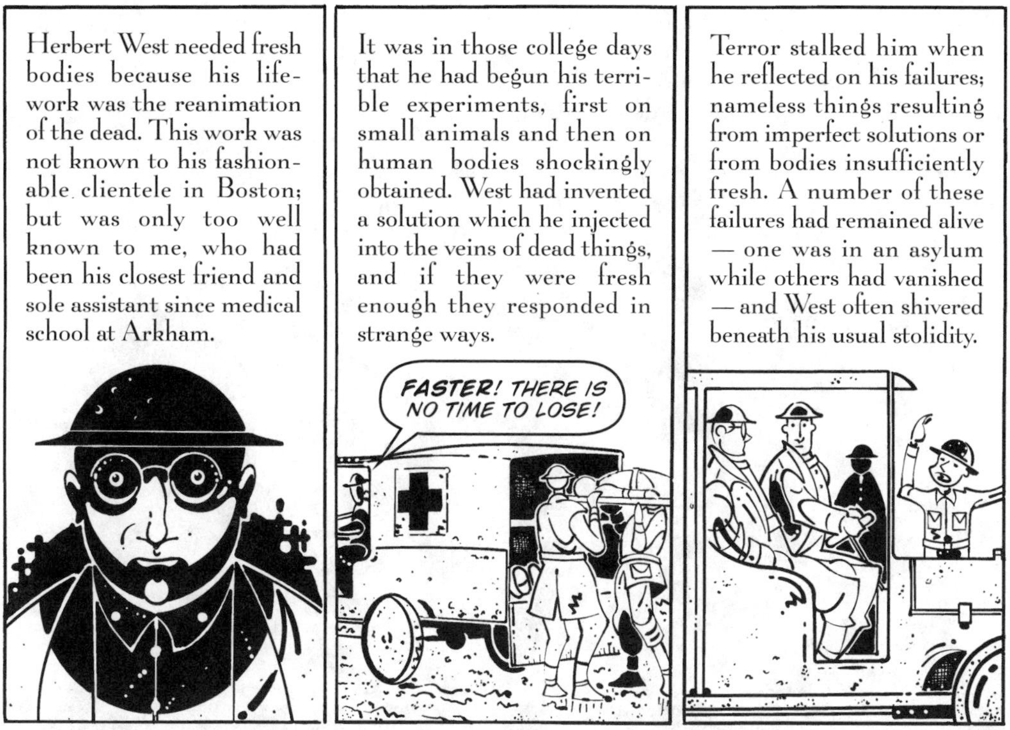
Herbert West needed fresh bodies because his life-work was the reanimation of the dead. This work was not known to his fashionable clientele in Boston; but was only too well known to me, who had been his closest friend and sole assistant since medical school at Arkham.
It was in those college days that he had begun his terrible experiments, first on small animals and then on human bodies shockingly obtained. West had invented a solution which he injected into the veins of dead things, and if they were fresh enough they responded in strange ways.
FASTER! THERE IS NO TIME TO LOSE!
Terror stalked him when he reflected on his failures; nameless things resulting from imperfect solutions or from bodies insufficiently fresh. A number of these failures had remained alive — one was in an asylum while others had vanished — and West often shivered beneath his usual stolidity.

West had soon learned that absolute freshness was the prime requisite for useful specimens, and had resorted to frightful expedients in body-snatching.

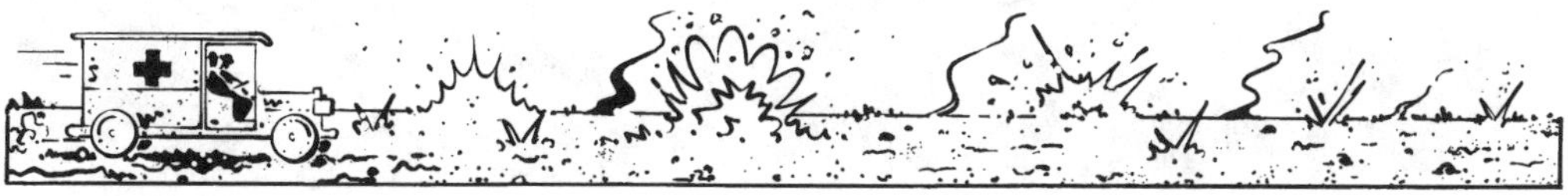

As his boldness in methods grew, I began to develop a gnawing fear. And then there came a nightmarish session when I learned that a specimen had been living being when he secured it.

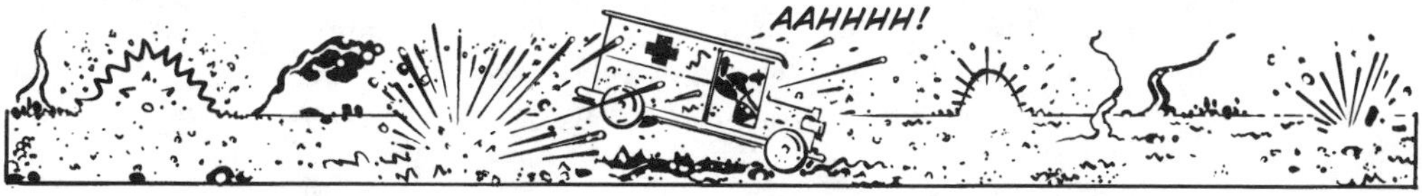
AAHHHH!

That was the first time he had ever been able to revive the quality of rational thought in a corpse; and his success had completely hardened him.

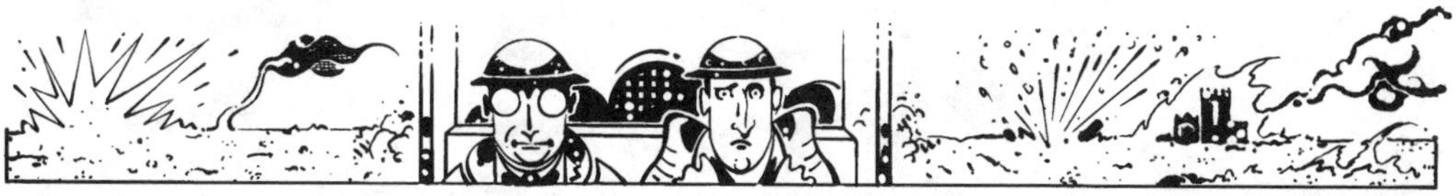

Gradually I came to find Herbert West himself more horrible than anything he did — his zeal for prolonging life had degenerated into a perverse addiction to the repellently abnormal.

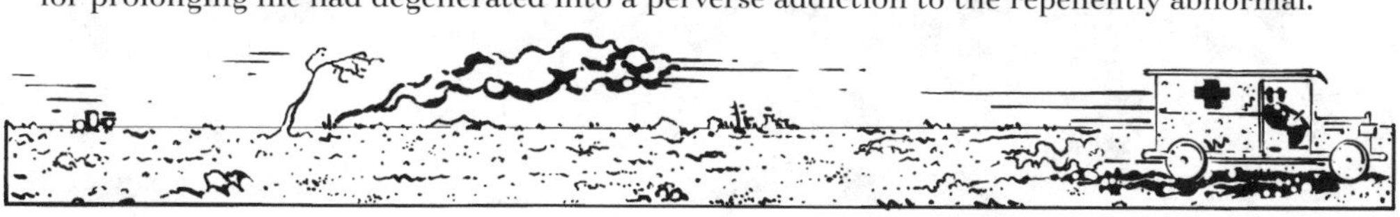

West had proved his point that rational life can be restored, and sought new worlds to conquer by experimenting on the reanimation of detached parts of bodies. He had achieved some hideous preliminary results in the form of never-dying, artificially nourished tissue obtained from the eggs of a tropical reptile. Two points he was exceedingly anxious to settle — first, whether consciousness was possible without the brain; and second, whether any intangible relation may exist to link the separated parts of what had previously been a single living organism. All this research work required a prodigious supply of freshly slaughtered human flesh — and that was why Herbert West had entered the Great War.

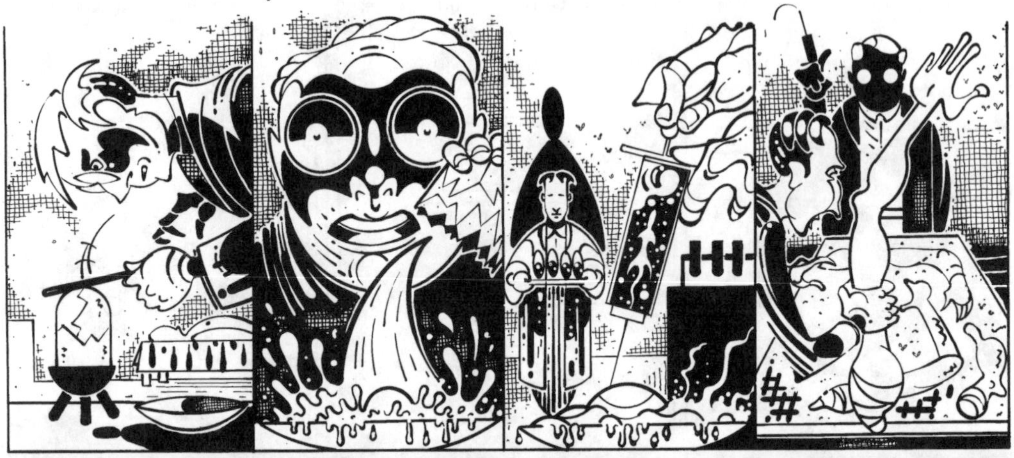

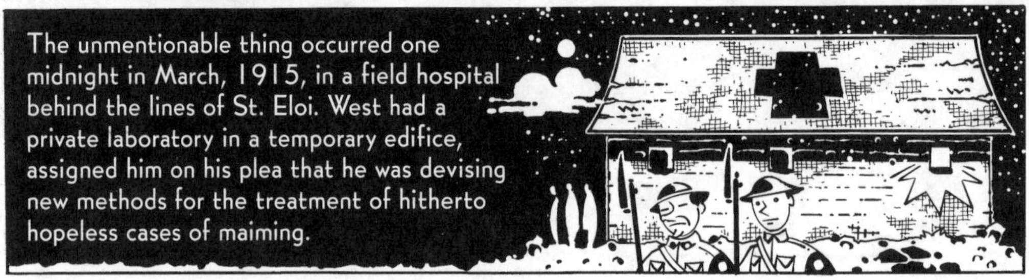
The unmentionable thing occurred one midnight in March, 1915, in a field hospital behind the lines of St. Eloi. West had a private laboratory in a temporary edifice, assigned him on his plea that he was devising new methods for the treatment of hitherto hopeless cases of maiming.

There he worked like a butcher in the midst of his gory wares. At times he actually did perform marvels of surgery for the soldiers; but his chief delights were of a less philanthropic kind, requiring many explanations of sounds which seemed peculiar even amidst that babel of the damned. Besides human tissue, West employed much of the reptile embryo tissue which he had cultivated with such singular results. In a dark corner of the laboratory, over a burner, he kept a large covered vat full of this reptilian cell-matter; which grew puffily and hideously.

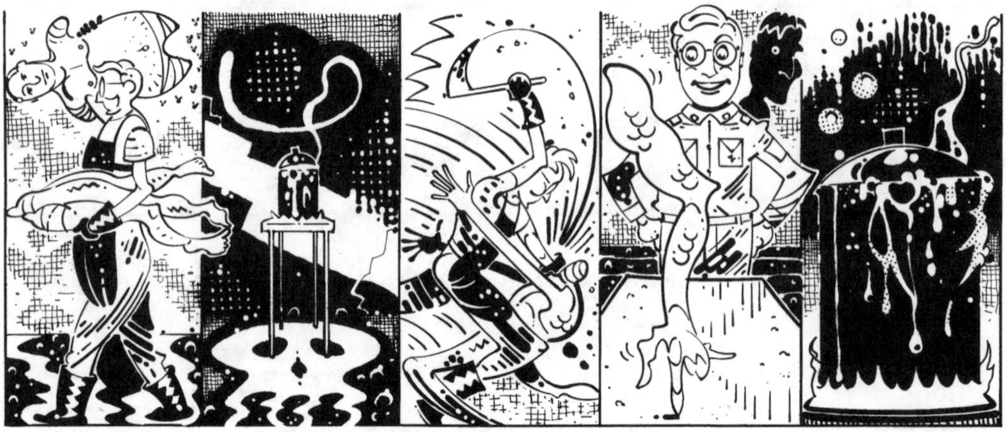

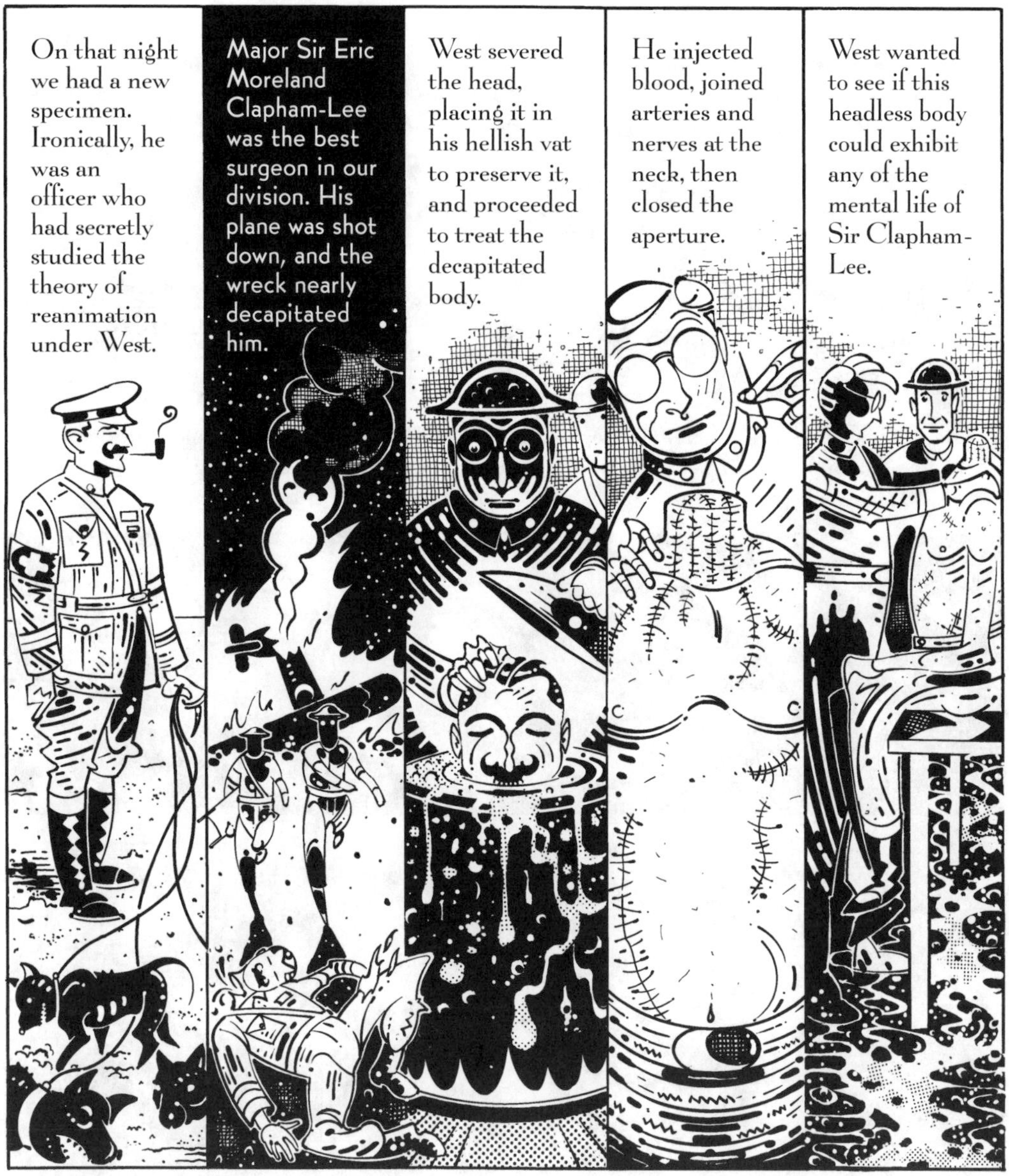
On that night we had a new specimen. Ironically, he was an officer who had secretly studied the theory of reanimation under West.
Major Sir Eric Moreland Clapham-Lee was the best surgeon in our division. His plane was shot down, and the wreck nearly decapitated him.
West severed the head, placing it in his hellish vat to preserve it, and proceeded to treat the decapitated body.
He injected blood, joined arteries and nerves at the neck, then closed the aperture.
West wanted to see if this headless body could exhibit any of the mental life of Sir Clapham-Lee.

I can still see Herbert West as he injected his reanimating solution into the arm of the headless body, with hideous reptilian abnormalities bubbling over a dim flame in the shadows.

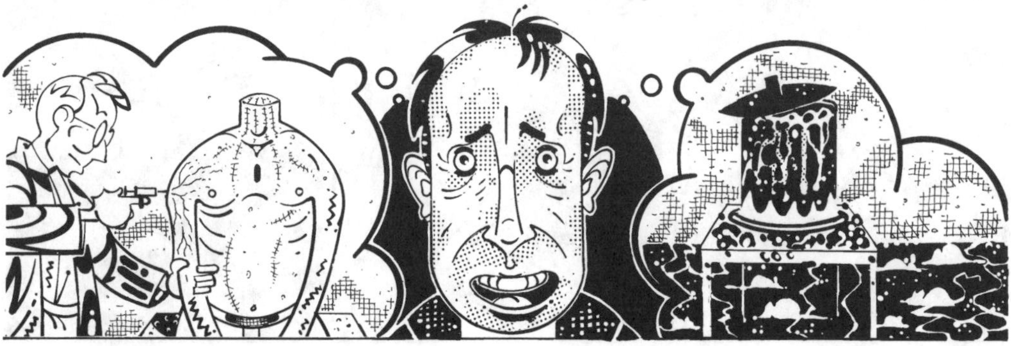

The specimen, as West observed, had a splendid nervous system. As a few twitching motions began to appear, I could see the feverish interest on West's face. In one triumphant demonstration he was about to relegate the mystery of life to the category of myth. The body now twitched more vigorously, and beneath our avid eyes commenced to heave in a frightful way.

The various muscles contracted in a repulsive kind of writhing. Then the headless thing threw out its arms in a gesture which was unmistakably one of desperation — the nerves were recalling the man's last act in life; the struggle to get free of the falling aeroplane.

What followed, I shall never positively know. It may have been wholly an hallucination from the shock caused at that instant by the sudden and complete destruction of the building in a cataclysm of German shell-fire — who can say, since West and I were the only proved survivors?

The body on the table had risen with a blind and terrible groping, and we had heard an awful sound. Its timbre was not the most awful thing about it. Neither was its message — the awful thing was its source.

JUMP, RONALD. FOR GOD'S SAKE, JUMP!

For it had come from the large covered vat in that ghoulish corner of crawling black shadows!

Part Four: **The Tomb-Legions**
adapted & illustrated by **Mark A. Nelson**

When Dr. Herbert West disappeared a year ago, the Boston police questioned me closely. They suspected that I was holding something back, and perhaps suspected graver things; but I could not tell them the truth because they would not have believed it. From the first I had shared West's terrible researches. He had tried to perfect a solution which, injected into the veins of the newly deceased, would restore life; a labour demanding an abundance of fresh corpses. Still more shocking were the products of some of the experiments — grisly masses of flesh that had been dead, but that West waked to a blind, brainless, nauseous animation. These were the usual results, for in order to reawaken the mind it was necessary to have specimens so absolutely fresh that no decay could possibly affect the delicate brain cells.

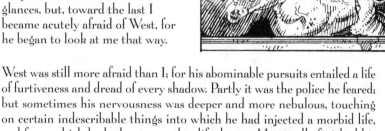

ANOTHER FAILURE! BUT NO MATTER...

West now harbored a soul calloused and seared, and a hardened eye which sometimes glanced with a hideous and calculating appraisal at men of especially sensitive brain and especially vigorous physique. People did not seem to notice his glances, but, toward the last I became acutely afraid of West, for he began to look at me that way.

West was still more afraid than I; for his abominable pursuits entailed a life of furtiveness and dread of every shadow. Partly it was the police he feared; but sometimes his nervousness was deeper and more nebulous, touching on certain indescribable things into which he had injected a morbid life, and from which he had not seen that life depart. He usually finished his experiments with a revolver, but a few times he had not been quick enough.

There was that first specimen on whose rifled grave marks of clawing were later seen. There was also that Arkham professor's body which had done cannibal things before it had been captured and thrust unidentified into a madhouse cell at Sefton. In later years West's scientific zeal had degenerated to an unhealthy and fantastic mania, and he had spent his chief skill in vitalising not entire human bodies but isolated parts of bodies, or parts joined to organic matter other than human.

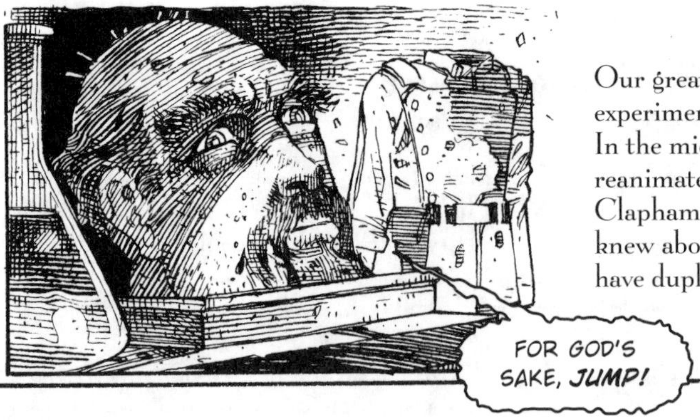
FOR GOD'S SAKE, JUMP!

Our greatest fear stemmed from an experiment in the Canadian army in 1915. In the midst of a severe battle, West had reanimated Major Sir Eric Moreland Clapham-Lee, a fellow-physician who knew about his experiments and could have duplicated them.

The head had been removed, so that the possibilities of quasi-intelligent life in the trunk might be investigated. Just as the building was wiped out by a German shell, the trunk had moved intelligently; and we were both sickeningly sure that articulate sounds had come from the detached head as it lay in a shadowy corner of the laboratory. West could never feel as certain as he wished, that we two were the only survivors. He used to make shuddering conjectures about the possible actions of a headless physician with the power of reanimating the dead.

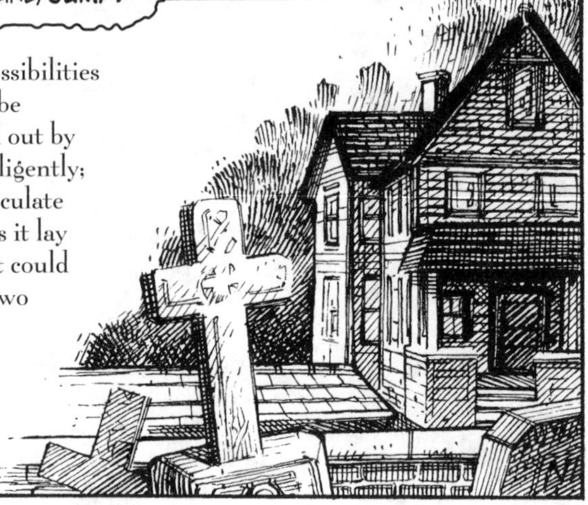

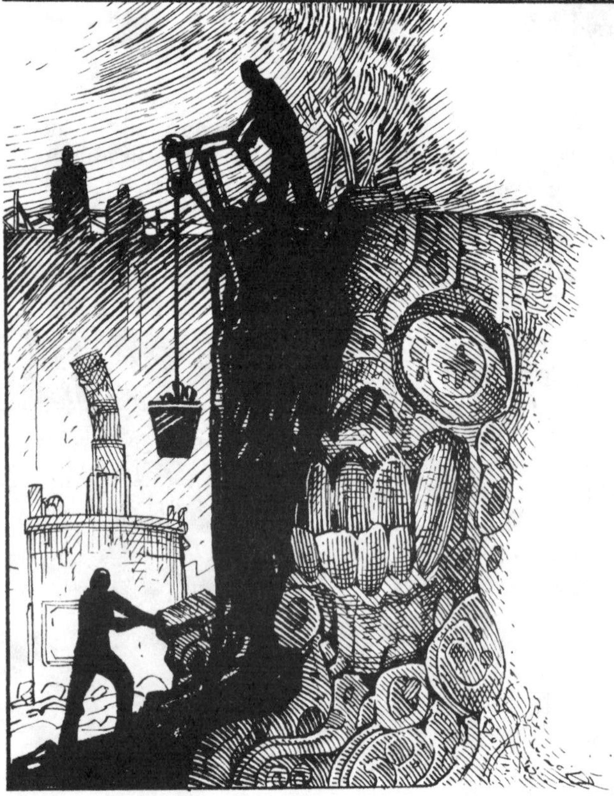

West's last quarters were in a venerable house overlooking one of the oldest burying-grounds in Boston. Most of the interments were of the colonial period and therefore of little use to a scientist seeking fresh bodies. The laboratory was in a sub-cellar secretly constructed by imported workmen, and contained a huge incinerator for the quiet disposal of such bodies, or fragments and mockeries of bodies, as might remain from the morbid experiments of the owner. During the excavation of this cellar the workmen had struck some ancient masonry; undoubtedly connected with the old burying-ground. For the first time West's new timidity conquered his natural curiosity, and he betrayed his degenerating fibre by ordering the masonry left intact and plastered over.

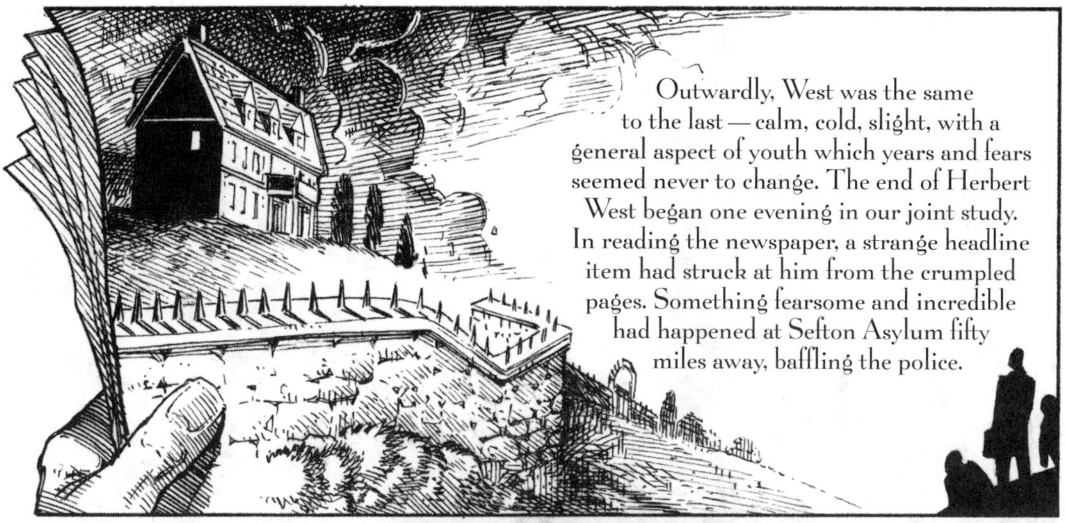
Outwardly, West was the same to the last — calm, cold, slight, with a general aspect of youth which years and fears seemed never to change. The end of Herbert West began one evening in our joint study. In reading the newspaper, a strange headline item had struck at him from the crumpled pages. Something fearsome and incredible had happened at Sefton Asylum fifty miles away, baffling the police.

In the small hours of the morning a body of silent men had entered the grounds, and their leader had aroused the attendants. He was a menacing military figure who talked without moving his lips and whose voice seemed strangely connected with an immense black case he carried.

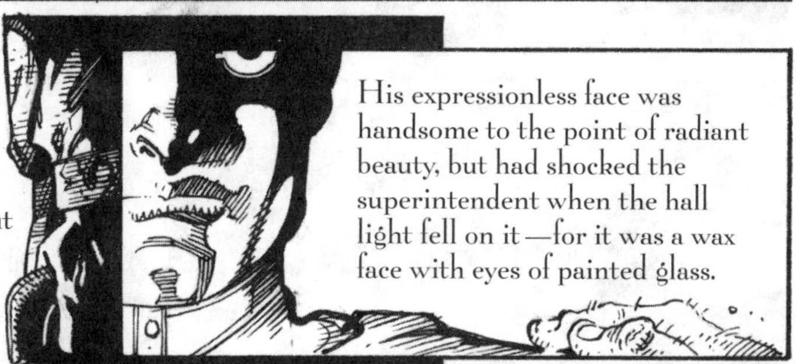
His expressionless face was handsome to the point of radiant beauty, but had shocked the superintendent when the hall light fell on it —for it was a wax face with eyes of painted glass.

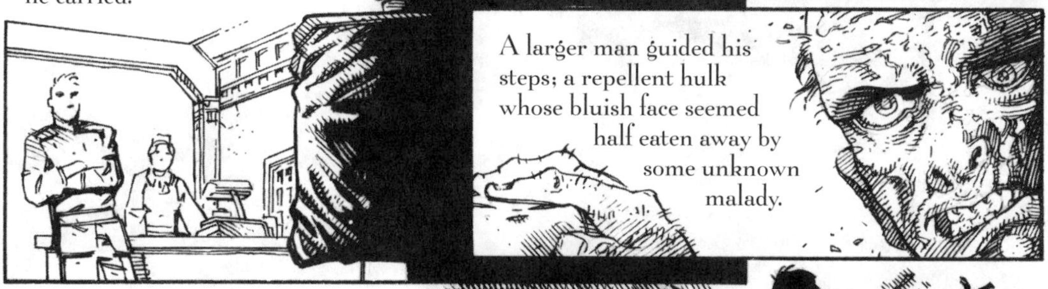
A larger man guided his steps; a repellent hulk whose bluish face seemed half eaten away by some unknown malady.

The speaker had asked for the custody of the cannibal monster committed from Arkham sixteen years before; and when refused, precipitated a shocking riot. The fiends had beaten, trampled, and bitten every attendant who did not flee; killing four and succeeding in the liberation of the monster. Those victims who could recall the event without hysteria swore that the creatures had acted like unthinkable automata guided by the wax-faced leader. By the time help could be summoned, every trace of the men and of their mad charge had vanished.

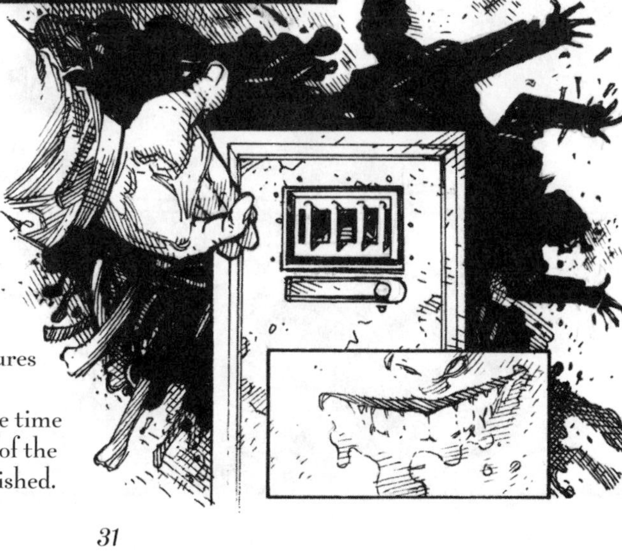

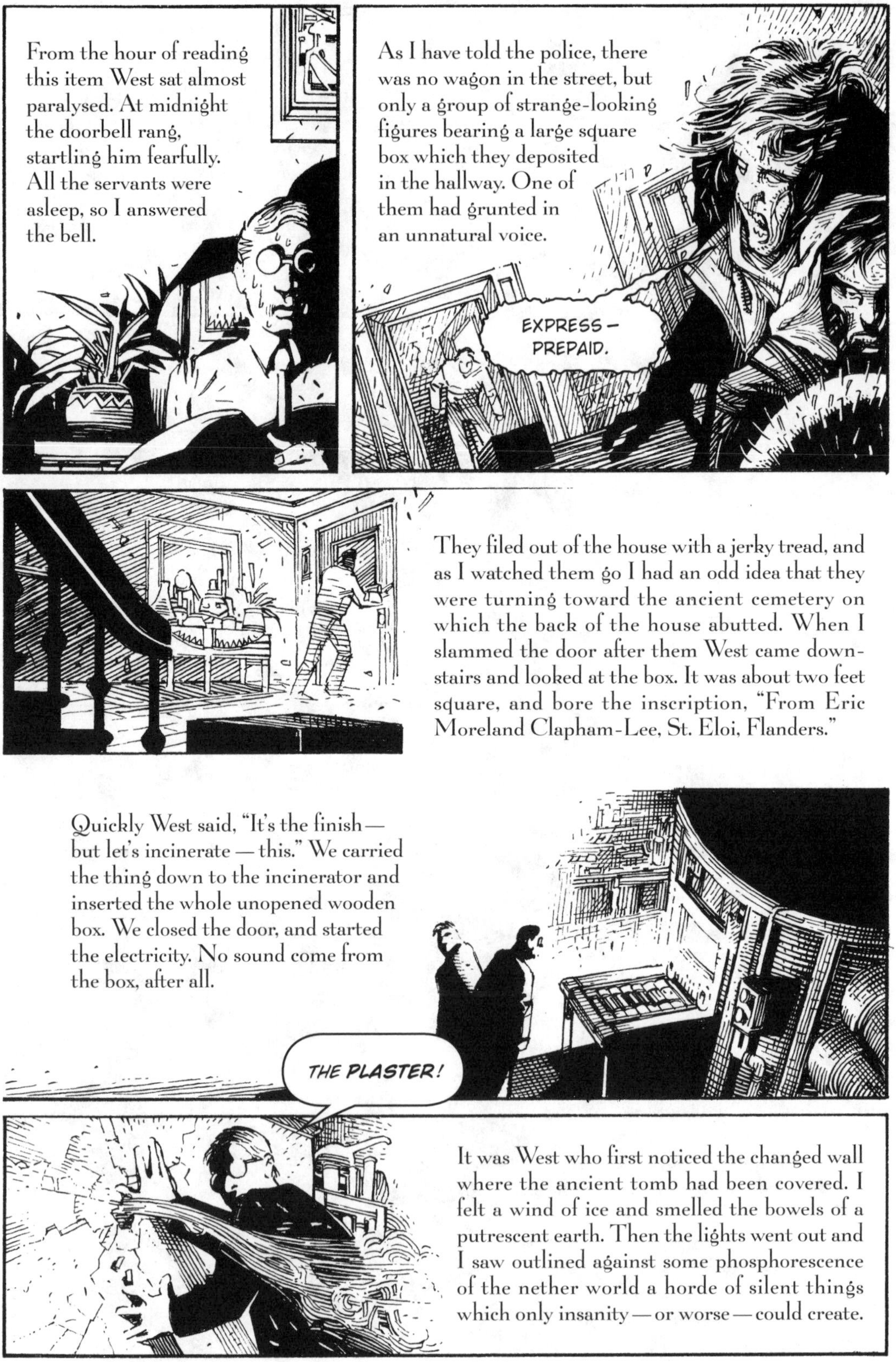
From the hour of reading this item West sat almost paralysed. At midnight the doorbell rang, startling him fearfully. All the servants were asleep, so I answered the bell.
As I have told the police, there was no wagon in the street, but only a group of strange-looking figures bearing a large square box which they deposited in the hallway. One of them had grunted in an unnatural voice.
EXPRESS — PREPAID.
They filed out of the house with a jerky tread, and as I watched them go I had an odd idea that they were turning toward the ancient cemetery on which the back of the house abutted. When I slammed the door after them West came downstairs and looked at the box. It was about two feet square, and bore the inscription, "From Eric Moreland Clapham-Lee, St. Eloi, Flanders."
Quickly West said, "It's the finish — but let's incinerate — this." We carried the thing down to the incinerator and inserted the whole unopened wooden box. We closed the door, and started the electricity. No sound come from the box, after all.
THE PLASTER!
It was West who first noticed the changed wall where the ancient tomb had been covered. I felt a wind of ice and smelled the bowels of a putrescent earth. Then the lights went out and I saw outlined against some phosphorescence of the nether world a horde of silent things which only insanity — or worse — could create.

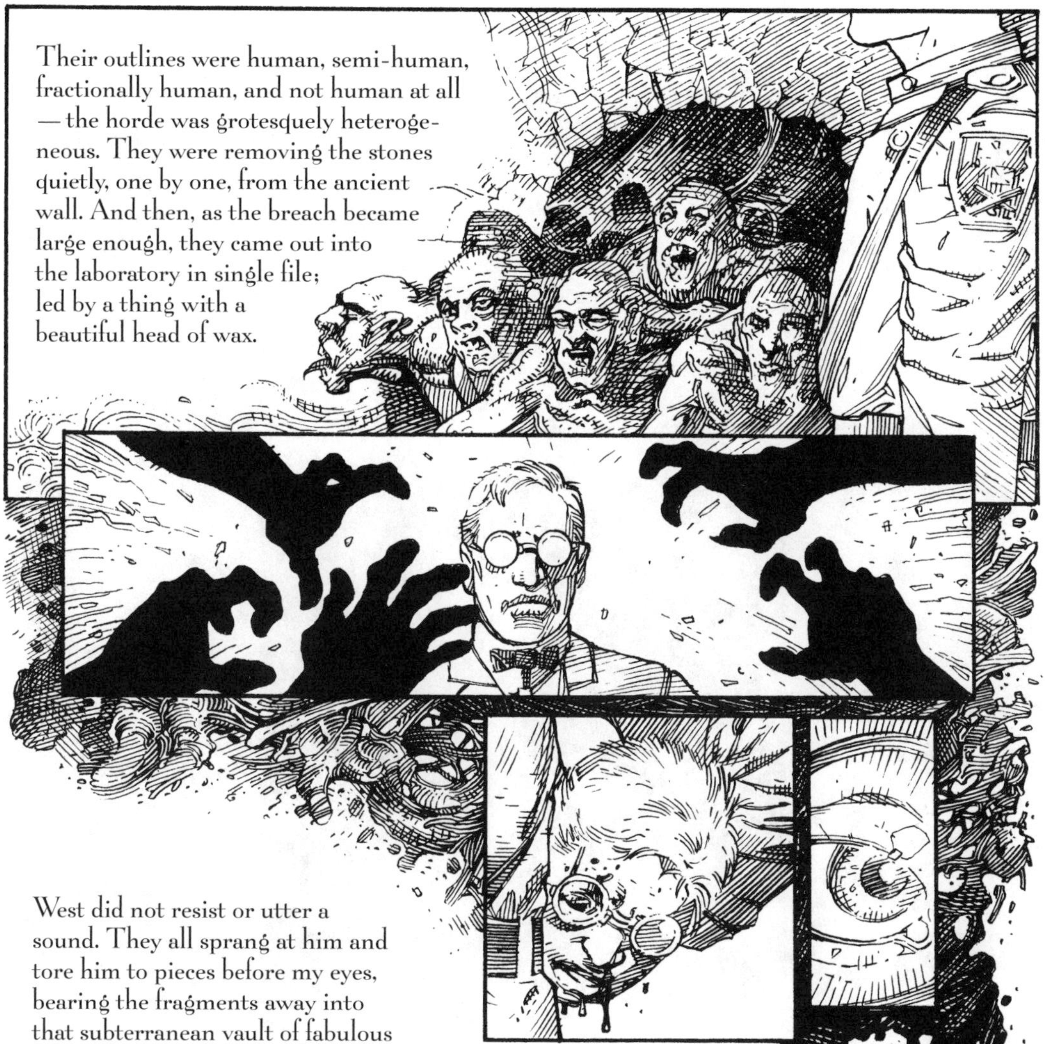

Their outlines were human, semi-human, fractionally human, and not human at all — the horde was grotesquely heterogeneous. They were removing the stones quietly, one by one, from the ancient wall. And then, as the breach became large enough, they came out into the laboratory in single file; led by a thing with a beautiful head of wax.

West did not resist or utter a sound. They all sprang at him and tore him to pieces before my eyes, bearing the fragments away into that subterranean vault of fabulous abominations. West's head was carried off by the wax-headed leader, who wore a Canadian officer's uniform. As it disappeared I saw that the blue eyes behind the spectacles were hideously blazing with their first touch of frantic, visible emotion.

Servants found me unconscious in the morning. West was gone. The incinerator contained only unidentifiable ashes. Detectives have questioned me, but what can I say? I told them of the vault, and they pointed to the unbroken plaster wall and laughed. So I told them no more. They imply that I am either a madman or a murderer — probably I *am* mad. But I might not be mad if not for one thing...

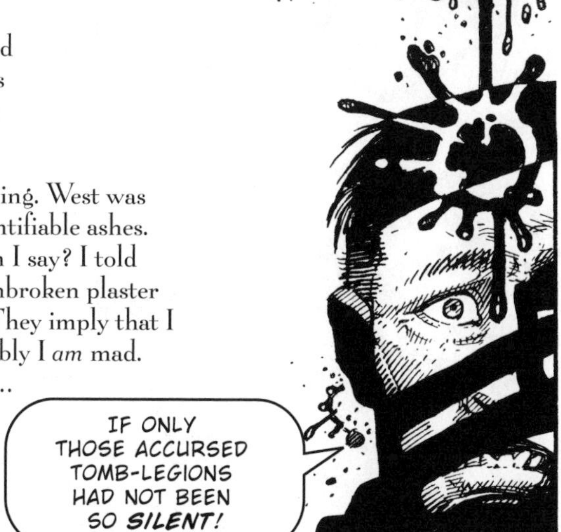
IF ONLY THOSE ACCURSED TOMB-LEGIONS HAD NOT BEEN SO SILENT!

The Dream-Quest of Unknown Kadath

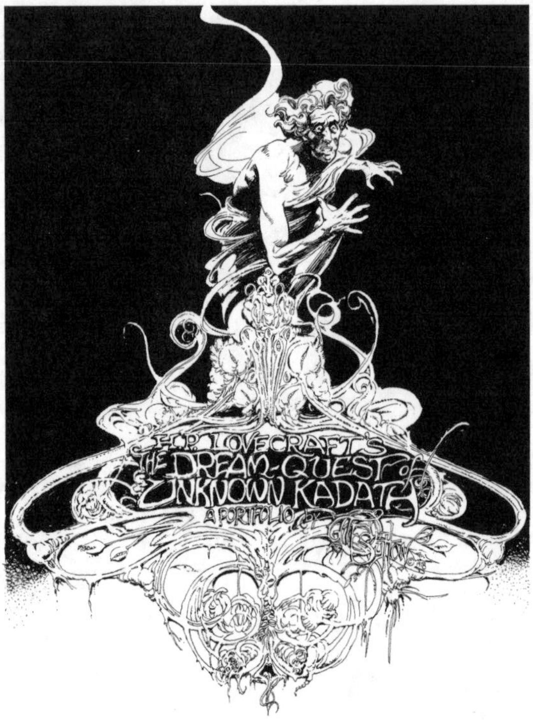
H.P. LOVECRAFT'S
THE DREAM-QUEST of
UNKNOWN KADATH
A PORTFOLIO

A portfolio based on the H.P. Lovecraft novel illustrated by

TOM SUTTON

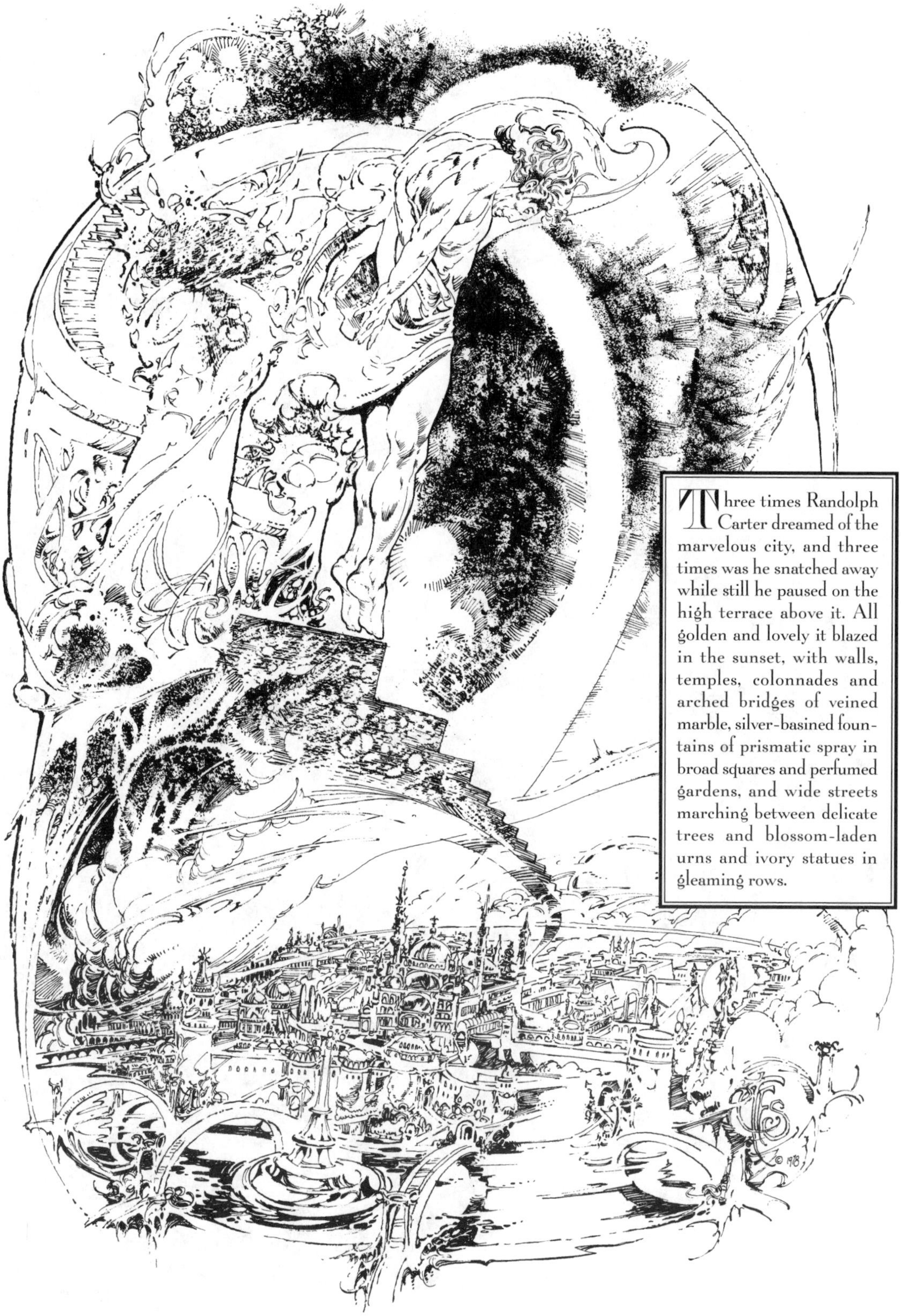
© 1978

Three times Randolph Carter dreamed of the marvelous city, and three times was he snatched away while still he paused on the high terrace above it. All golden and lovely it blazed in the sunset, with walls, temples, colonnades and arched bridges of veined marble, silver-basined fountains of prismatic spray in broad squares and perfumed gardens, and wide streets marching between delicate trees and blossom-laden urns and ivory statues in gleaming rows.

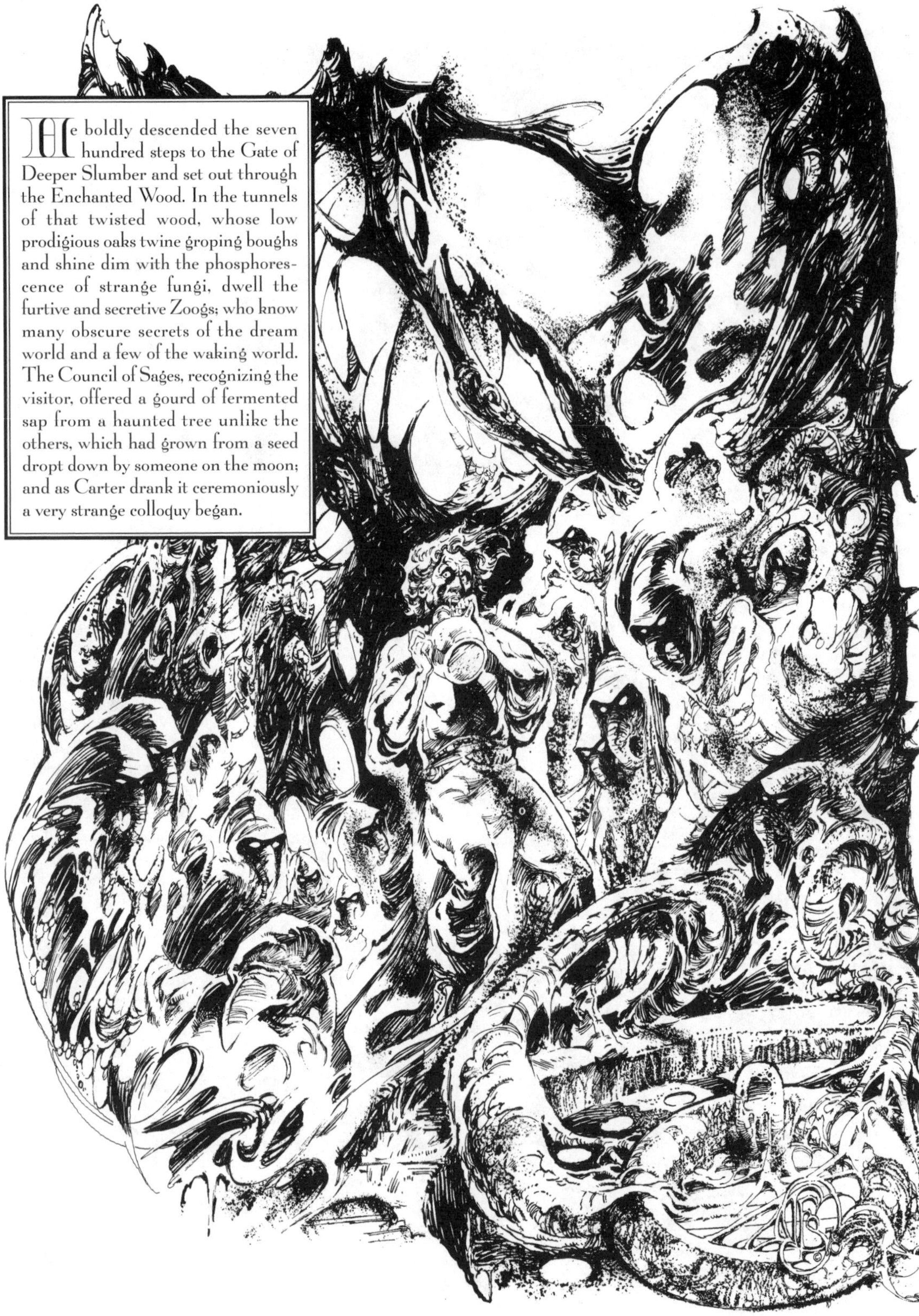
He boldly descended the seven hundred steps to the Gate of Deeper Slumber and set out through the Enchanted Wood. In the tunnels of that twisted wood, whose low prodigious oaks twine groping boughs and shine dim with the phosphorescence of strange fungi, dwell the furtive and secretive Zoogs; who know many obscure secrets of the dream world and a few of the waking world. The Council of Sages, recognizing the visitor, offered a gourd of fermented sap from a haunted tree unlike the others, which had grown from a seed dropt down by someone on the moon; and as Carter drank it ceremoniously a very strange colloquy began.

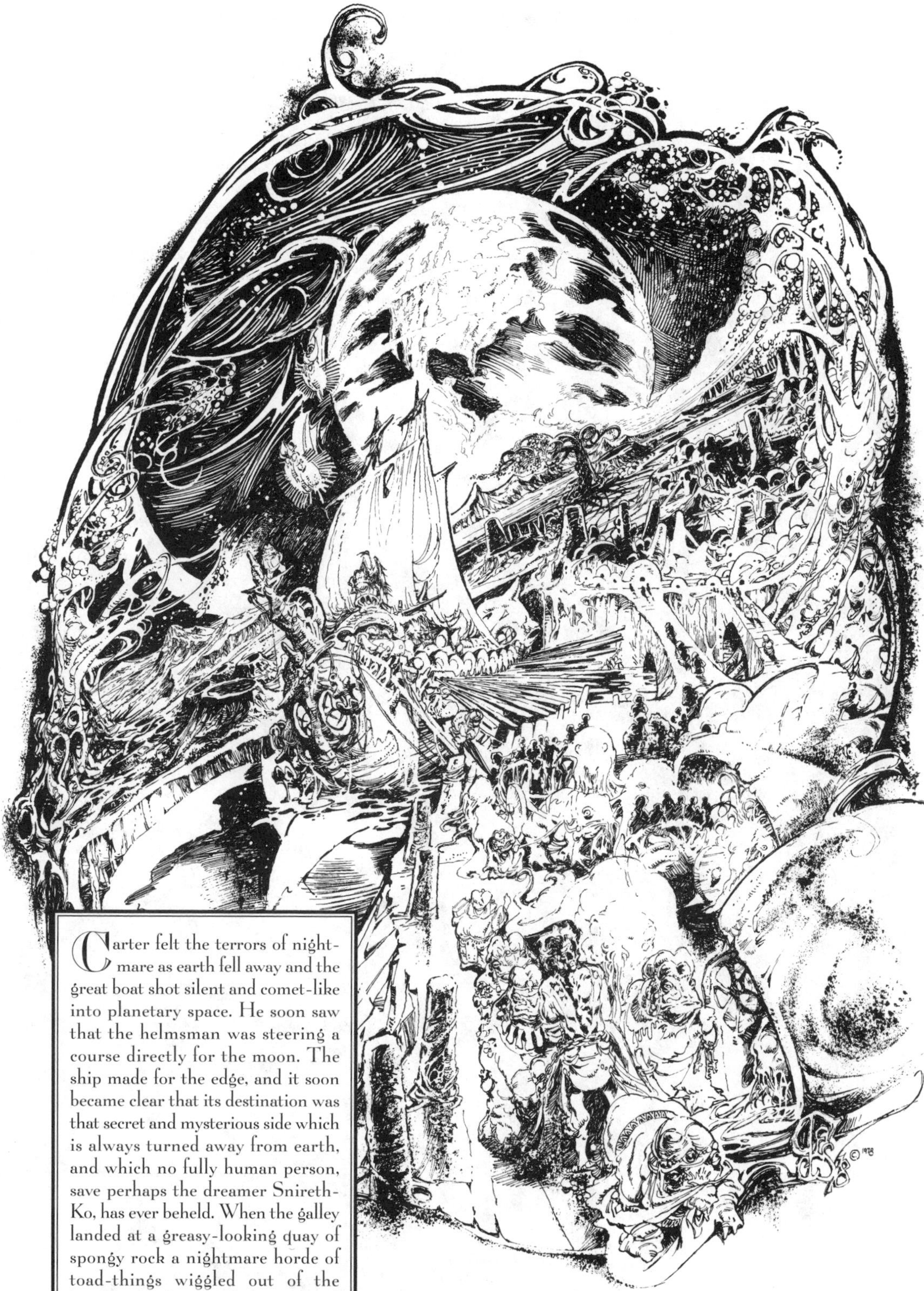

Carter felt the terrors of nightmare as earth fell away and the great boat shot silent and comet-like into planetary space. He soon saw that the helmsman was steering a course directly for the moon. The ship made for the edge, and it soon became clear that its destination was that secret and mysterious side which is always turned away from earth, and which no fully human person, save perhaps the dreamer Snireth-Ko, has ever beheld. When the galley landed at a greasy-looking quay of spongy rock a nightmare horde of toad-things wiggled out of the hatches, and two of them seized Carter and dragged him ashore.

The speech of cats was known to Randolph Carter, and in this far terrible place he uttered the cry that was suitable. The call of the clan had been given, and before the foul procession had time even to be frightened a cloud of smothering fur and a phalanx of murderous claws were tidally and tempestuously upon it. Dying almost-humans screamed, and cats spit and yowled and roared, but the toad-things made never a sound as their stinking green ichor oozed fatally upon that porous earth with the obscene fungi. It was a stupendous sight while the torches lasted, and Carter had never before seen so many cats. He had seized a torch from a stricken slave, but was soon overborne by the surging waves of his loyal defenders. Then he lay in the utter blackness hearing the clangour of war and the shouts of the victors, and feeling the soft paws of his friends as they rushed to and fro over him in the fray.

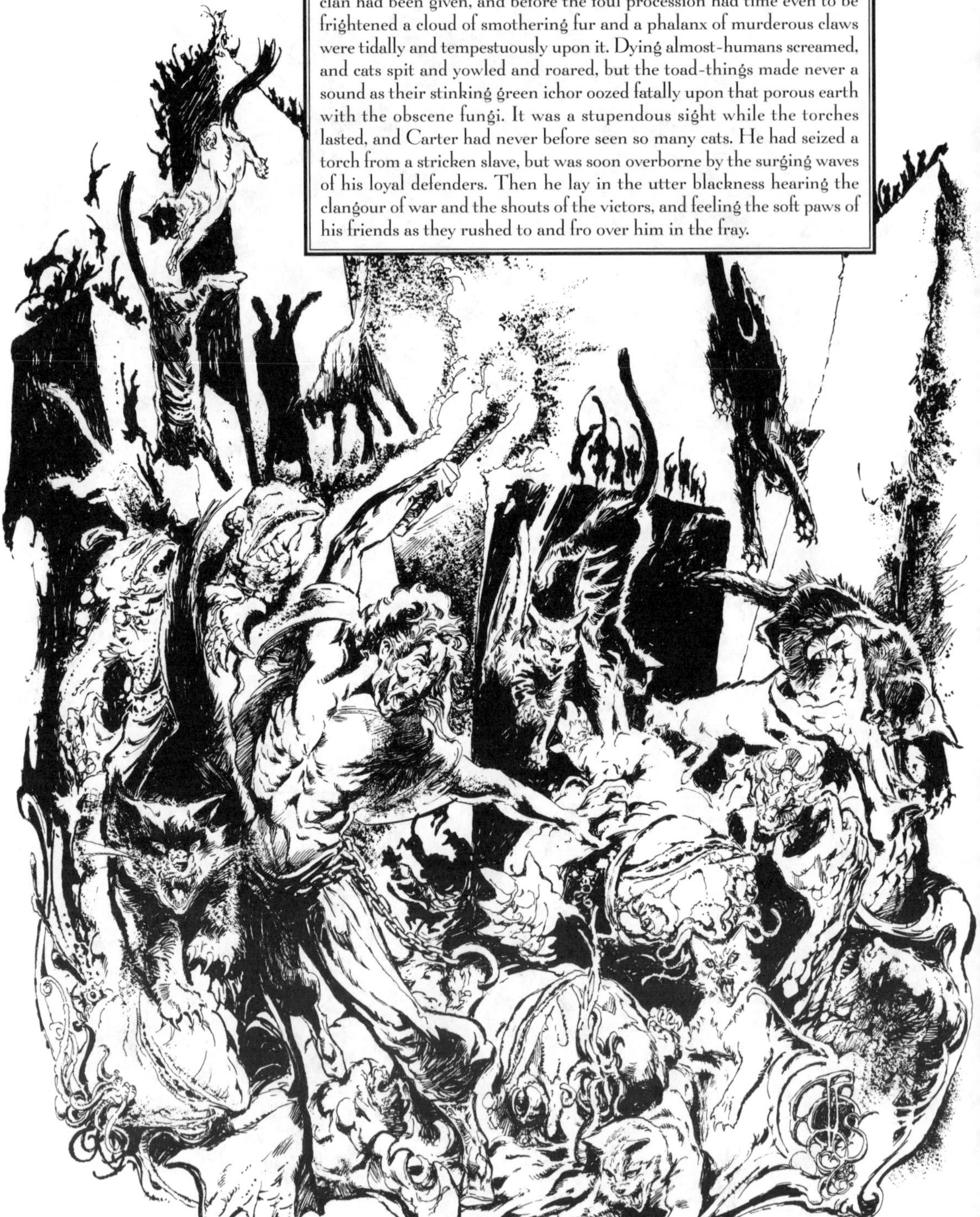

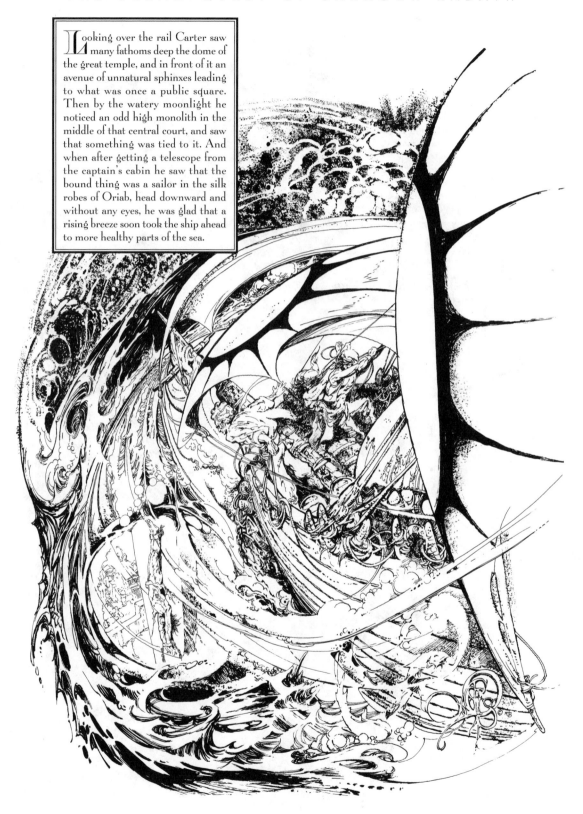

Looking over the rail Carter saw many fathoms deep the dome of the great temple, and in front of it an avenue of unnatural sphinxes leading to what was once a public square. Then by the watery moonlight he noticed an odd high monolith in the middle of that central court, and saw that something was tied to it. And when after getting a telescope from the captain's cabin he saw that the bound thing was a sailor in the silk robes of Oriab, head downward and without any eyes, he was glad that a rising breeze soon took the ship ahead to more healthy parts of the sea.

39

The slant-eyed merchant motioned Carter to mount one of the repugnant Shantaks, helping him up as his judgement struggled with his loathing. Once he was seated, the man hopped up behind him and there followed a hideous whirl through frigid space, endlessly up and eastward toward the gaunt grey flanks of those impassable mountains beyond which Leng was said to be. Far above the clouds they flew, till at last there lay beneath them those fabled summits which the folk of Inquanok have never seen, and which lie always in high vortices of gleaming mist.

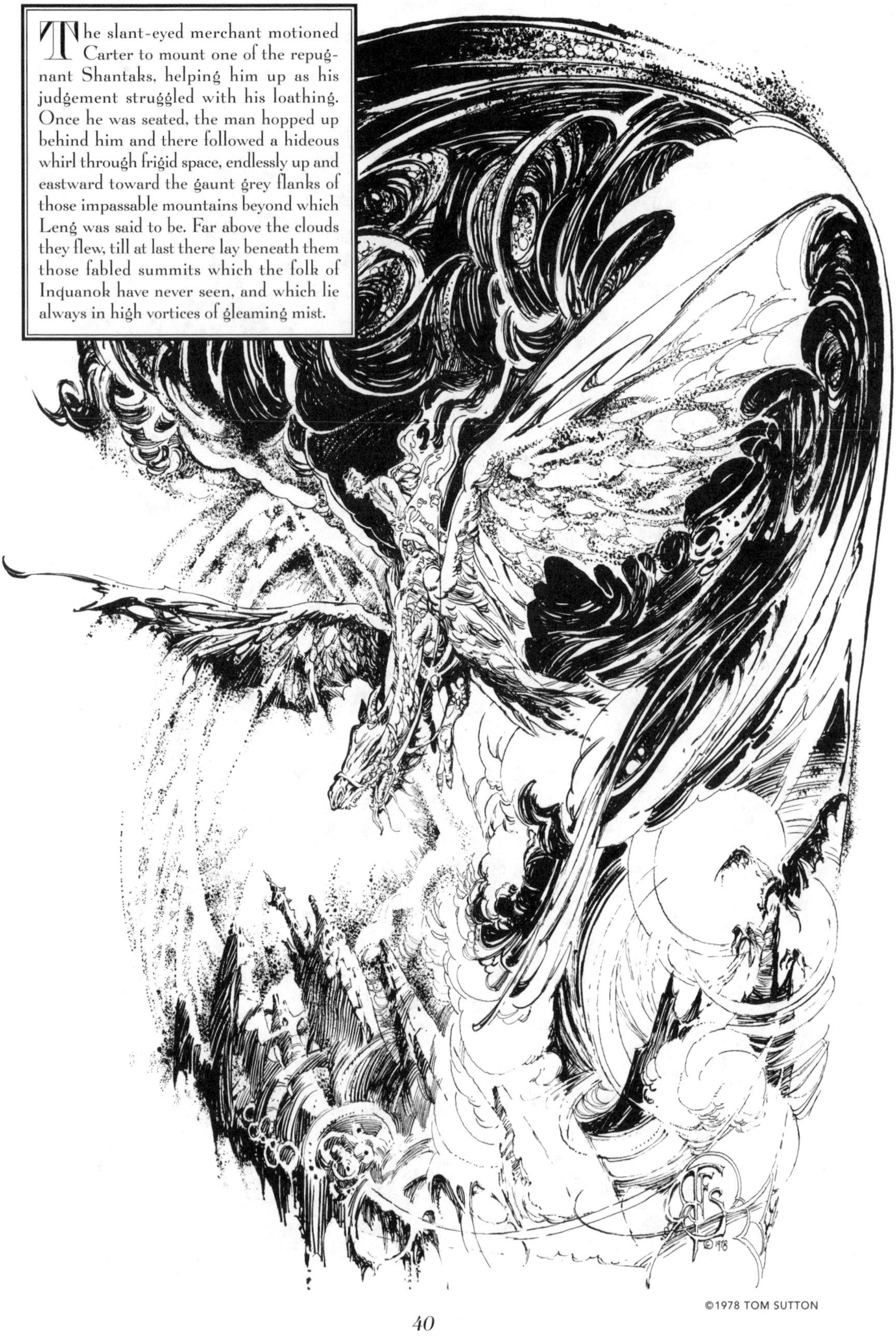

THE OUTSIDER

illustrated by

DEVON DEVEREAUX

story by

H.P. LOVECRAFT

edited and abridged by Tom Pomplun

Unhappy is he to whom the memories of childhood bring only fear and sadness. I know not where I was born, save that the castle was infinitely old and infinitely horrible. The stones in the crumbling corridors seemed always hideously damp, and there was an accursed smell everywhere. It was never light, since the terrible trees grew high above the topmost towers. There was but one black tower which reached above the trees, but that was partly ruined and could not be ascended save by a nearly impossible climb up the sheer wall.

I cannot recall any person except myself, or anything alive but the noiseless rats and bats and spiders. Skeletons strewed the stone crypts deep down among the foundations. I thought them more natural than the pictures of living beings which I found in many of the mouldy books from which I learned all that I know. I regarded myself by instinct as akin to the youthful figures I saw painted in the books.

So through endless twilights I dreamed, and at last I resolved to scale the black tower, fall though I might; since it were better to glimpse the sky and perish than to live without ever beholding day.

I climbed the aged stairs till they ceased, and thereafter clung perilously to small footholds leading upward. Ghastly and terrible was the slowness of my progress, but after an infinity of sightless crawling up that desperate precipice, I felt my head touch a solid thing, and I knew I must have gained the roof. In the darkness I tested the barrier, pushing the stone slab with my head as I used both hands in my fearful ascent. The slab was a trapdoor leading to a level stone surface of great circumference. I crawled through carefully, and tried to prevent the heavy slab from falling back into place, but failed in the attempt.

Believing I was now far above the accursed branches of the wood, I fumbled about for windows, that I might look for the first time upon the sky. But all that I found were vast shelves of marble, bearing oblong boxes of disturbing size. Then my hands came upon a doorway, where hung a portal of stone. With a burst of strength I dragged it open. As I did so there came to me the

purest ecstasy I have ever known; for shining through an ornate grating was the radiant full moon, which I had never before seen save in vague visions I dared not call memories.

Fancying that I had finally attained the pinnacle of the castle, I commenced to rush up the few steps beyond the door. Nothing could compare in terror with what I now saw. Instead of treetops, seen from a lofty eminence, there stretched around me nothing less than the solid ground, decked by marble slabs and columns and overshadowed by an ancient stone church.

I opened the grating and staggered out upon the white gravel path. My mind still held the frantic craving for light. I knew not who I was or what I was, though as I continued to stumble along I became conscious of a kind of fearsome latent memory that made my progress not wholly fortuitous. I passed under an arch out of that region of slabs and columns and wandered through the open country.

Over two hours must have passed before I reached what seemed to be my goal, a castle maddeningly familiar, yet full of perplexing strangeness to me. But what I observed with chief interest were the open windows – ablaze with light and sending forth sound of the gayest revelry. Advancing to one of these I looked in and saw an oddly dressed company making merry and speaking brightly to one another.

I stepped through the low window into the brilliantly lighted room. Scarcely had I crossed the sill when there descended upon the whole company a sudden fear of hideous intensity, evoking the most horrible screams from nearly every throat. Many covered their eyes with their hands, and plunged blindly and awkwardly in their race to escape through one of the many doors.

As I stood alone and dazed, I trembled at the thought of what might be lurking near me unseen. The room seemed deserted, but when I moved towards one of the alcoves I thought I detected a presence – a hint of motion beyond the arched doorway leading to a similar room. As I

approached the arch I
began to perceive the
presence more clearly;
and then I beheld in
frightful vividness
the inconceivable mon-
strosity which had by
its simple appearance
changed a merry com-
pany to a herd of
delirious fugitives.

I cannot even hint
what it was like, for it
was a compound of
all that is unclean,
abnormal, and detest-
able. Yet to my horror
I saw in its outlines
an abhorrent travesty
on the human shape;
and in its disintegrating
apparel an unspeakable
quality that chilled me
even more.

I threw out a hand
to ward off the foetid
apparition which pressed
so close; when in one
cataclysmic second
of hellish accident my
fingers touched the
rotting outstretched
paw of the monster
beneath the golden arch.

In that same second
there crashed down
upon my mind a fleet-
ing avalanche of
memory. I remembered
beyond the frightful
castle and the trees,
and recognized the
edifice in which I now
stood; I recognized,
most terrible of all,
the unholy abomina-
tion that stood before
me as I withdrew my
sullied fingers from
its own.

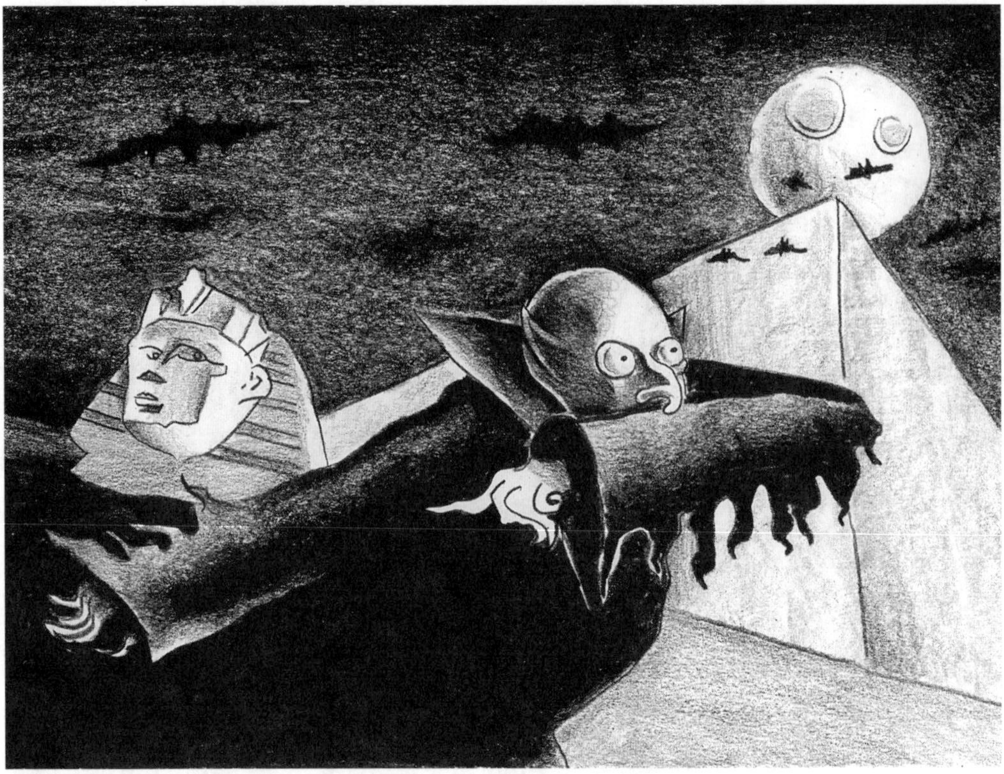

©2002 DEVON DEVEREAUX

But in the cosmos there is balm as well as bitterness, and that balm is nepenthe. In the supreme horror of that second I forgot what had horrified me, and the burst of black memory vanished in a chaos of echoing images. In a dream I fled from that accursed pile, and ran swiftly and silently in the moonlight. When I returned to the churchyard place of marble and went down the steps I found the stone trapdoor immovable; but I was not sorry, for I had hated the antique castle and the trees. Now I ride with the ghouls on the night wind, and play by day amongst the catacombs of Nephren-Ka in the sealed and unknown valley of Hadoth by the Nile. I know that light is not for me, nor any gaiety save the unnamed feasts of Nitokris beneath the Great Pyramid; yet in my new wildness and freedom I almost welcome the bitterness of alienage.

For I know always that I am an outsider; a stranger in this century and among those who are still men. This I have known ever since I stretched out my fingers to the abomination within that great gilded frame; stretched out my fingers and touched a cold and unyielding surface of polished glass. §

The Shadow Out of Time

adapted & illustrated by

MATT HOWARTH

story by

H.P. LOVECRAFT

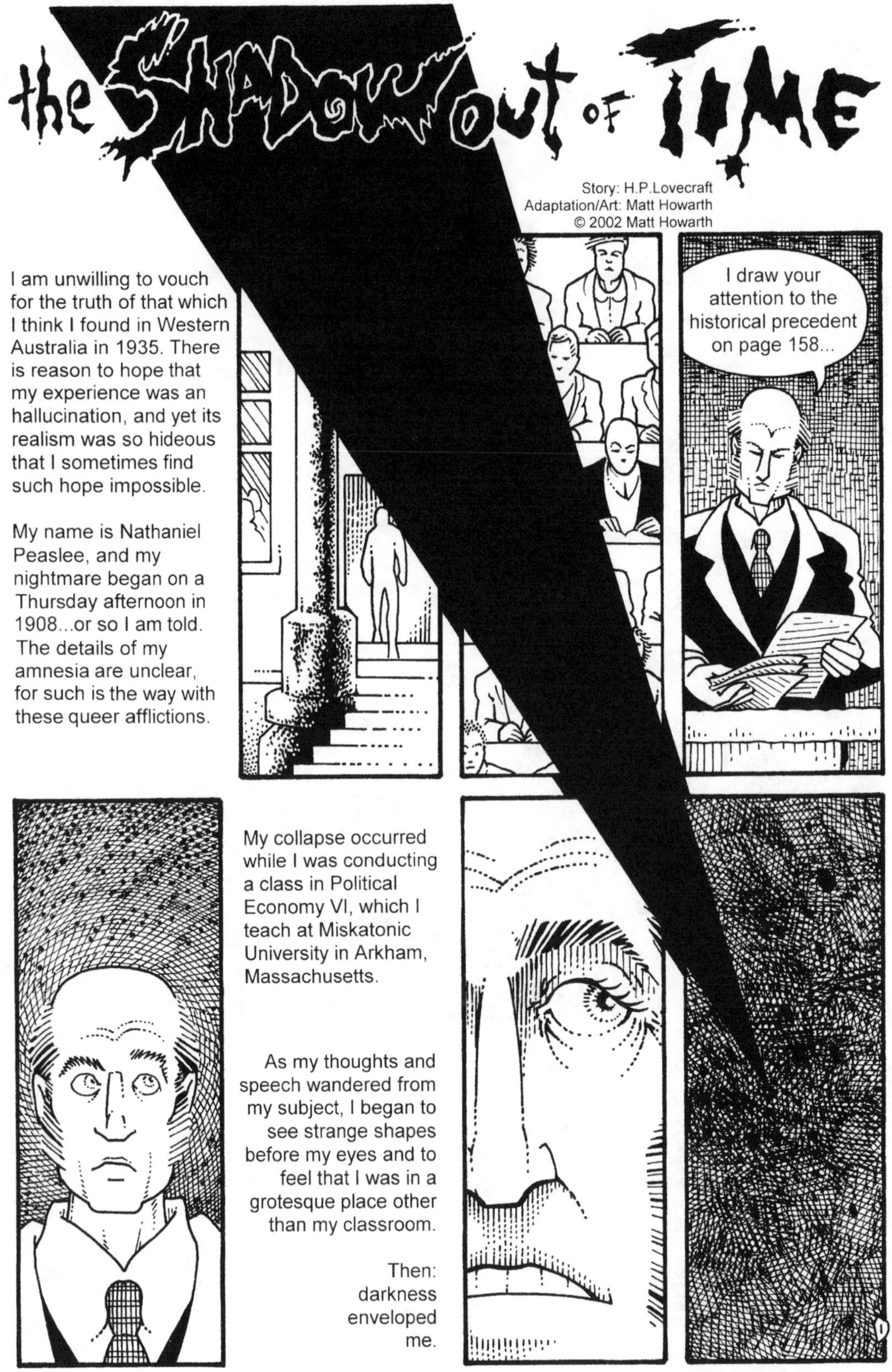
the SHADOW out of TIME
Story: H.P.Lovecraft
Adaptation/Art: Matt Howarth
© 2002 Matt Howarth
I am unwilling to vouch for the truth of that which I think I found in Western Australia in 1935. There is reason to hope that my experience was an hallucination, and yet its realism was so hideous that I sometimes find such hope impossible.
My name is Nathaniel Peaslee, and my nightmare began on a Thursday afternoon in 1908...or so I am told. The details of my amnesia are unclear, for such is the way with these queer afflictions.
I draw your attention to the historical precedent on page 158...
My collapse occurred while I was conducting a class in Political Economy VI, which I teach at Miskatonic University in Arkham, Massachusetts.
As my thoughts and speech wandered from my subject, I began to see strange shapes before my eyes and to feel that I was in a grotesque place other than my classroom.
Then: darkness enveloped me.

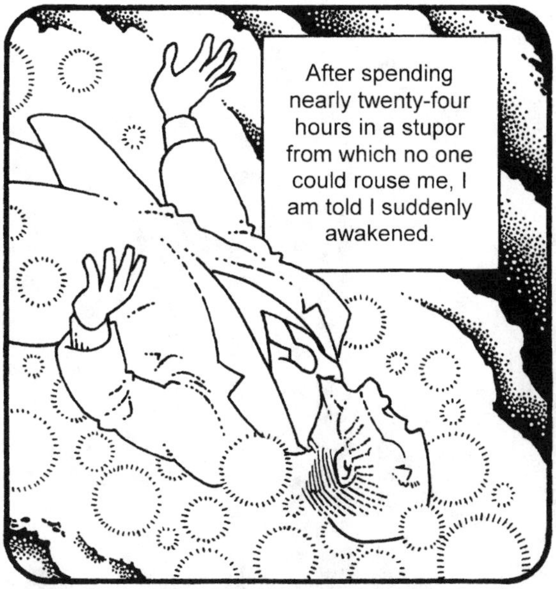
After spending nearly twenty-four hours in a stupor from which no one could rouse me, I am told I suddenly awakened.

It is, of course, from others that I have learned what followed. I have no recollection of the next five years.

Apparently, my recovery was problematic. My coordination was awkward, and my tongue was foreign. I laboriously learned the English language from books, but my pronunciation was barbarously alien.

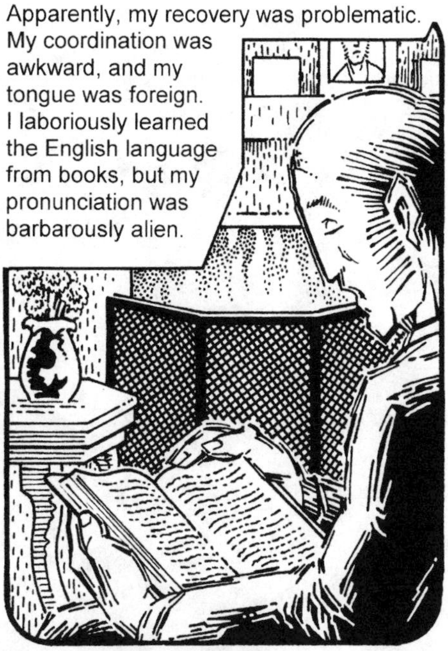

My travels were equally extreme, involving long visits to remote and desolate places.

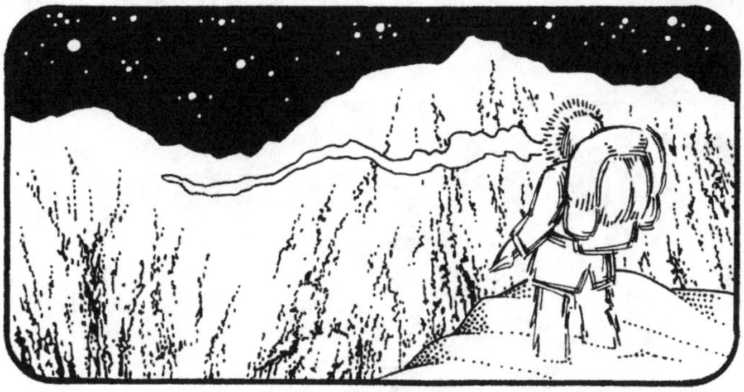

In 1909, I spent a month in the Himalayas.

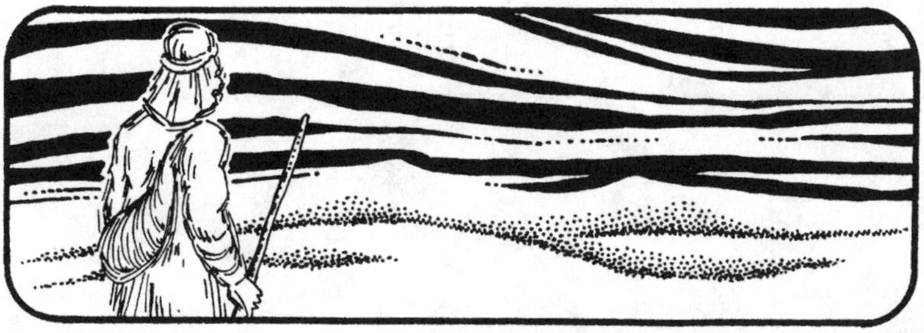

In 1911, I aroused much attention by traveling into the unknown deserts of Arabia. What happened on those journeys I have never been able to learn.

During the summer of 1912, I chartered a ship and sailed in the Arctic, afterward showing signs of disappointment.

There were rumors concerning my intimacy with leaders of occultist groups.

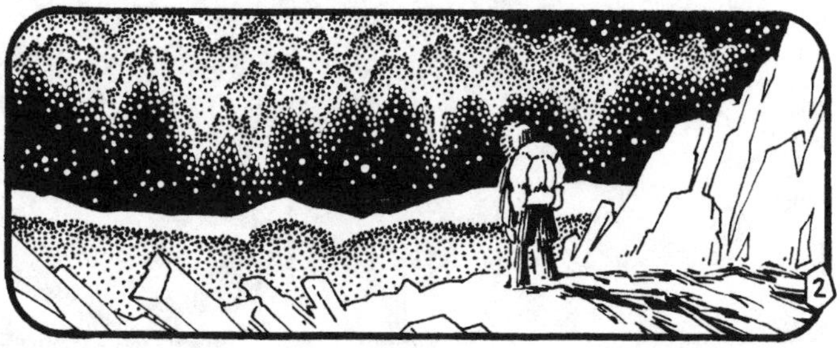
2

By 1913, I had returned to Arkham to assemble in secret a mechanism of the most curious aspect, constructed piecemeal by different makers of scientific apparatus in Europe.

After dismissing my housekeeper one evening that September, I was visited by a strange foreigner.

In the morning, my amnesia was gone.

—Jevon's attempt to link the economic cycle of prosperity and depression with the celestial cycle of sunspot activity forms a—

—what— Where am I? Where has my class gone?

Also gone was every scrap of evidence concerning my actions during the last five years. Of the curious mechanism, there was no trace.

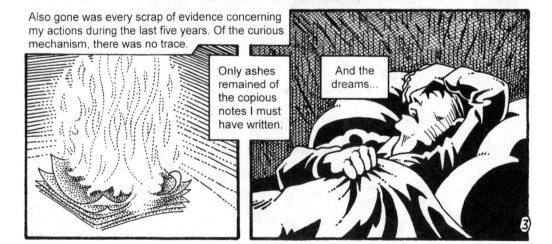

Only ashes remained of the copious notes I must have written.

And the dreams...

3

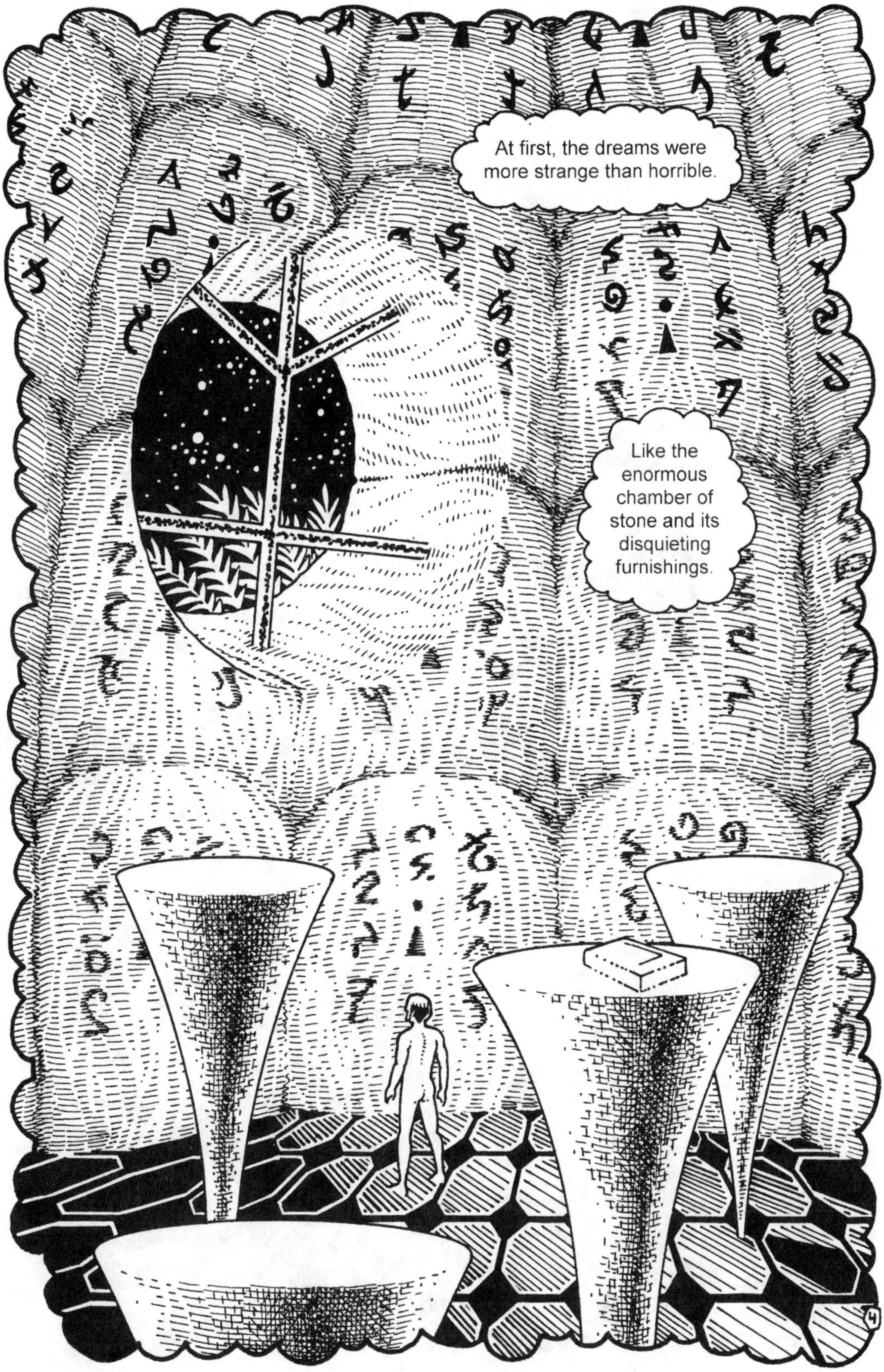
At first, the dreams were more strange than horrible.
Like the enormous chamber of stone and its disquieting furnishings.

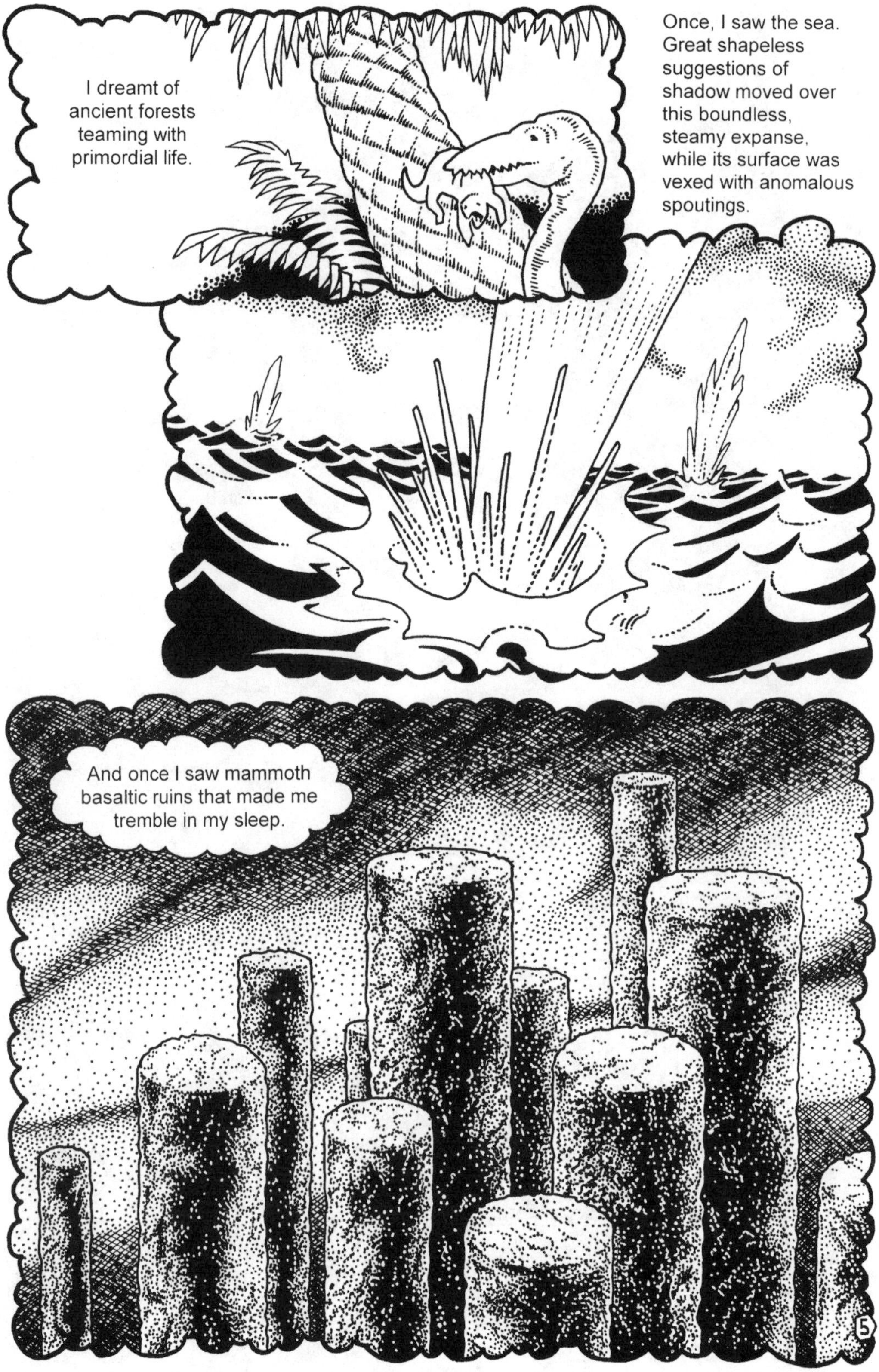
I dreamt of ancient forests teaming with primordial life.
Once, I saw the sea. Great shapeless suggestions of shadow moved over this boundless, steamy expanse, while its surface was vexed with anomalous spoutings.
And once I saw mammoth basaltic ruins that made me tremble in my sleep.
5

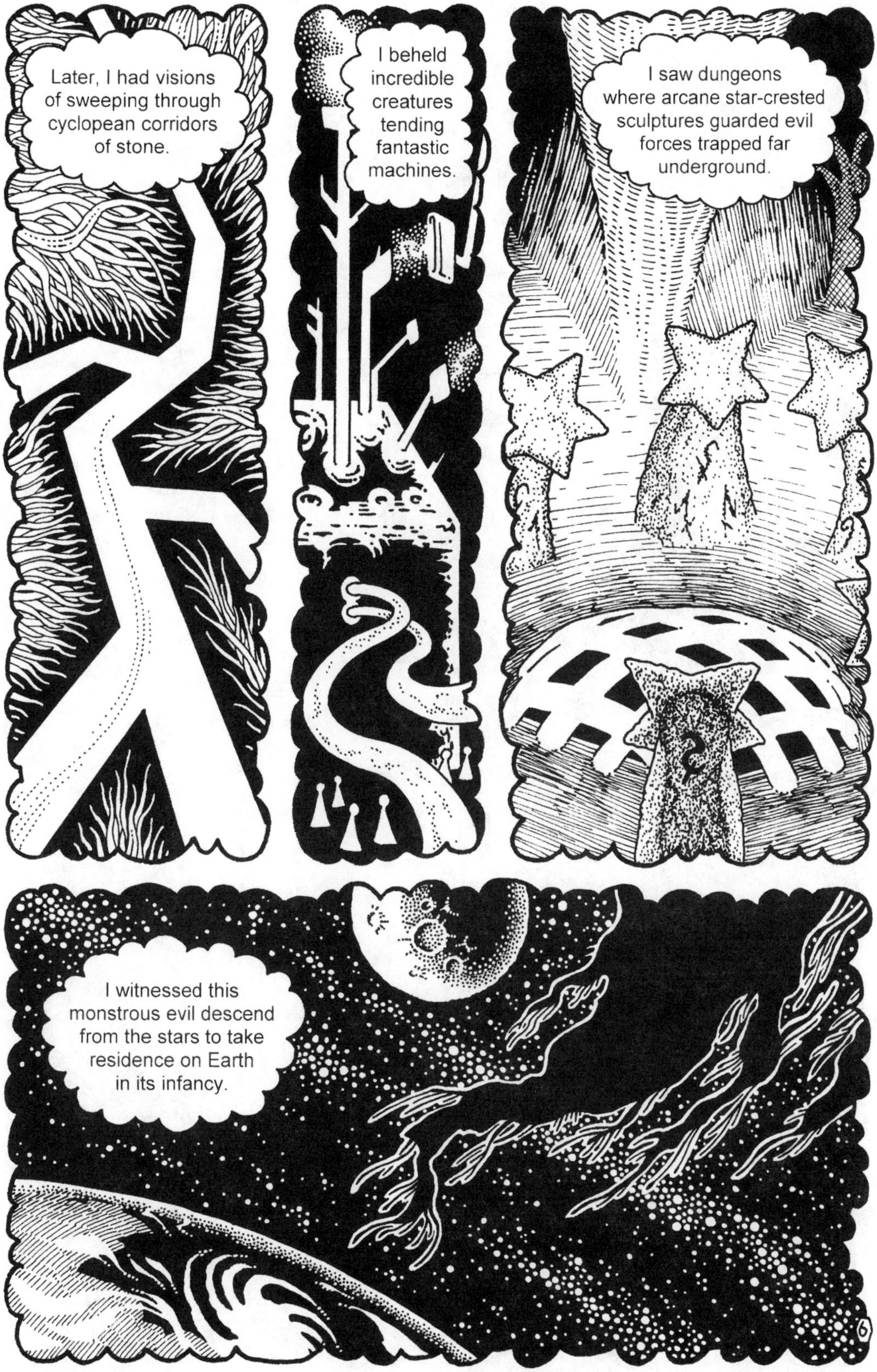
Later, I had visions of sweeping through cyclopean corridors of stone.
I beheld incredible creatures tending fantastic machines.
I saw dungeons where arcane star-crested sculptures guarded evil forces trapped far underground.
I witnessed this monstrous evil descend from the stars to take residence on Earth in its infancy.

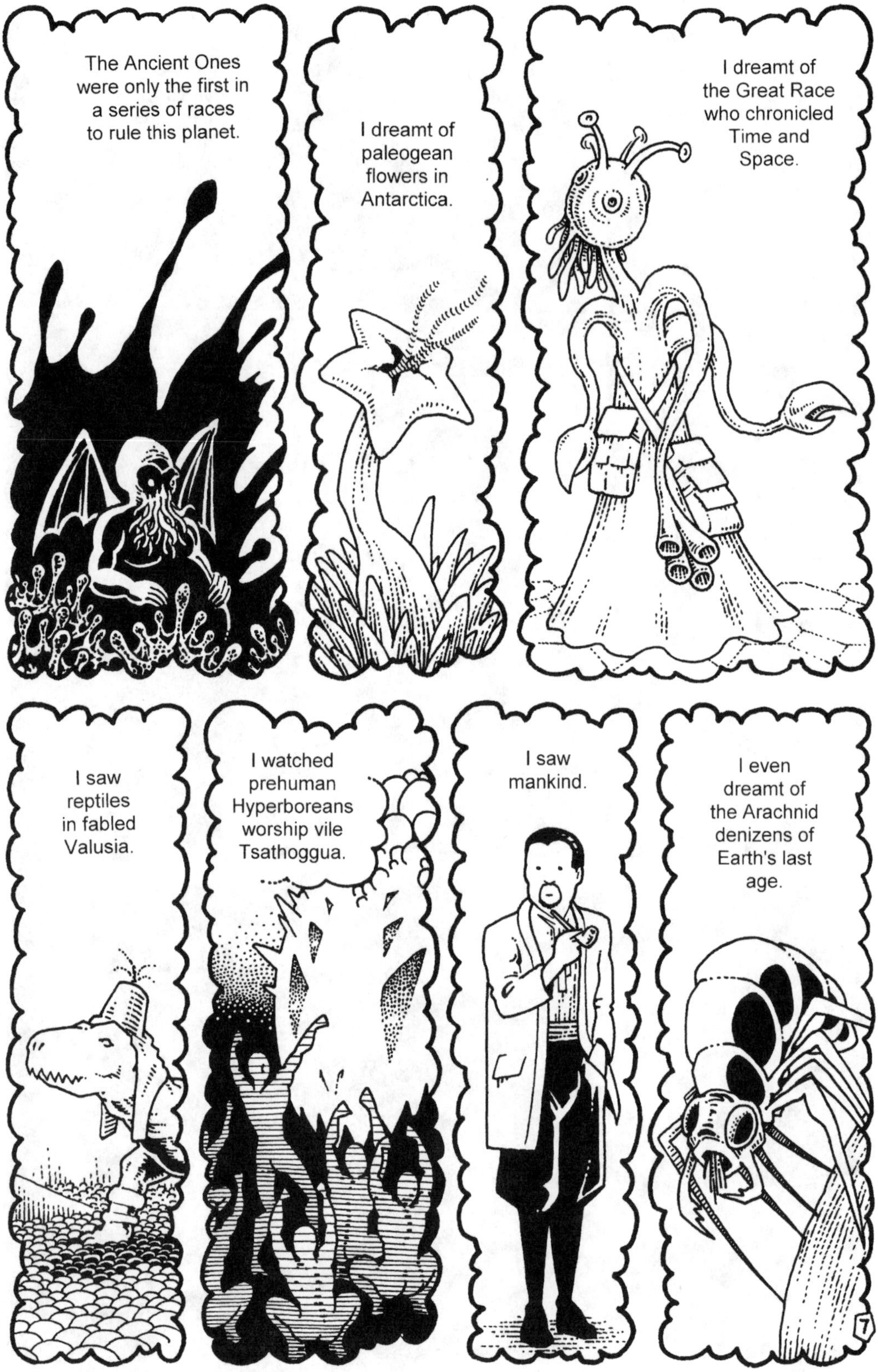
The Ancient Ones were only the first in a series of races to rule this planet.
I dreamt of paleogean flowers in Antarctica.
I dreamt of the Great Race who chronicled Time and Space.
I saw reptiles in fabled Valusia.
I watched prehuman Hyperboreans worship vile Tsathoggua.
I saw mankind.
I even dreamt of the Arachnid denizens of Earth's last age.
7

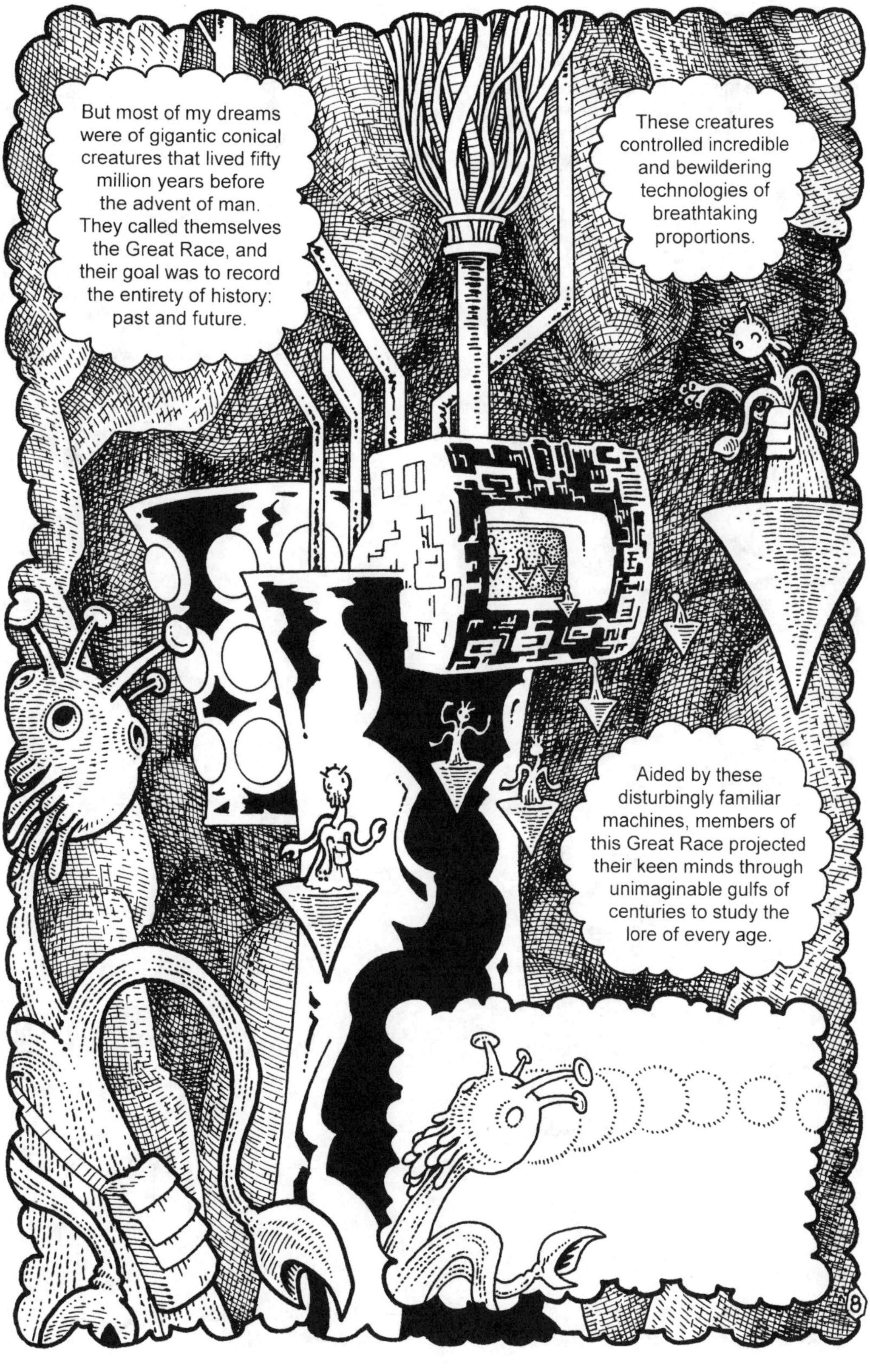
But most of my dreams were of gigantic conical creatures that lived fifty million years before the advent of man. They called themselves the Great Race, and their goal was to record the entirety of history: past and future.
These creatures controlled incredible and bewildering technologies of breathtaking proportions.
Aided by these disturbingly familiar machines, members of this Great Race projected their keen minds through unimaginable gulfs of centuries to study the lore of every age.
8

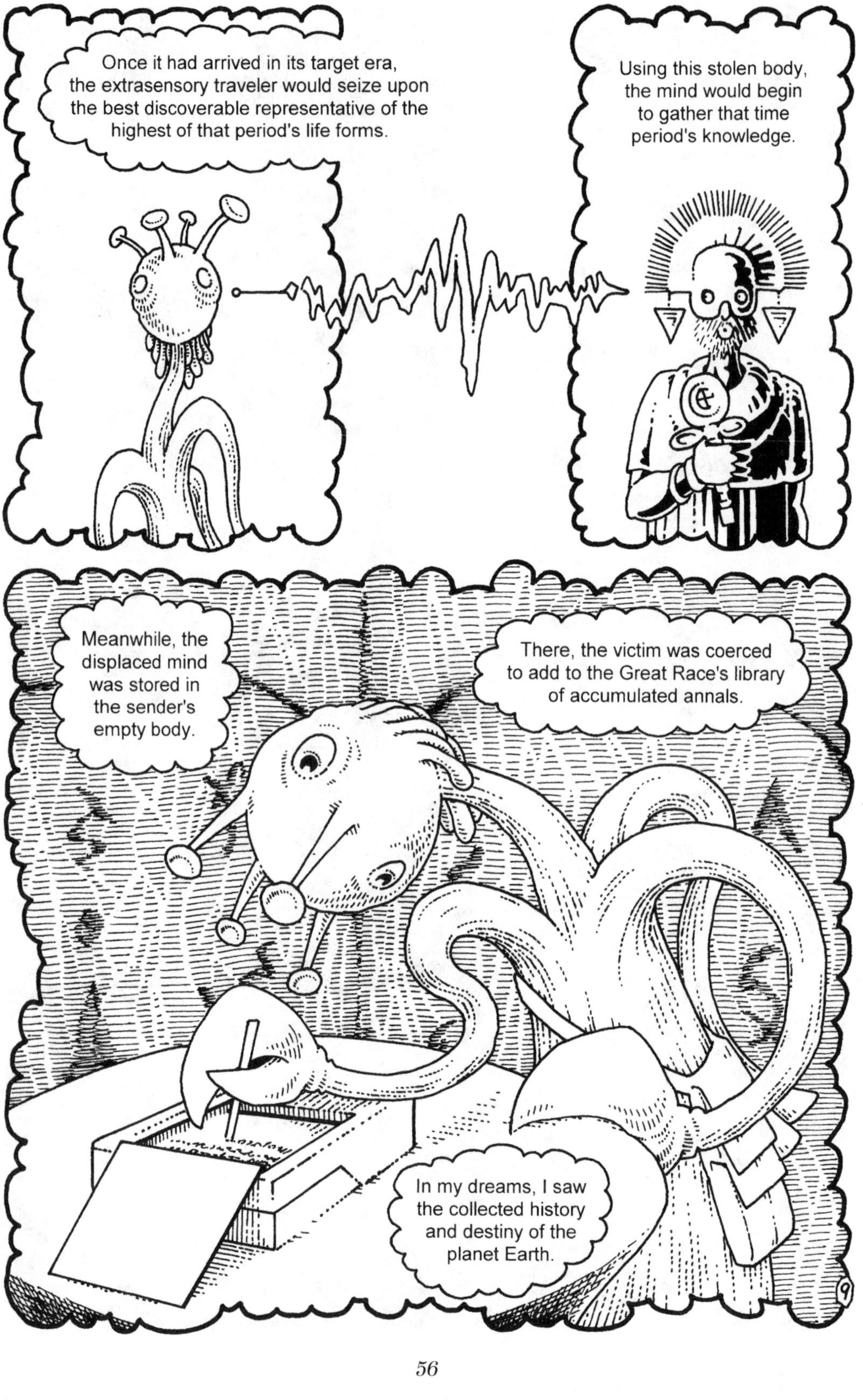
Once it had arrived in its target era, the extrasensory traveler would seize upon the best discoverable representative of the highest of that period's life forms.
Using this stolen body, the mind would begin to gather that time period's knowledge.
Meanwhile, the displaced mind was stored in the sender's empty body.
There, the victim was coerced to add to the Great Race's library of accumulated annals.
In my dreams, I saw the collected history and destiny of the planet Earth.

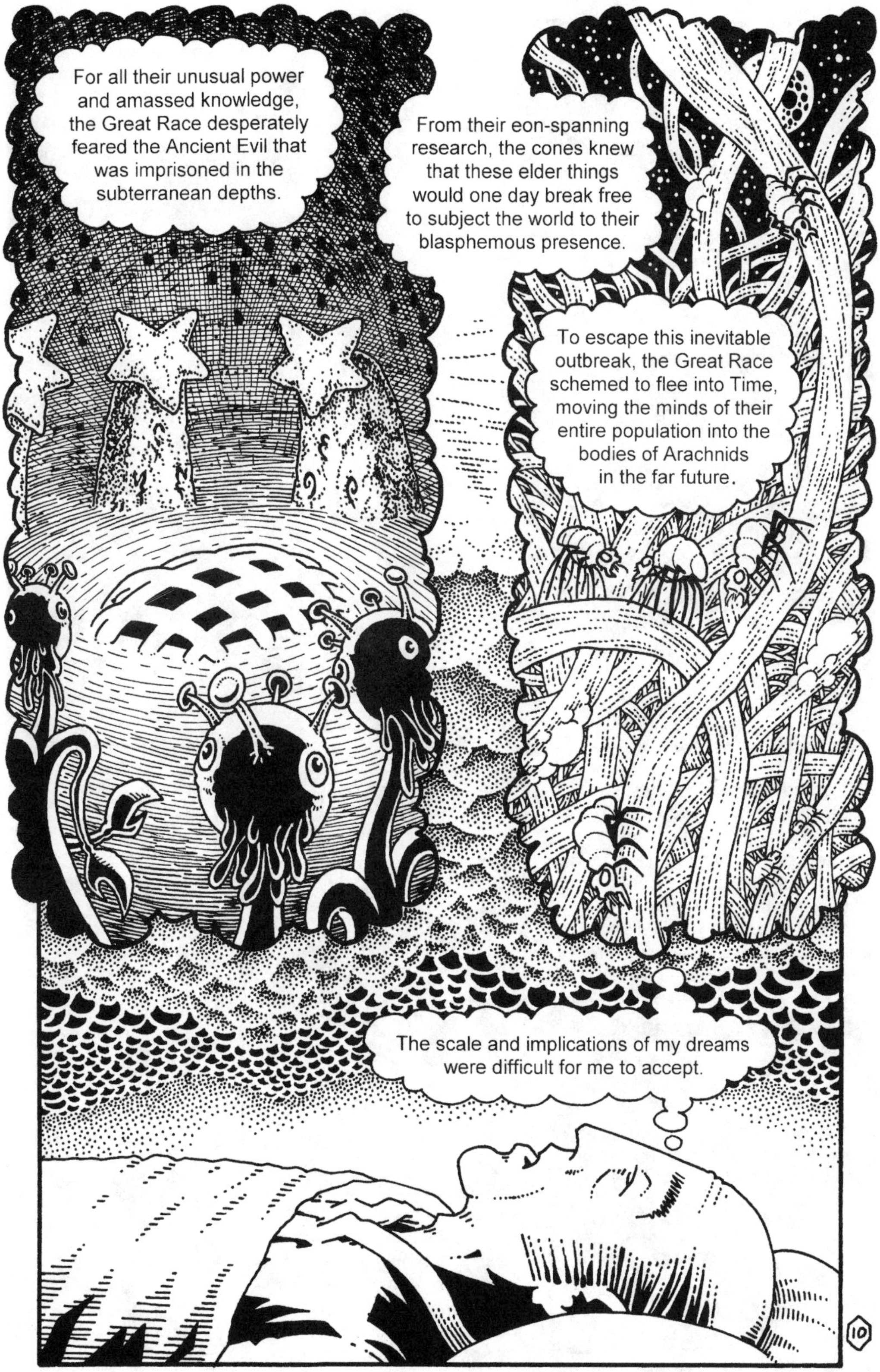
For all their unusual power and amassed knowledge, the Great Race desperately feared the Ancient Evil that was imprisoned in the subterranean depths.
From their eon-spanning research, the cones knew that these elder things would one day break free to subject the world to their blasphemous presence.
To escape this inevitable outbreak, the Great Race schemed to flee into Time, moving the minds of their entire population into the bodies of Arachnids in the far future.
The scale and implications of my dreams were difficult for me to accept.
10

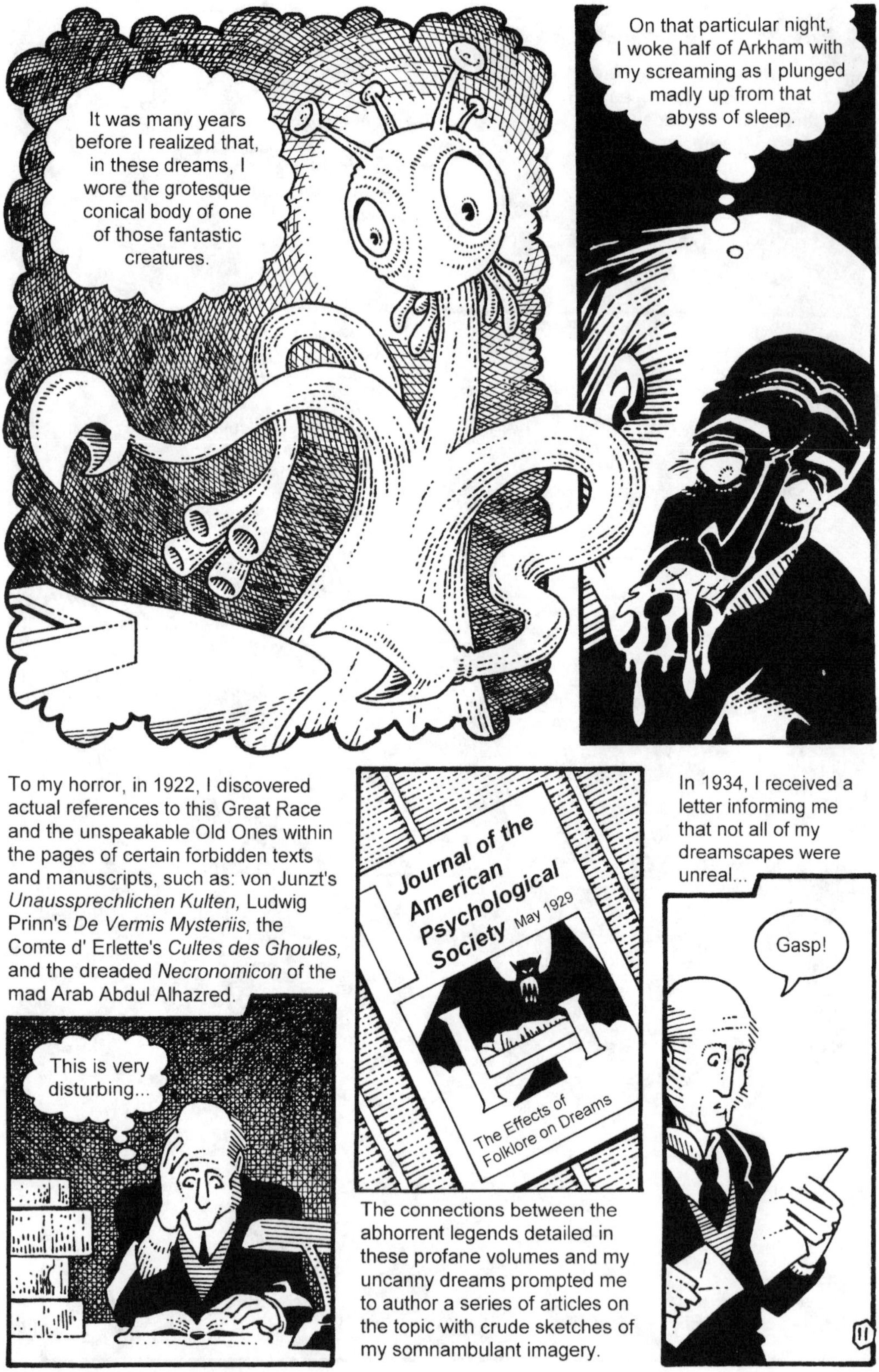

It was many years before I realized that, in these dreams, I wore the grotesque conical body of one of those fantastic creatures.
On that particular night, I woke half of Arkham with my screaming as I plunged madly up from that abyss of sleep.
To my horror, in 1922, I discovered actual references to this Great Race and the unspeakable Old Ones within the pages of certain forbidden texts and manuscripts, such as: von Junzt's *Unaussprechlichen Kulten,* Ludwig Prinn's *De Vermis Mysteriis,* the Comte d' Erlette's *Cultes des Ghoules,* and the dreaded *Necronomicon* of the mad Arab Abdul Alhazred.
This is very disturbing...
Journal of the American Psychological Society May 1929
The Effects of Folklore on Dreams
The connections between the abhorrent legends detailed in these profane volumes and my uncanny dreams prompted me to author a series of articles on the topic with crude sketches of my somnambulant imagery.
In 1934, I received a letter informing me that not all of my dreamscapes were unreal...
Gasp!

With funding generously provided by Miskatonic University, I was able to travel to Pilbarra, Australia, in order to meet and confer with Robert Mackenzie, the geologist who had written me about the anomalies he had unearthed in Australia's barren outback.

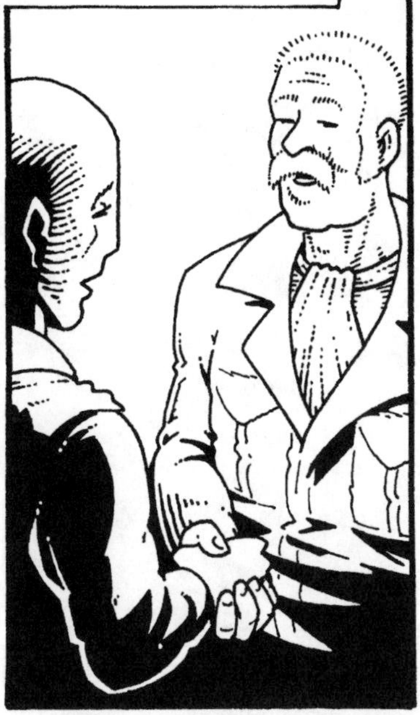

As we drove out to his excavation site in the desert, Mackenzie explained his interest in the aboriginal myth of Buddai, the gigantic old man who lies asleep for ages underground, who will someday awake and eat up the world. While searching for evidence of this tribal legend, he had unearthed some blocks of stone bearing curious carvings. According to Mackenzie, these markings bore an exceptional resemblance to the drawings that had accompanied my articles, which had been brought to the geologist's attention by an associate. Contacting me about this strange coincidence had been a professional courtesy.

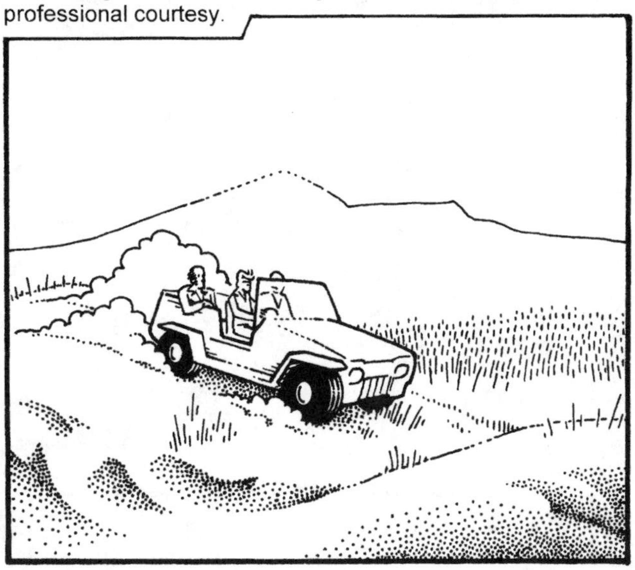

Mackenzie was unaware of my emotional agitation as we approached the excavation. His interest in the blocks was purely scientific, while my own curiosity was shaded with a dark trepidation.

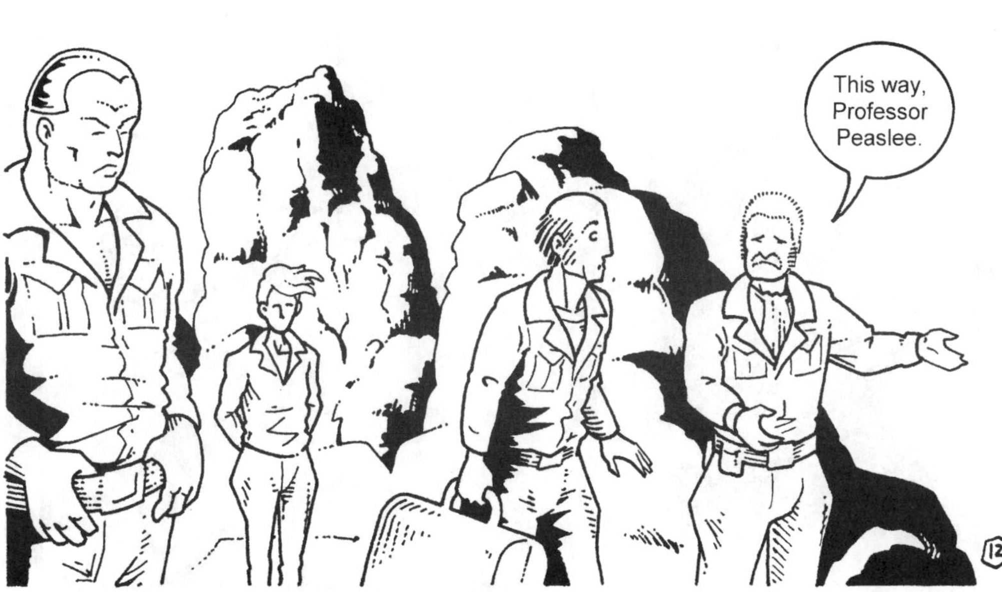
This way, Professor Peaslee.
12

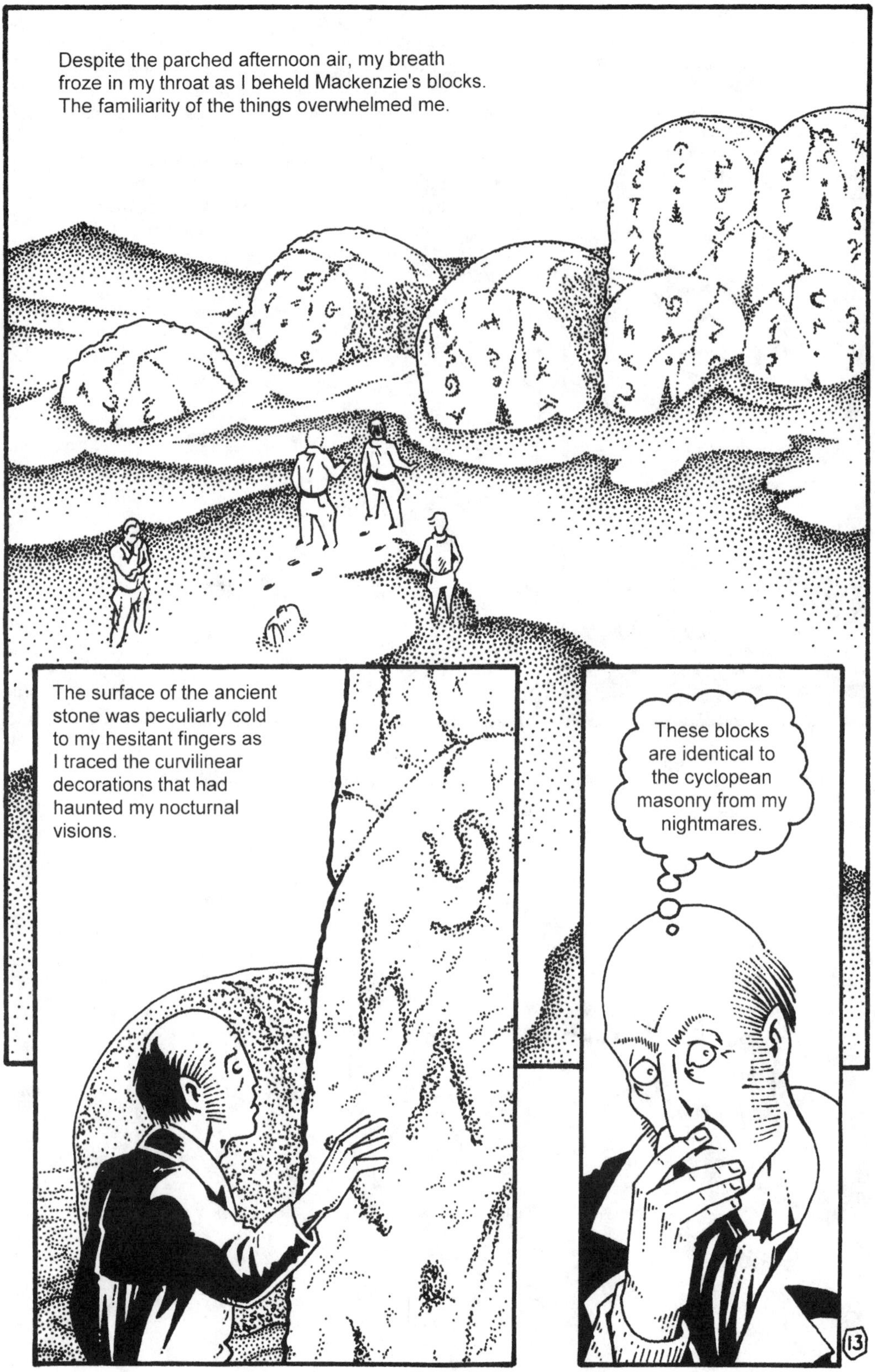
Despite the parched afternoon air, my breath froze in my throat as I beheld Mackenzie's blocks. The familiarity of the things overwhelmed me.
The surface of the ancient stone was peculiarly cold to my hesitant fingers as I traced the curvilinear decorations that had haunted my nocturnal visions.
These blocks are identical to the cyclopean masonry from my nightmares.
13

As the sun set on this desolate wasteland, my thoughts were deeply troubled.

These blocks that Mackenzie has unearthed are undeniable proof...but of what? That my dreams are *real*? That cannot be.

For if the stones exist, what does that imply for the other parts of my nightmares?

I did not share my ruminations with Mackenzie lest he think me insane. Instead, I took a long solitary walk to consider the dreadful implications of what the geologist had found in the Australian outback.

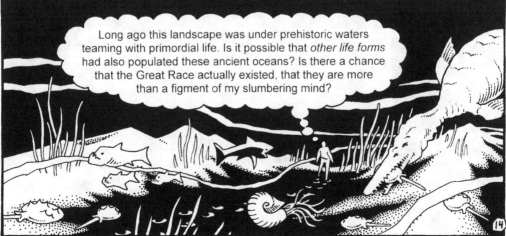

Long ago this landscape was under prehistoric waters teaming with primordial life. Is it possible that *other life forms* had also populated these ancient oceans? Is there a chance that the Great Race actually existed, that they are more than a figment of my slumbering mind?

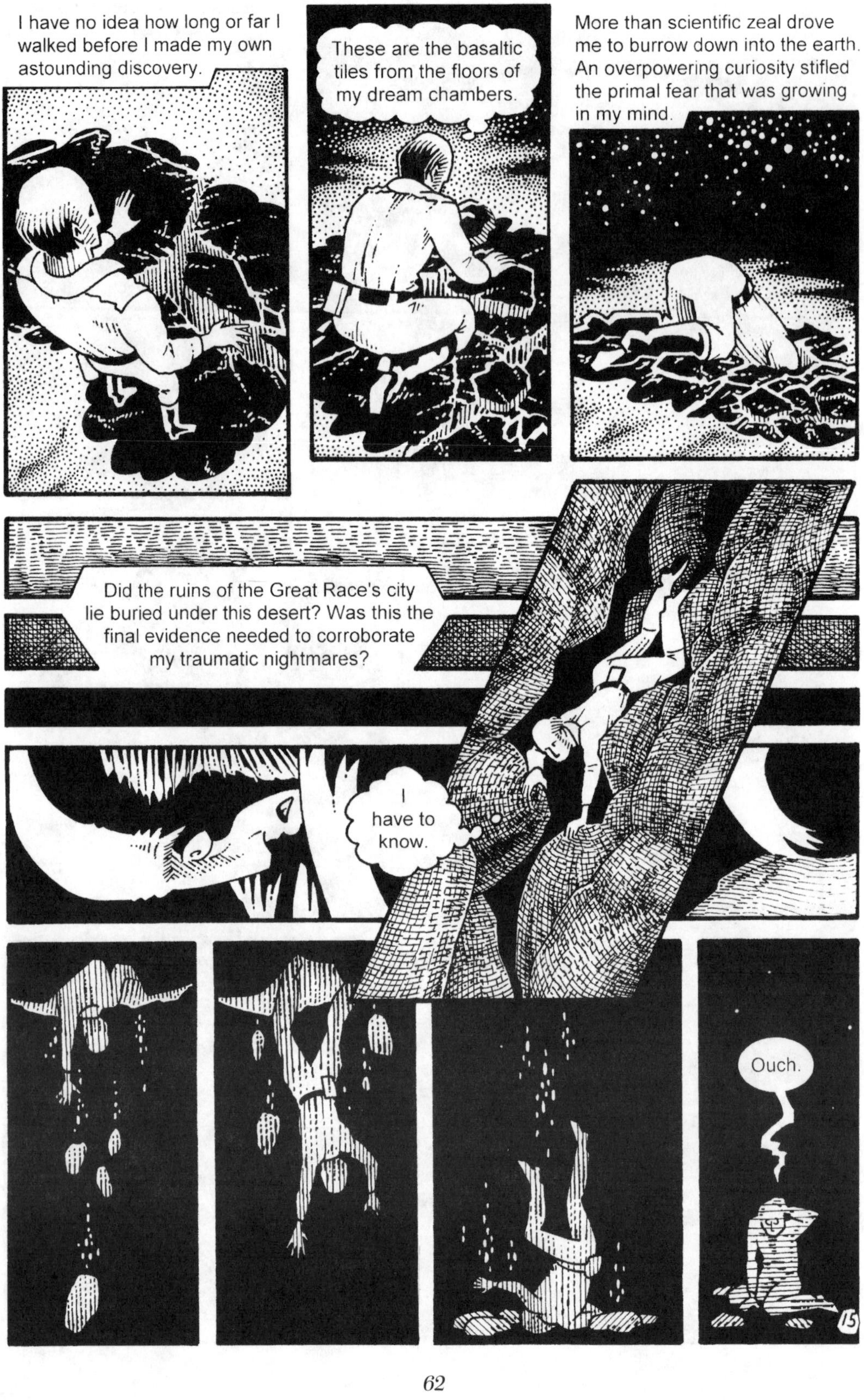
I have no idea how long or far I walked before I made my own astounding discovery.
These are the basaltic tiles from the floors of my dream chambers.
More than scientific zeal drove me to burrow down into the earth. An overpowering curiosity stifled the primal fear that was growing in my mind.
Did the ruins of the Great Race's city lie buried under this desert? Was this the final evidence needed to corroborate my traumatic nightmares?
I have to know.
Ouch.

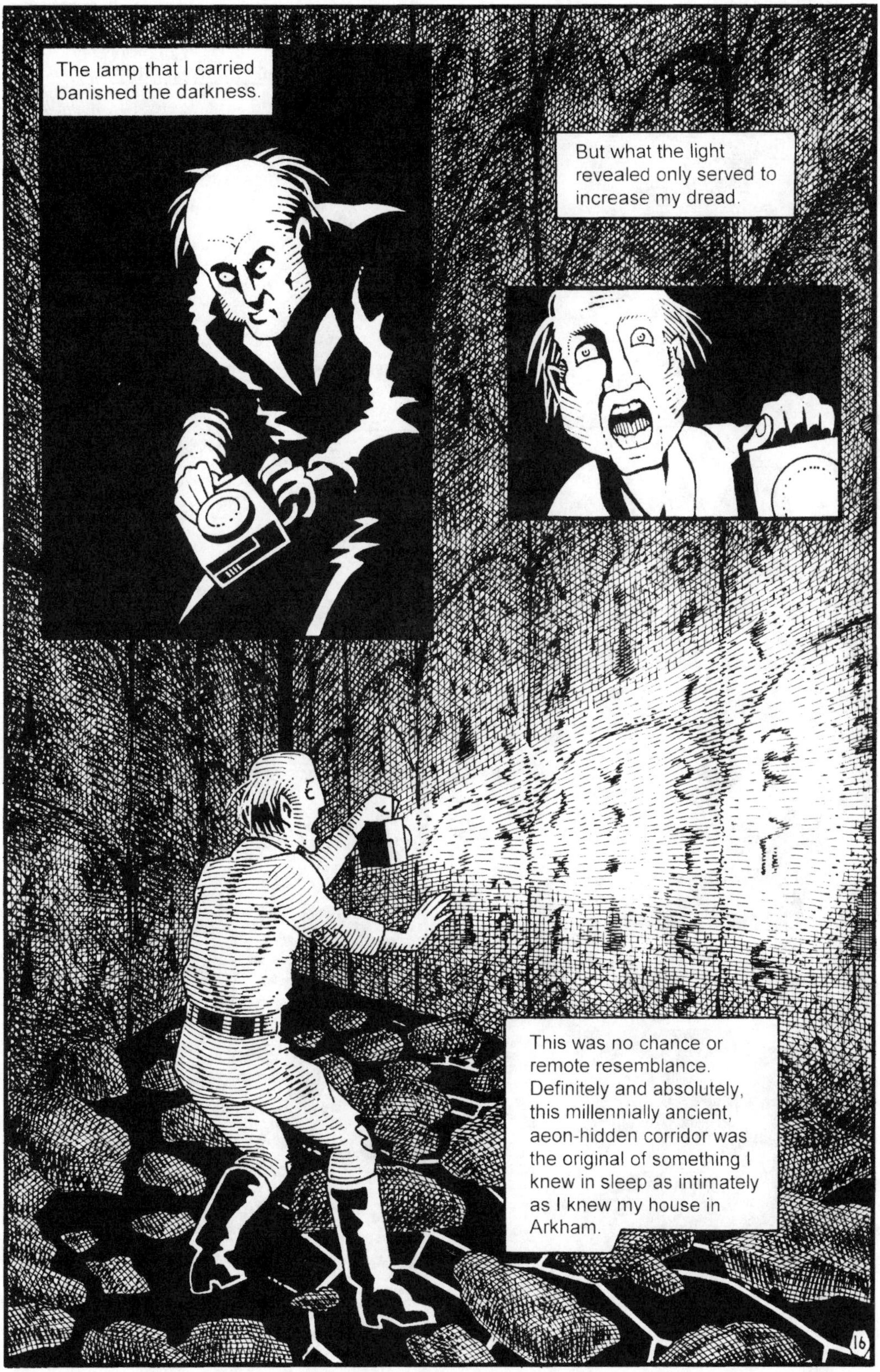
The lamp that I carried banished the darkness.
But what the light revealed only served to increase my dread.
This was no chance or remote resemblance. Definitely and absolutely, this millennially ancient, aeon-hidden corridor was the original of something I knew in sleep as intimately as I knew my house in Arkham.
16

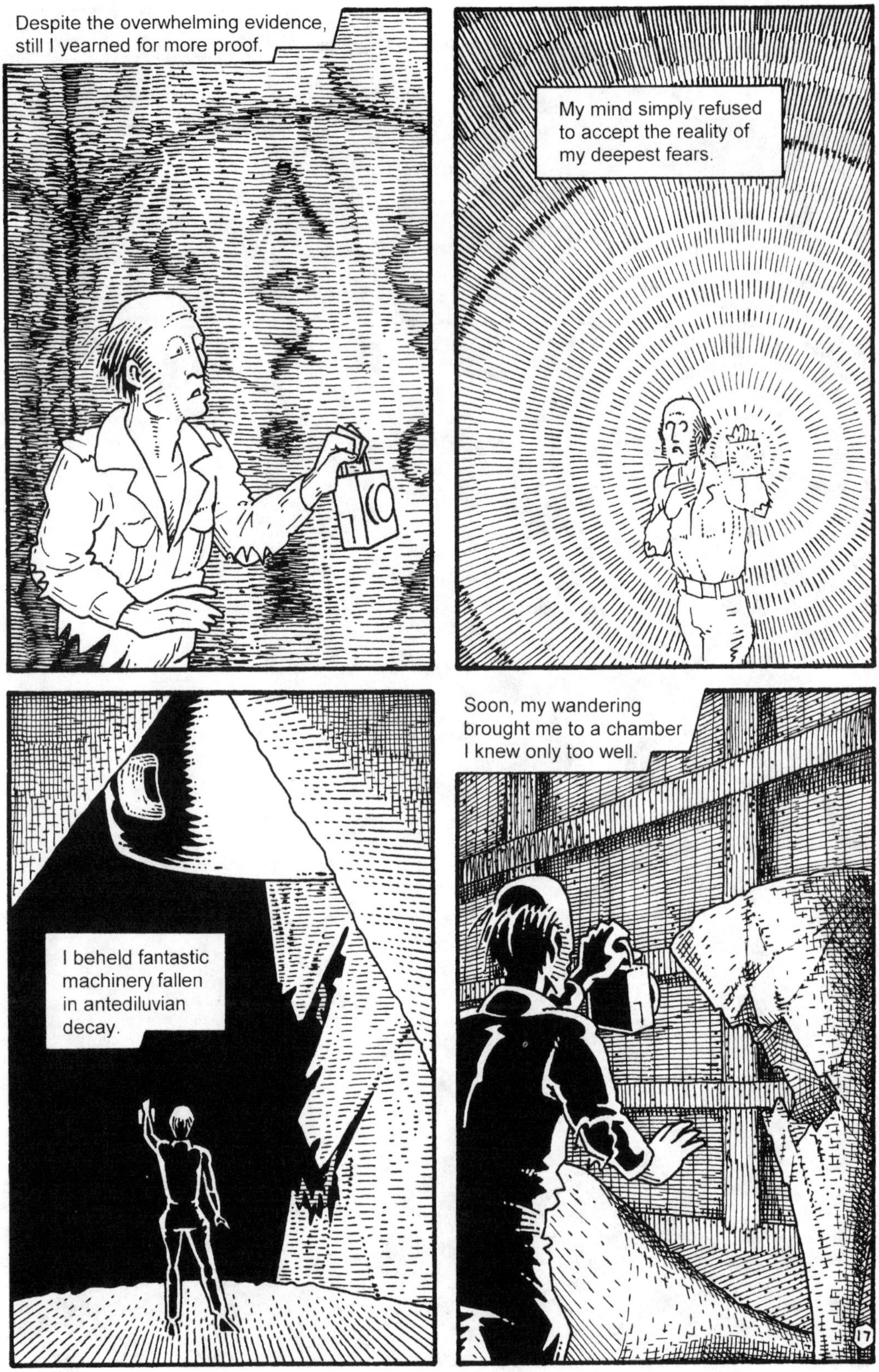
Despite the overwhelming evidence, still I yearned for more proof.
My mind simply refused to accept the reality of my deepest fears.
I beheld fantastic machinery fallen in antediluvian decay.
Soon, my wandering brought me to a chamber I knew only too well.
17

This was the library from my dreams. Here, the Great Race had archived the past- and future-history of the Earth gathered during their telepathic journeys along the planet's timeline.

While the volumes scribed by minds which had been displaced by the Great Race's chronological voyages, those would be stored here too.

I have to know...

According to my tormented dreams, I had supposedly filled several of these alien texts with my own accounts. The location of these tomes was hideously fresh in my numbed mind.

Gasp!

There was no mistaking the penultimate proof of my own penmanship on these cellulose sheets.

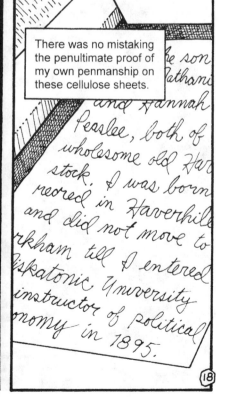

he son
athani
and Hannah
Peaslee, both of
wholesome old Ha
stock. I was born
reored in Haverhill
and did not move to
rkham till I entered
iskatonic University
instructor of political
onomy in 1895.

(18)

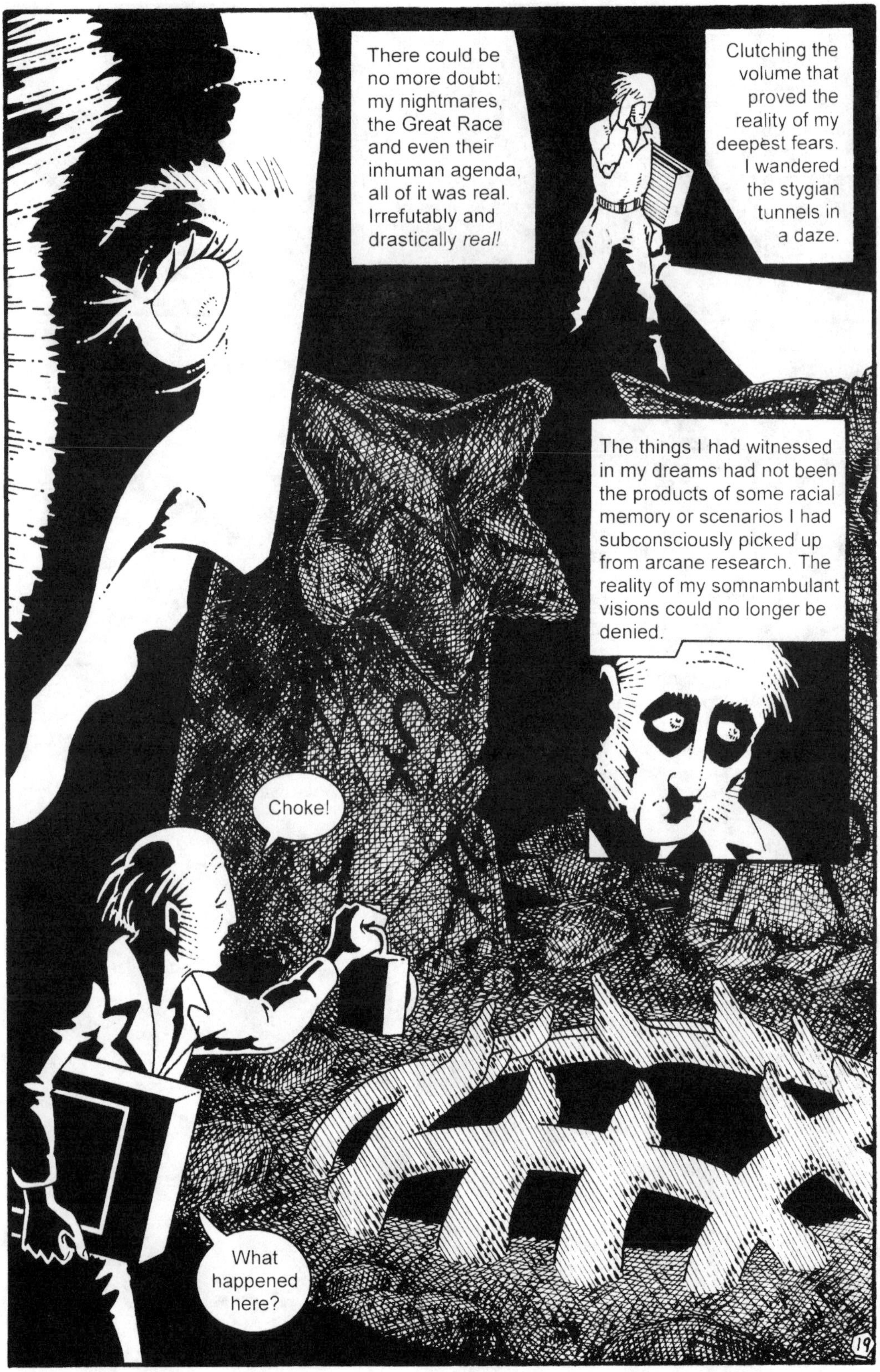
There could be no more doubt: my nightmares, the Great Race and even their inhuman agenda, all of it was real. Irrefutably and drastically *real!*
Clutching the volume that proved the reality of my deepest fears. I wandered the stygian tunnels in a daze.
The things I had witnessed in my dreams had not been the products of some racial memory or scenarios I had subconsciously picked up from arcane research. The reality of my somnambulant visions could no longer be denied.
Choke!
What happened here?
19

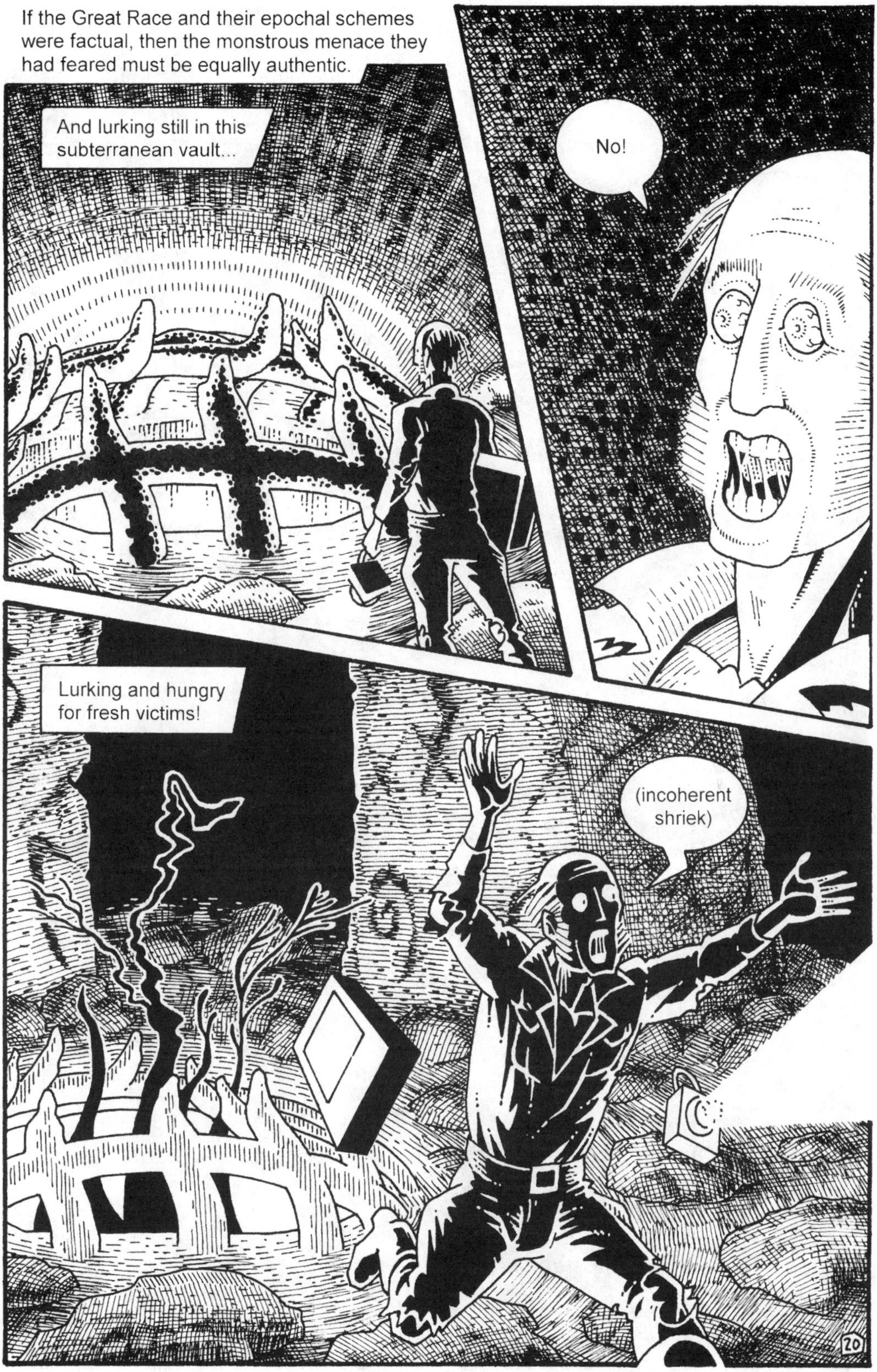
If the Great Race and their epochal schemes were factual, then the monstrous menace they had feared must be equally authentic.
And lurking still in this subterranean vault...
No!
Lurking and hungry for fresh victims!
(incoherent shriek)
20

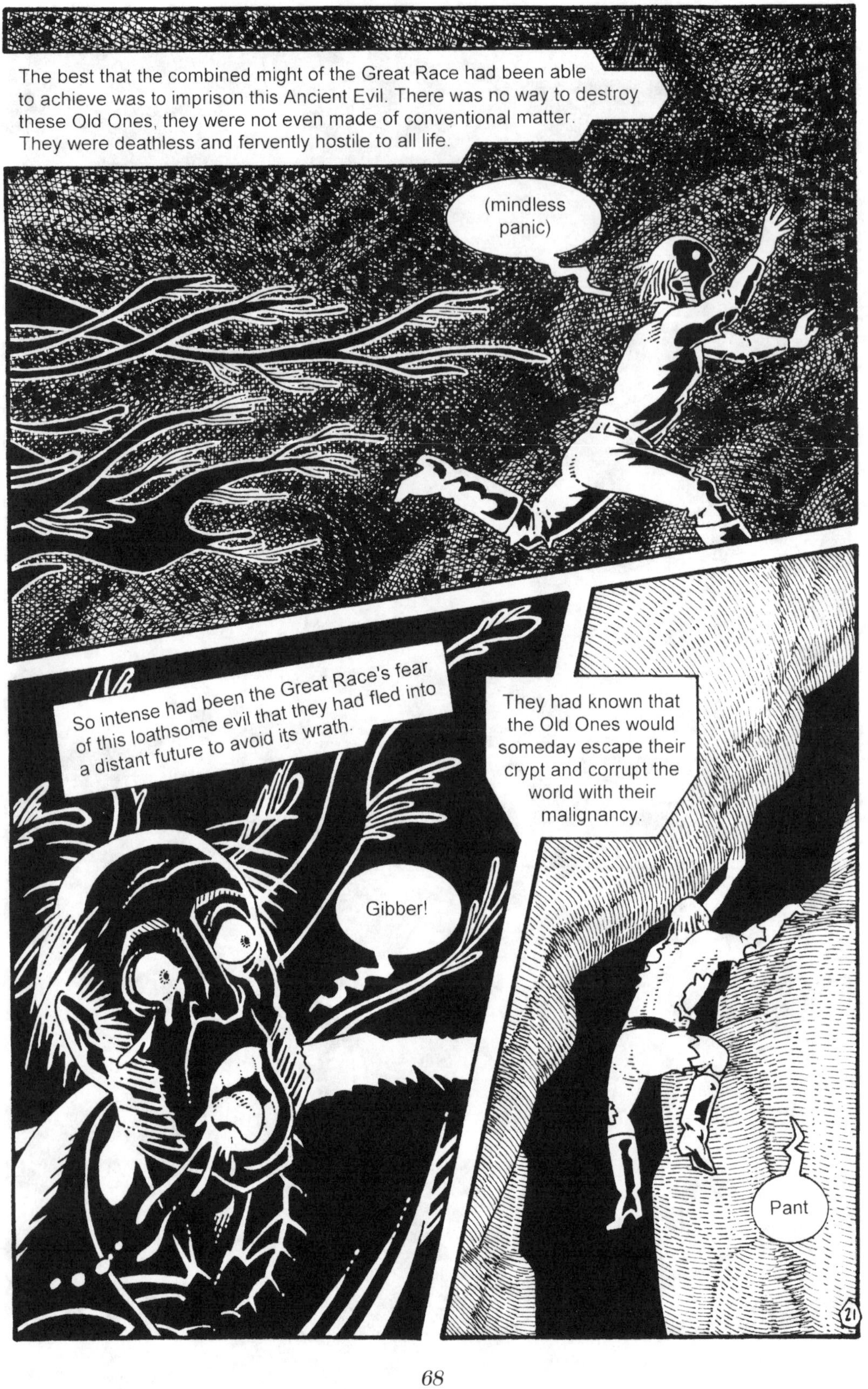
The best that the combined might of the Great Race had been able to achieve was to imprison this Ancient Evil. There was no way to destroy these Old Ones, they were not even made of conventional matter. They were deathless and fervently hostile to all life.
(mindless panic)
So intense had been the Great Race's fear of this loathsome evil that they had fled into a distant future to avoid its wrath.
Gibber!
They had known that the Old Ones would someday escape their crypt and corrupt the world with their malignancy.
Pant
21

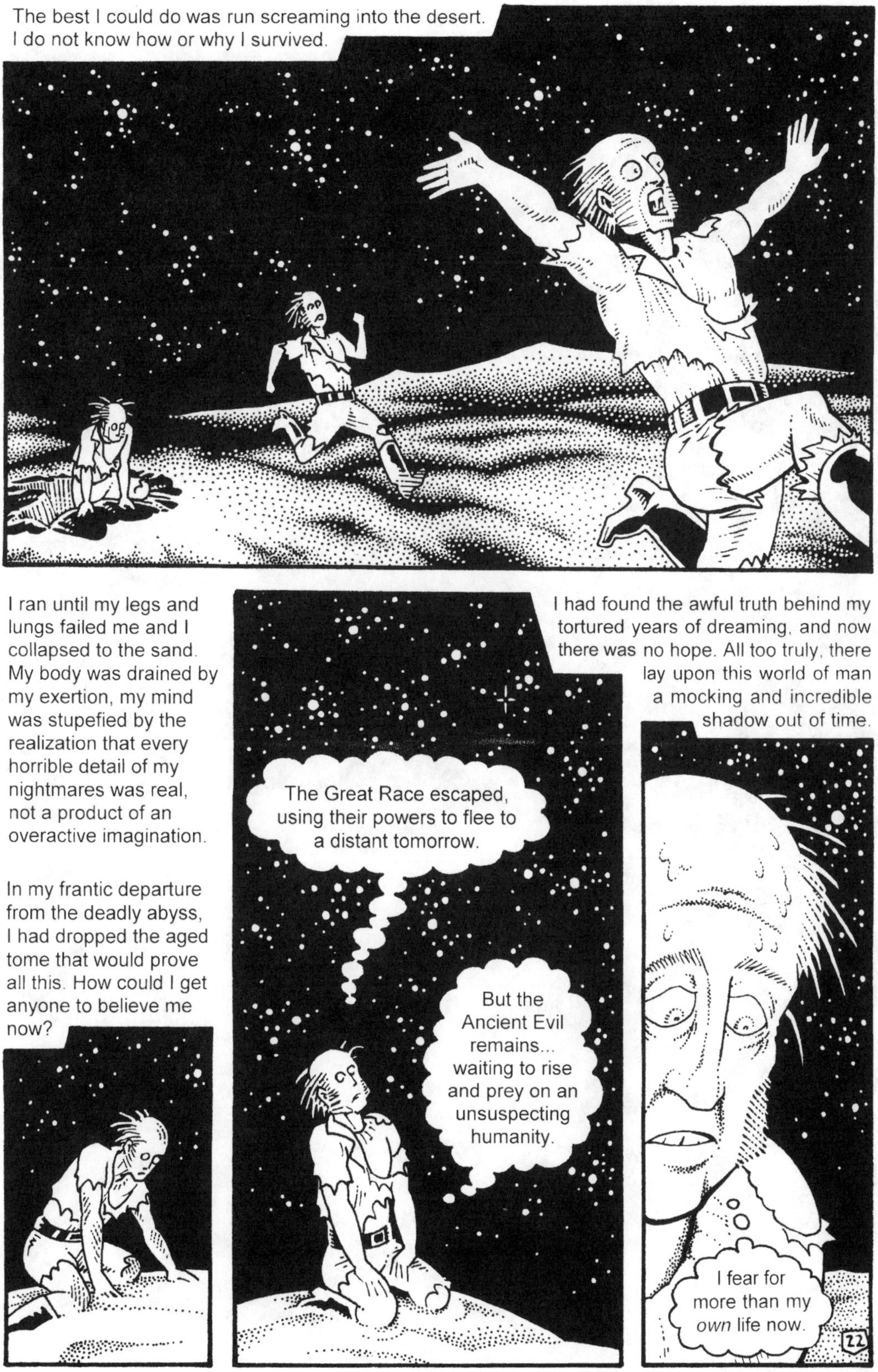
The best I could do was run screaming into the desert.
I do not know how or why I survived.
I ran until my legs and lungs failed me and I collapsed to the sand. My body was drained by my exertion, my mind was stupefied by the realization that every horrible detail of my nightmares was real, not a product of an overactive imagination.
In my frantic departure from the deadly abyss, I had dropped the aged tome that would prove all this. How could I get anyone to believe me now?
The Great Race escaped, using their powers to flee to a distant tomorrow.
But the Ancient Evil remains... waiting to rise and prey on an unsuspecting humanity.
I had found the awful truth behind my tortured years of dreaming, and now there was no hope. All too truly, there lay upon this world of man a mocking and incredible shadow out of time.
I fear for more than my *own* life now.

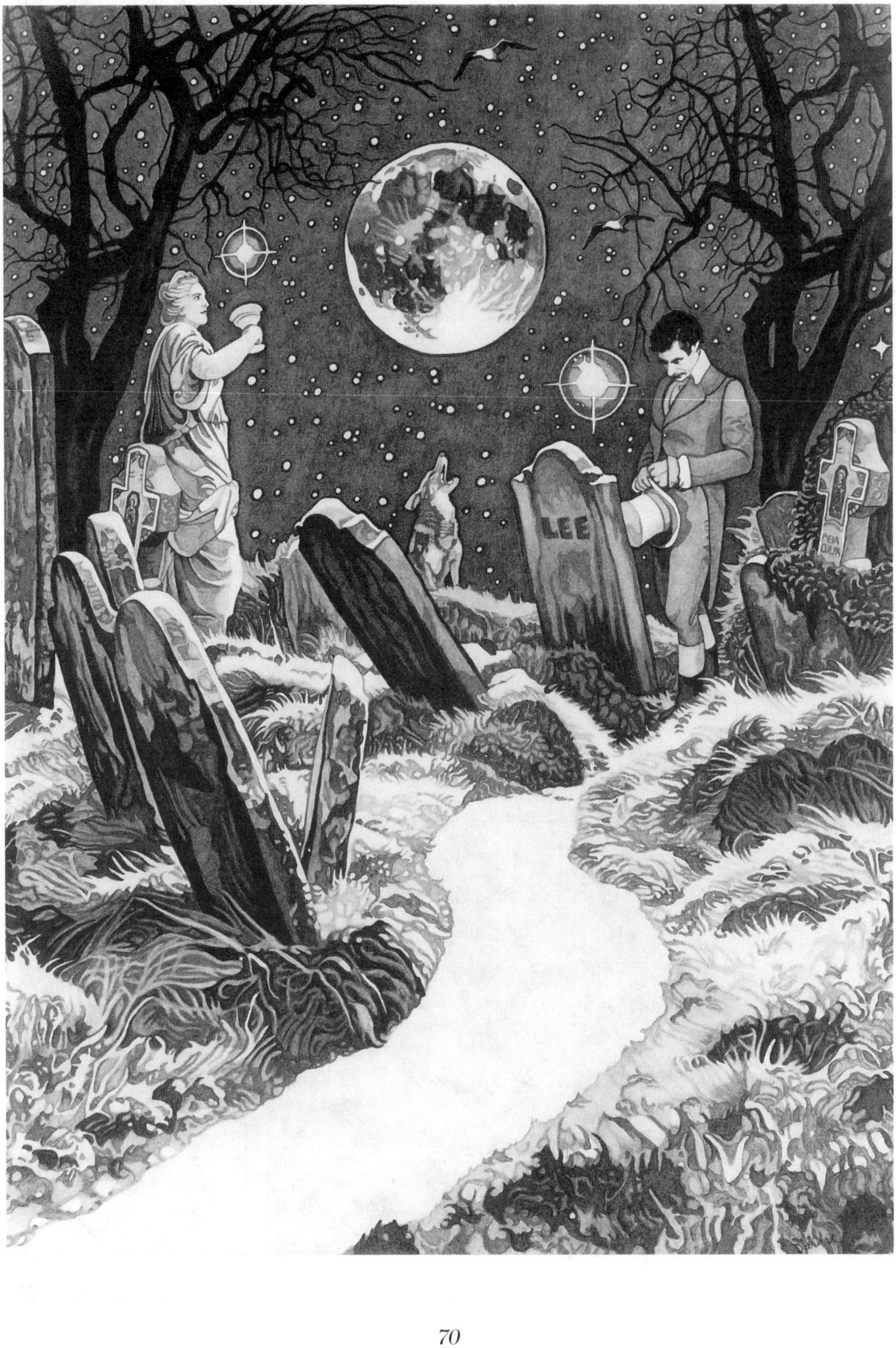
LEE
MEIA CULPA

In a Sequester'd Providence Churchyard Where Once Poe Walk'd

by H.P. LOVECRAFT

Eternal brood the shadows on this ground,
Dreaming of centuries that have gone before;
Great elms rise solemnly by slab and mound,
Arched high above a hidden world of yore.
Round all the scene a light of memory plays,
And dead leaves whisper of departed days,
Longing for sights and sounds that are no more.

Lonely and sad, a specter glides along
Aisles where of old his living footsteps fell;
No common glance discerns him, though his song
Peals down through time with a mysterious spell.
Only the few who sorcery's secret know,
Espy amidst these tombs the shade of Poe.

art by DIERDRE LUZWICK

The Terrible Old Man

illustrated by

ONSMITH JEREMI

story by

H.P. LOVECRAFT

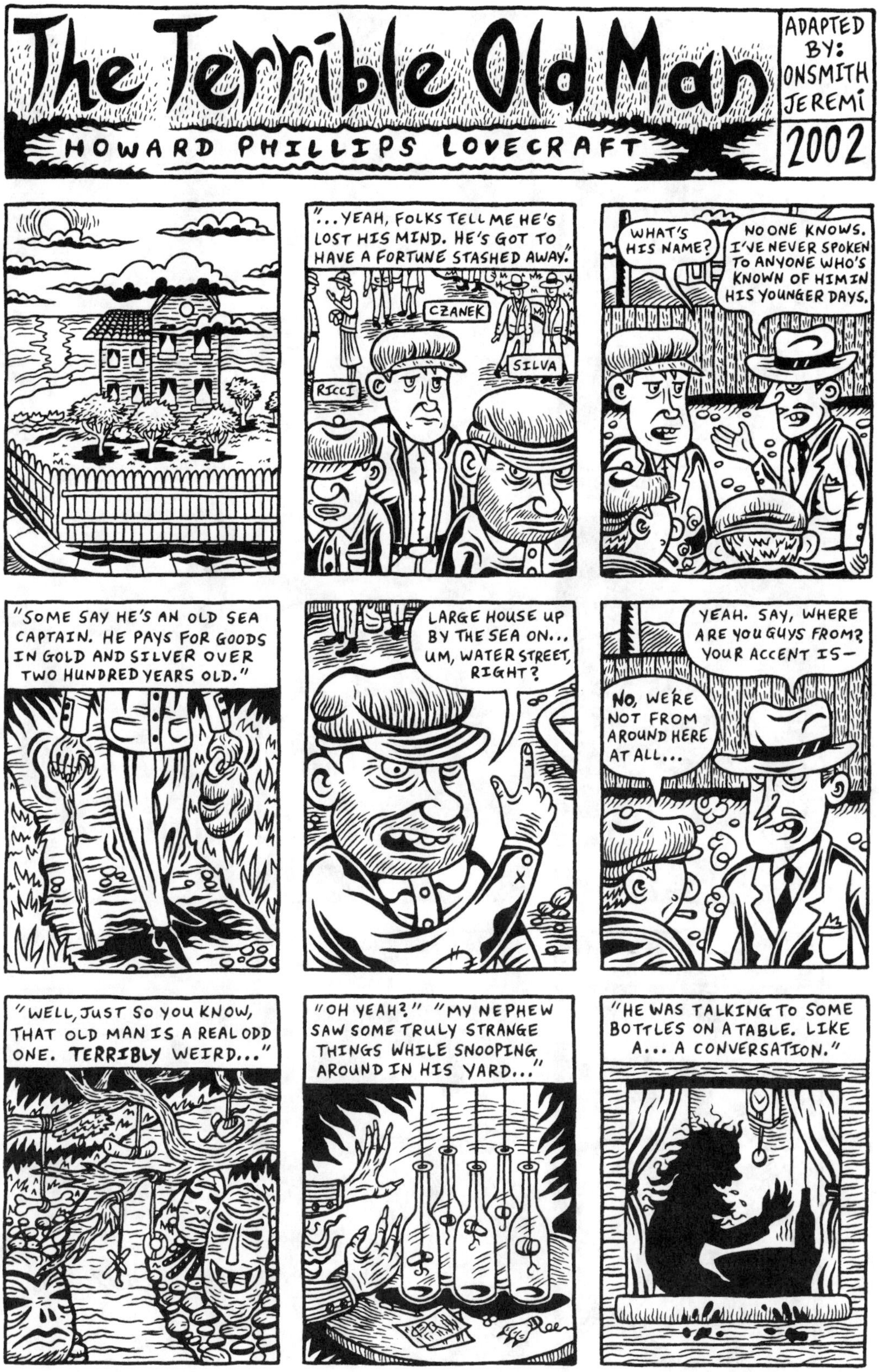
The Terrible Old Man
HOWARD PHILLIPS LOVECRAFT
ADAPTED BY: ONSMITH JEREMI
2002
"...YEAH, FOLKS TELL ME HE'S LOST HIS MIND. HE'S GOT TO HAVE A FORTUNE STASHED AWAY."
CZANEK
SILVA
RICCI
WHAT'S HIS NAME?
NO ONE KNOWS. I'VE NEVER SPOKEN TO ANYONE WHO'S KNOWN OF HIM IN HIS YOUNGER DAYS.
"SOME SAY HE'S AN OLD SEA CAPTAIN. HE PAYS FOR GOODS IN GOLD AND SILVER OVER TWO HUNDRED YEARS OLD."
LARGE HOUSE UP BY THE SEA ON... UM, WATER STREET, RIGHT?
YEAH. SAY, WHERE ARE YOU GUYS FROM? YOUR ACCENT IS—
NO, WE'RE NOT FROM AROUND HERE AT ALL...
"WELL, JUST SO YOU KNOW, THAT OLD MAN IS A REAL ODD ONE. TERRIBLY WEIRD..."
"OH YEAH?" "MY NEPHEW SAW SOME TRULY STRANGE THINGS WHILE SNOOPING AROUND IN HIS YARD..."
"HE WAS TALKING TO SOME BOTTLES ON A TABLE. LIKE A... A CONVERSATION."

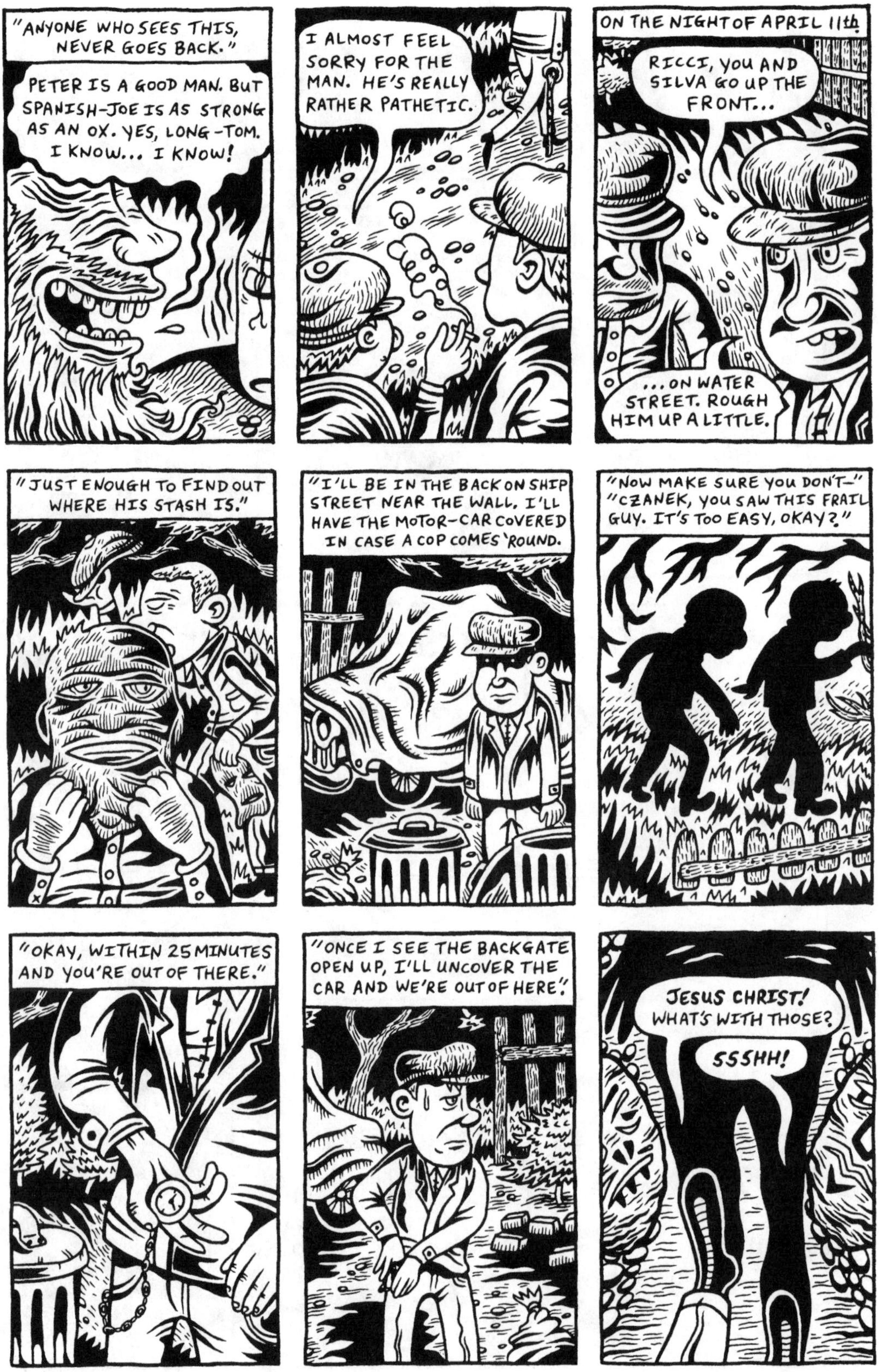
"ANYONE WHO SEES THIS, NEVER GOES BACK."
PETER IS A GOOD MAN. BUT SPANISH-JOE IS AS STRONG AS AN OX. YES, LONG-TOM. I KNOW... I KNOW!
I ALMOST FEEL SORRY FOR THE MAN. HE'S REALLY RATHER PATHETIC.
ON THE NIGHT OF APRIL 11th
RICCI, YOU AND SILVA GO UP THE FRONT...
...ON WATER STREET. ROUGH HIM UP A LITTLE.
"JUST ENOUGH TO FIND OUT WHERE HIS STASH IS."
"I'LL BE IN THE BACK ON SHIP STREET NEAR THE WALL. I'LL HAVE THE MOTOR-CAR COVERED IN CASE A COP COMES 'ROUND.
"NOW MAKE SURE YOU DON'T—"
"CZANEK, YOU SAW THIS FRAIL GUY. IT'S TOO EASY, OKAY?"
"OKAY, WITHIN 25 MINUTES AND YOU'RE OUT OF THERE."
"ONCE I SEE THE BACKGATE OPEN UP, I'LL UNCOVER THE CAR AND WE'RE OUT OF HERE."
JESUS CHRIST! WHAT'S WITH THOSE?
SSSHH!

KNOCK KNOCK KNOCK

"I WANT TO MAKE SURE THAT YOU TWO CAN FOLLOW ME ON THIS PLAN. I WANT IT TO GO SMOOTHLY, GOT ME?"

YYYESSS?

C'MON. ALREADY 15 MINUTES DOWN. C'MON! HURRY IT UP...

AAAAAHHH! NNNO NOOOO!

I TOLD THEM TO BE GENTLE WITH HIM...

THEY BETTER HAVE GOTTEN — THE...THE — LOCATION OF HIS S-S-STASH! IT SOUNDS LIKE THE TWO OF THEM ARE — K-K-JESUS! KILLING HIM!

AAHKKKA! AAA IGUHGU OONNN NNN AHAHAA GA! CKCKKCKA

40 MINUTES NOW. TOTALLY QUIET. WHERE ARE THEY?! ...I SHOULD REALLY GET OUT OF HERE...

WHERE THE HELL — I SHOULD GO! I SHOULD — WHA — !

RUSTLE RUSTLE RUSTLE

TOOK TWICE AS LONG AS I TOLD YOU TWO... W-WHAT HAPPENED?

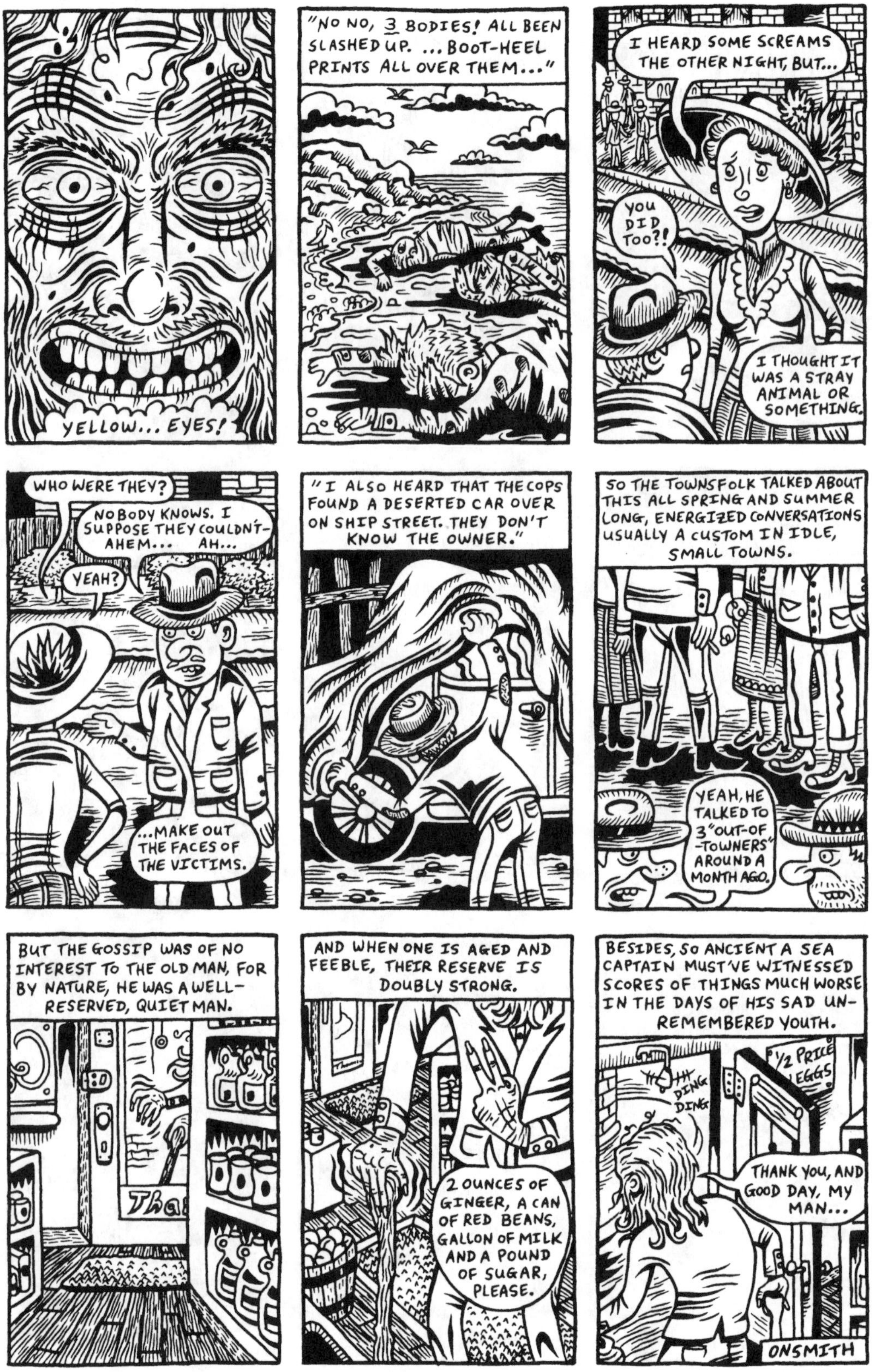
YELLOW... EYES!
"NO NO, 3 BODIES! ALL BEEN SLASHED UP. ...BOOT-HEEL PRINTS ALL OVER THEM..."
I HEARD SOME SCREAMS THE OTHER NIGHT, BUT...
YOU DID TOO?!
I THOUGHT IT WAS A STRAY ANIMAL OR SOMETHING.
WHO WERE THEY?
NOBODY KNOWS. I SUPPOSE THEY COULDN'T- AHEM... AH...
YEAH?
...MAKE OUT THE FACES OF THE VICTIMS.
"I ALSO HEARD THAT THE COPS FOUND A DESERTED CAR OVER ON SHIP STREET. THEY DON'T KNOW THE OWNER."
SO THE TOWNSFOLK TALKED ABOUT THIS ALL SPRING AND SUMMER LONG, ENERGIZED CONVERSATIONS USUALLY A CUSTOM IN IDLE, SMALL TOWNS.
YEAH, HE TALKED TO 3 "OUT-OF-TOWNERS" AROUND A MONTH AGO.
BUT THE GOSSIP WAS OF NO INTEREST TO THE OLD MAN, FOR BY NATURE, HE WAS A WELL-RESERVED, QUIET MAN.
AND WHEN ONE IS AGED AND FEEBLE, THEIR RESERVE IS DOUBLY STRONG.
2 OUNCES OF GINGER, A CAN OF RED BEANS, GALLON OF MILK AND A POUND OF SUGAR, PLEASE.
BESIDES, SO ANCIENT A SEA CAPTAIN MUST'VE WITNESSED SCORES OF THINGS MUCH WORSE IN THE DAYS OF HIS SAD UN-REMEMBERED YOUTH.
1/2 PRICE EGGS
DING DING
THANK YOU, AND GOOD DAY, MY MAN...
ONSMITH

The Cats of Ulthar

illustrated by

LISA K. WEBER

story by

H.P. LOVECRAFT

edited and abridged by Tom Pomplun

It is said that in Ulthar, which lies beyond the river Skai, no man may kill a cat; and this I can verily believe as I gaze upon him who sitteth purring before the fire. For the cat is cryptic, and close to strange things which men cannot see. The Sphinx is his cousin, and he speaks her language; but he is more ancient than the Sphinx, and remembers that which she hath forgotten.

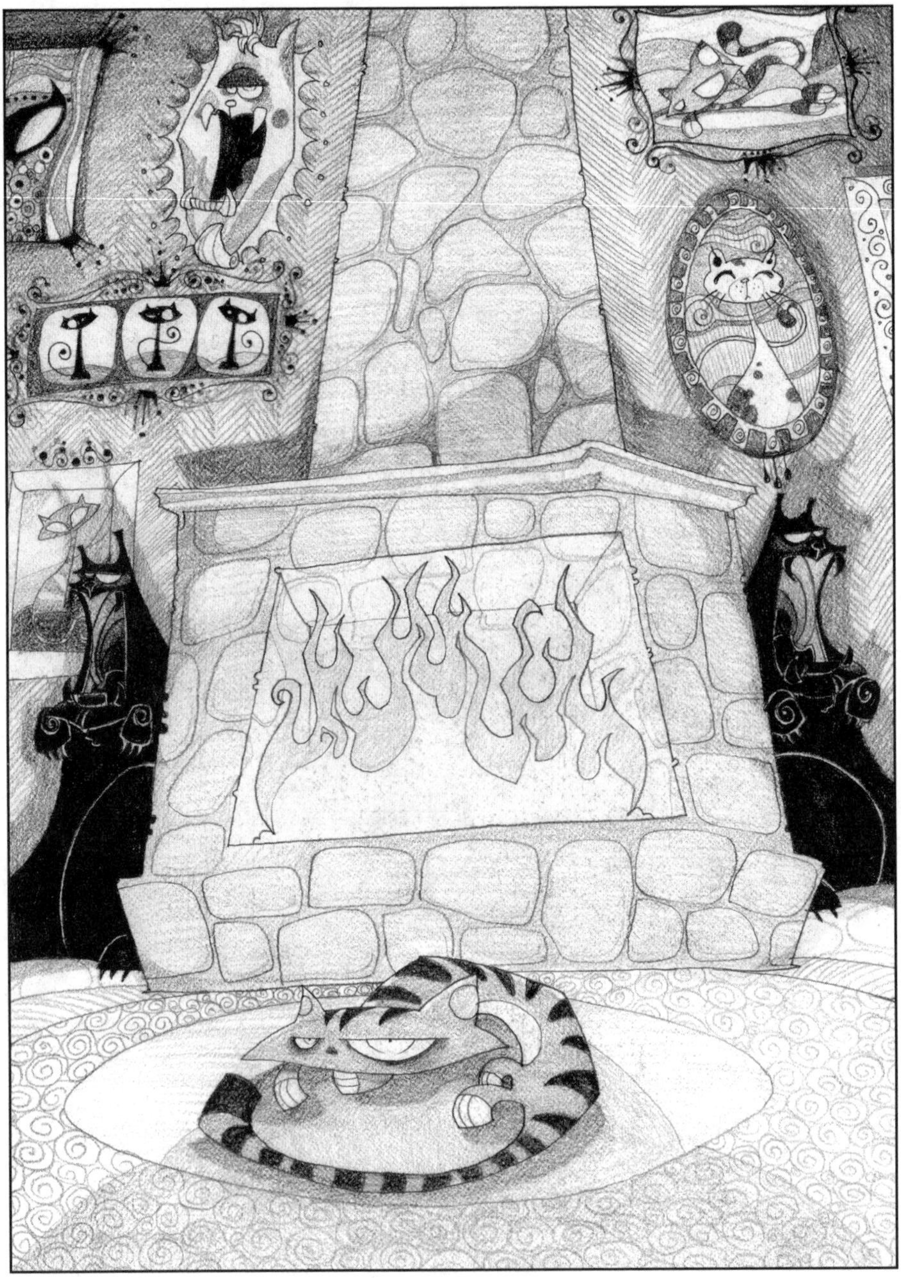

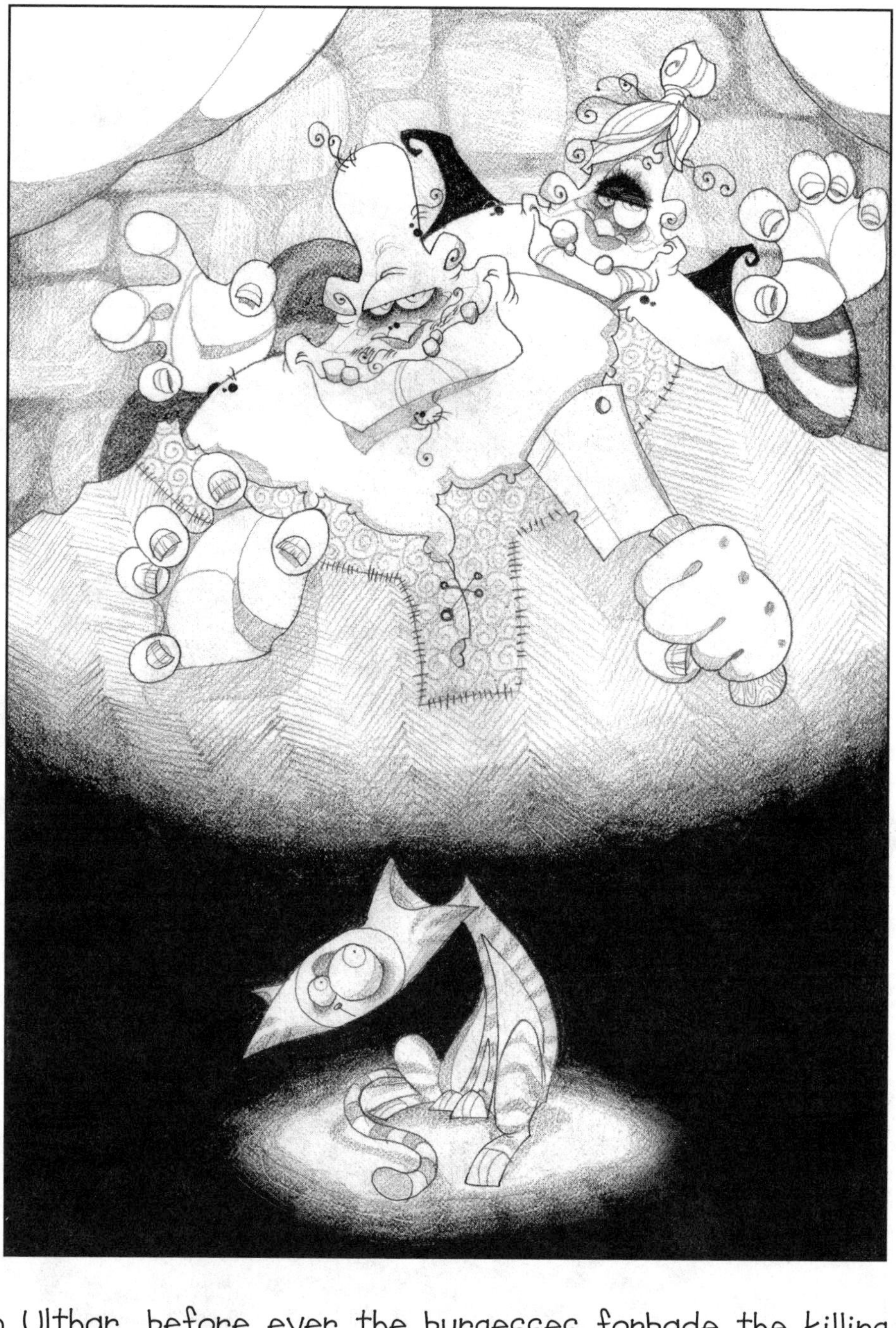

In Ulthar, before ever the burgesses forbade the killing of cats, there dwelt an old cotter and his wife who delighted to trap and slay the cats of their neighbors. Why they did this I know not; save that many hate the voice of the cat in the night, and take it ill that cats should run stealthily about yards and gardens at twilight.

Much as the owners of cats hated these odd folk, they feared them more. Instead of accusing them, they merely took care that no cherished pet should stray toward the remote hovel under the dark trees. When a cat was missed, the loser would lament impotently. For the people of Ulthar were simple, and knew not whence it is all cats first came.

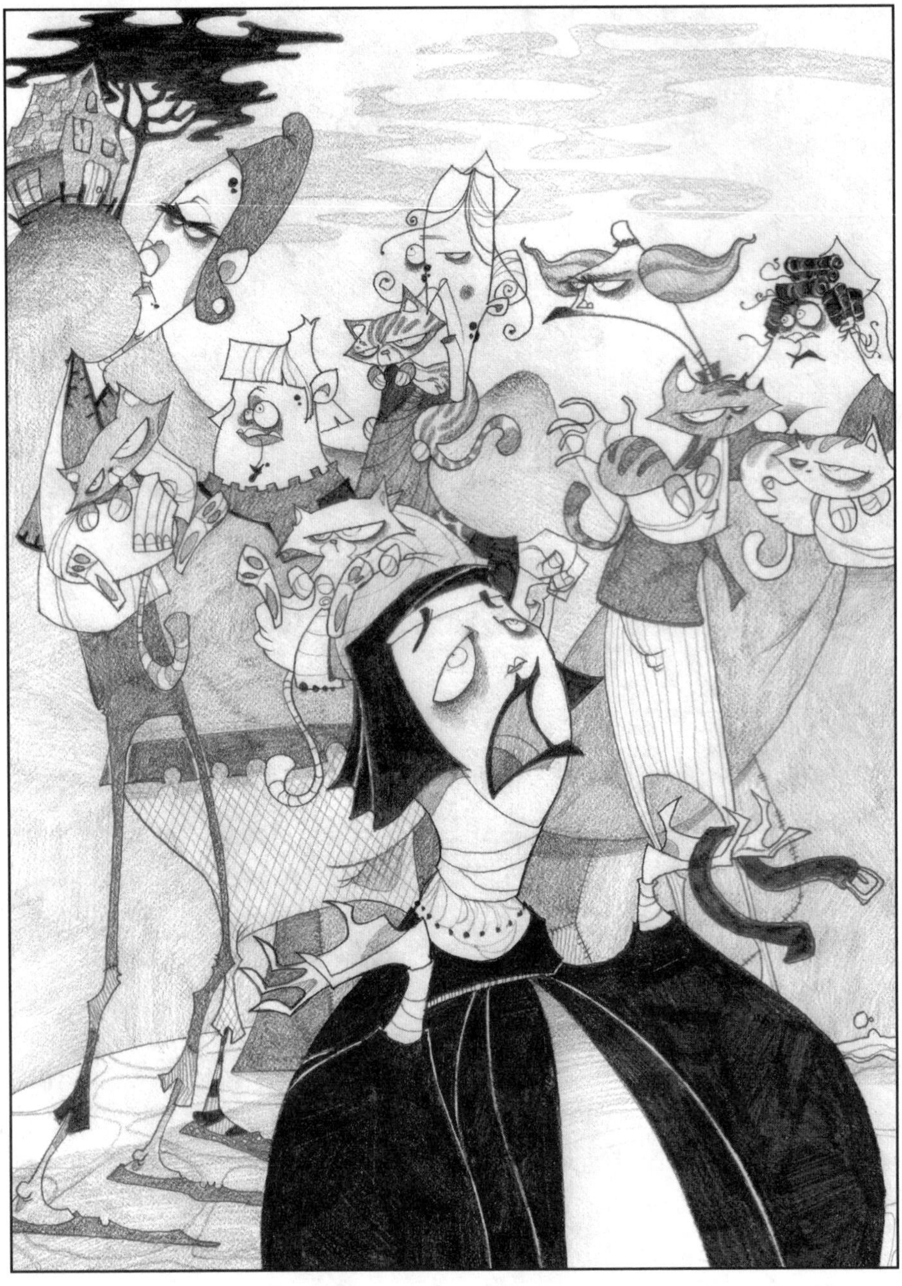

One day a caravan of wanderers entered the cobbled streets of Ulthar. What was the land of these wanderers none could tell; but it was seen that they were given to strange prayers, and that they had painted many strange figures on the sides of their wagons. The leader of the caravan wore a headdress with two horns and a curious disk betwixt the horns.

There was in this singular caravan a little boy with no father or mother, but only a tiny black kitten to cherish. The plague had not been kind to him, yet had left him this small thing to mitigate his sorrow. So the boy, whom the dark people called Menes, smiled more often than he wept as he sat playing with his graceful kitten on the steps of an oddly painted wagon.

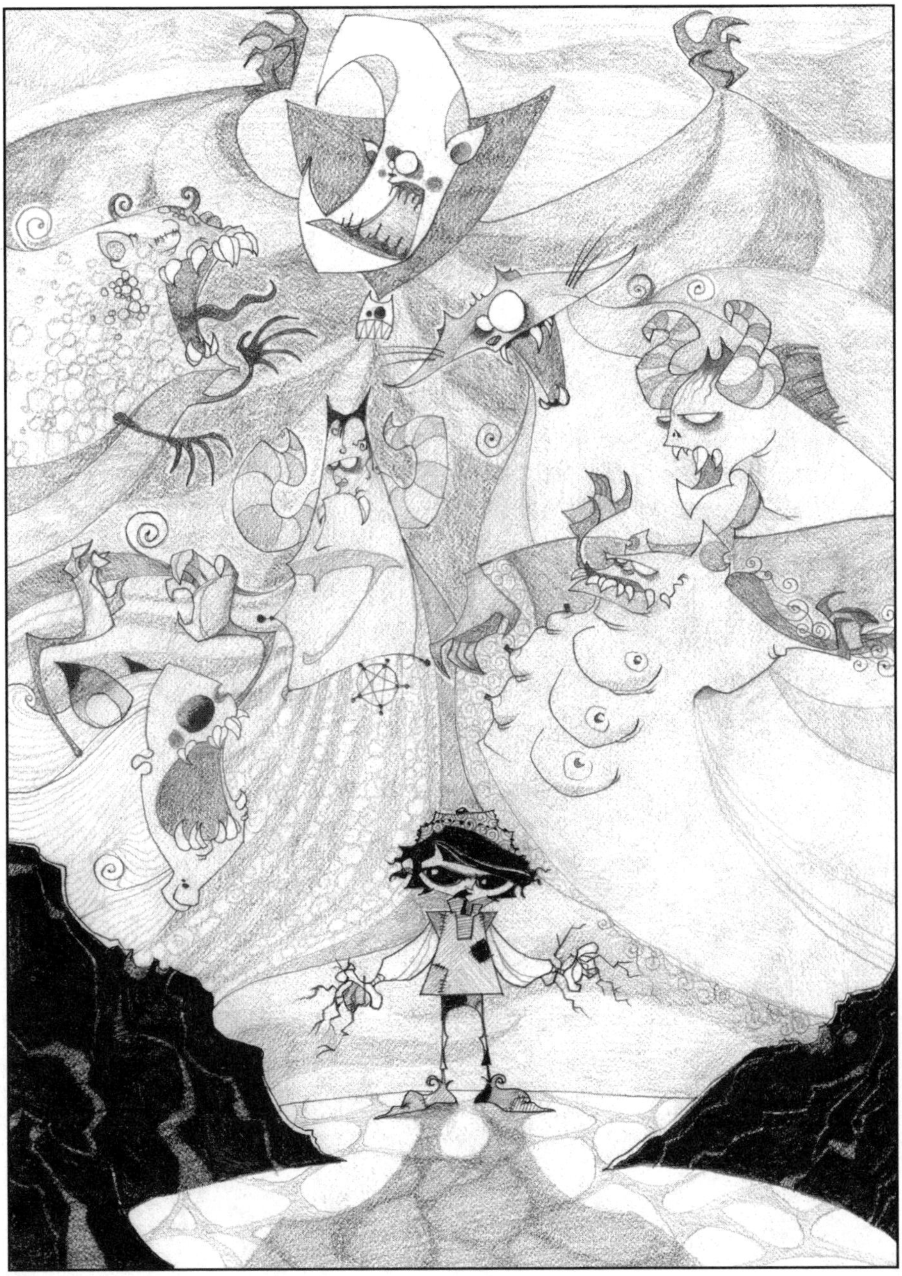

On the third morning of the wanderers' stay in Ulthar, Menes could not find his kitten; and as he sobbed in the marketplace the villagers told him of the old man and his wife. His sobbing soon gave place to prayer. He stretched out his arms, and as he prayed in a strange tongue there seemed to form overhead the shadowy figures of hybrid creatures.

That night the wanderers left Ulthar. And the householders were troubled when they noticed that in all the village there was not a cat to be found. From each hearth the familiar cat had vanished; cats large and small, black, grey, striped, yellow and white. Kranon the burgomaster swore that the dark folk had taken the cats away in revenge for the killing of Menes' kitten.

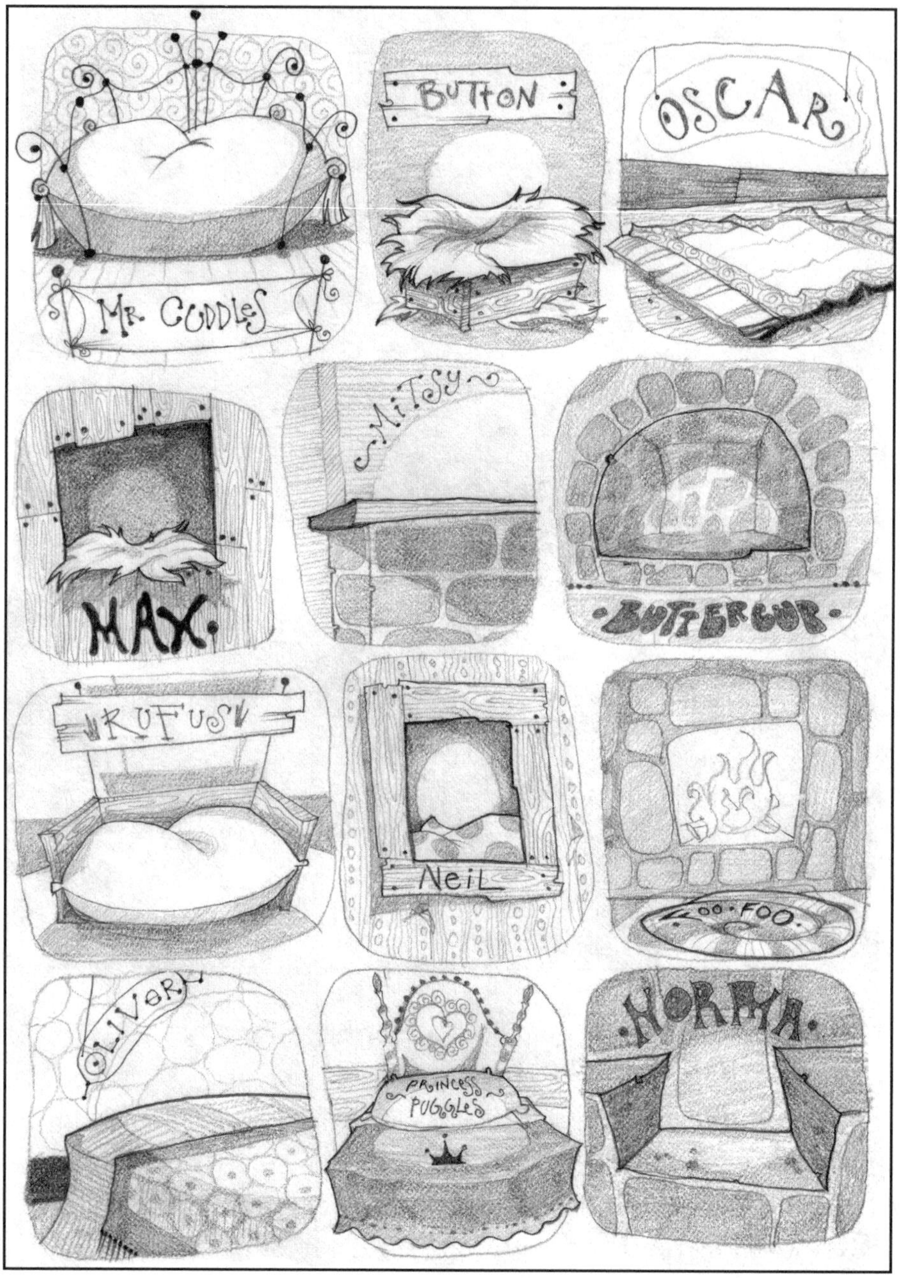
MR. CUDDLES
BUTTON
OSCAR
MITSY
MAX
BUTTERCUP
RUFUS
NEIL
FOO·FOO
OLIVER
PRINCESS PUGGLES
NORMA

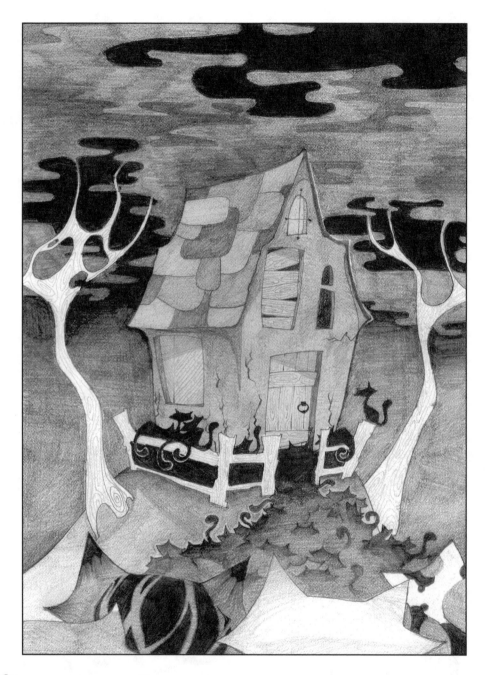

But Nith, the lean notary, declared that the old cotter and his wife were more likely persons to suspect. And little Atal, the innkeeper's son, vowed that he had at twilight seen all the cats of Ulthar in the cotter's yard under the trees, pacing very slowly and solemnly in a circle around the cottage, two abreast, as if in performance of some unheard-of rite of beasts.

So Ulthar went to sleep in anger; and when the people awakened at dawn every cat was back at his accustomed hearth! The refusal of all the cats to eat their portions of meat or drink their saucers of milk was exceedingly curious. And for two whole days the sleek, lazy cats of Ulthar would touch no food, but only doze by the fire or in the sun.

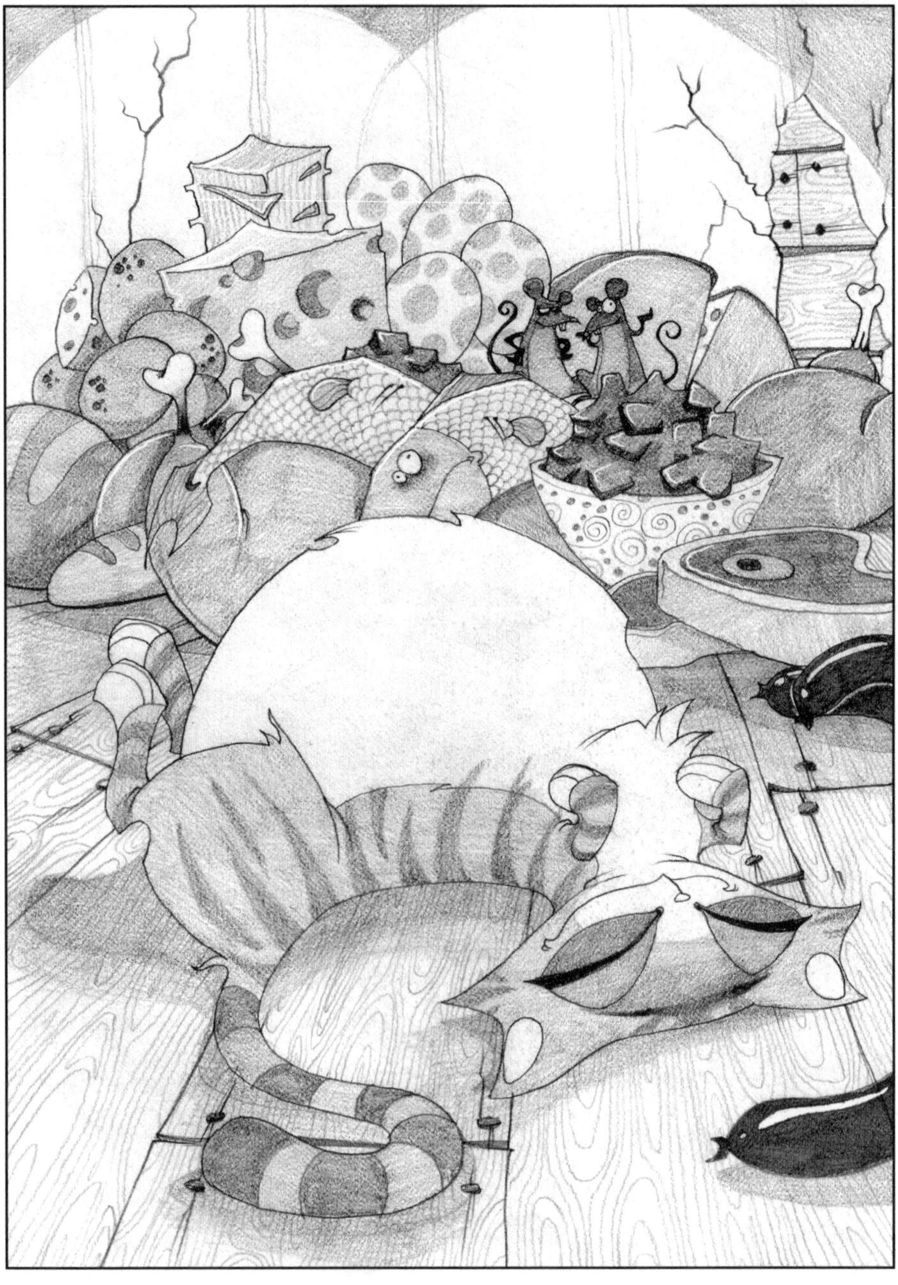

It was fully a week before the villagers noticed that no lights were appearing at dusk in the windows of the cottage under the trees. The burgomaster finally decided to overcome his fears and call at the strangely silent dwelling as a matter of duty. And when he, Shang and Thul had broken in the door they found only two cleanly picked skeletons on the earthen floor.

When news reached the village, there was subsequently much talk among the citizens and burgesses of Ulthar. Zath, the coroner, disputed at length with Nith, the lean notary; and old Kranon, Shang the blacksmith and Thul the stonecutter were overwhelmed with questions. Even little Atal was closely questioned and given a sweetmeat as reward.

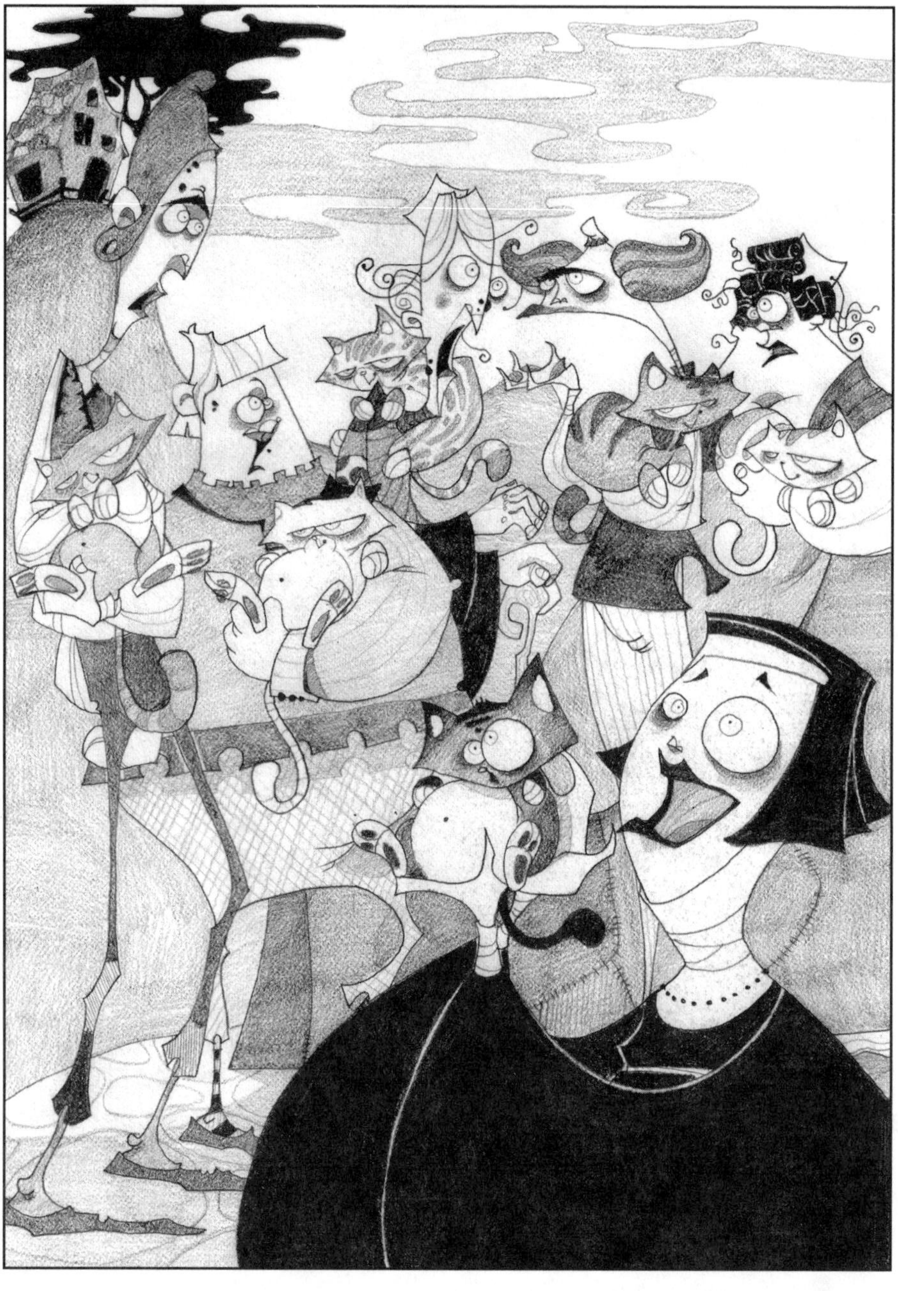

©2002 LISA K. WEBER

They talked of the old cotter and his wife, of the caravan of dark wanderers, of the prayer of Menes, and of what was later found in the cottage under the dark trees. And in the end the burgesses passed that remarkable law which is told of by traders in Hatheg and discussed by travelers in Nir; namely, that in Ulthar no man may kill a cat.

Cthulhu's Dreams:
Le Chaos Rapant

written & illustrated by

DOMINIQUE SIGNORET

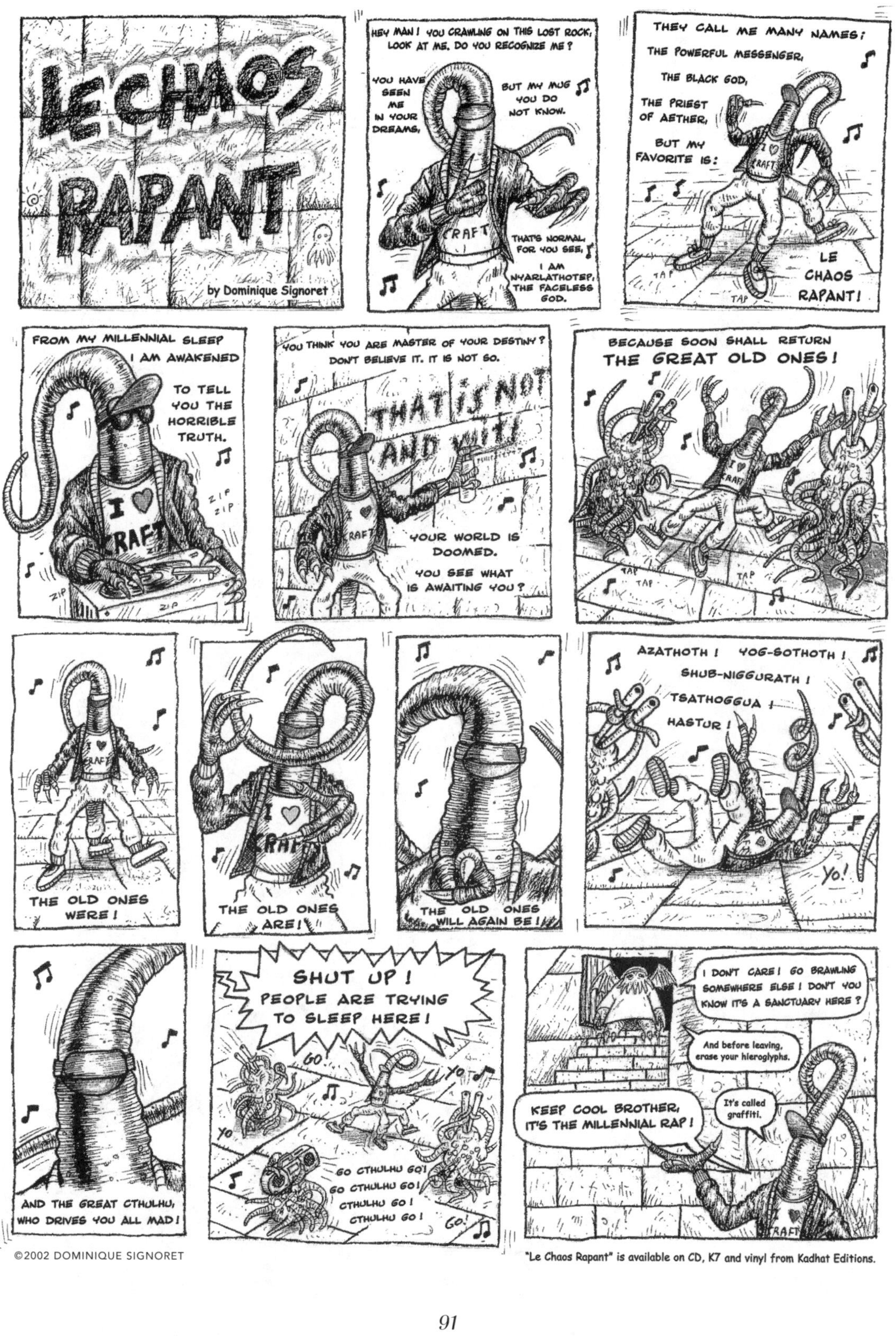
LE CHAOS RAPANT
by Dominique Signoret
HEY MAN! YOU CRAWLING ON THIS LOST ROCK, LOOK AT ME. DO YOU RECOGNIZE ME?
YOU HAVE SEEN ME IN YOUR DREAMS,
BUT MY MUG YOU DO NOT KNOW.
THAT'S NORMAL, FOR YOU SEE, I AM NYARLATHOTEP, THE FACELESS GOD.
THEY CALL ME MANY NAMES:
THE POWERFUL MESSENGER,
THE BLACK GOD,
THE PRIEST OF AETHER,
BUT MY FAVORITE IS:
TAP
TAP
LE CHAOS RAPANT!
FROM MY MILLENNIAL SLEEP I AM AWAKENED
TO TELL YOU THE HORRIBLE TRUTH.
ZIP ZIP
ZIP
ZIP
YOU THINK YOU ARE MASTER OF YOUR DESTINY? DON'T BELIEVE IT. IT IS NOT SO.
YOUR WORLD IS DOOMED.
YOU SEE WHAT IS AWAITING YOU?
BECAUSE SOON SHALL RETURN
THE GREAT OLD ONES!
TAP
TAP
TAP
THE OLD ONES WERE!
THE OLD ONES ARE!
THE OLD ONES WILL AGAIN BE!
AZATHOTH! YOG-SOTHOTH!
SHUB-NIGGURATH!
TSATHOGGUA!
HASTUR!
YO!
AND THE GREAT CTHULHU, WHO DRIVES YOU ALL MAD!
SHUT UP! PEOPLE ARE TRYING TO SLEEP HERE!
GO!
YO
YO
GO CTHULHU GO! GO CTHULHU GO! CTHULHU GO! CTHULHU GO!
GO!
I DON'T CARE! GO BRAWLING SOMEWHERE ELSE! DON'T YOU KNOW IT'S A SANCTUARY HERE?
And before leaving, erase your hieroglyphs.
KEEP COOL BROTHER, IT'S THE MILLENNIAL RAP!
It's called graffiti.

"Le Chaos Rapant" is available on CD, K7 and vinyl from Kadhat Editions.

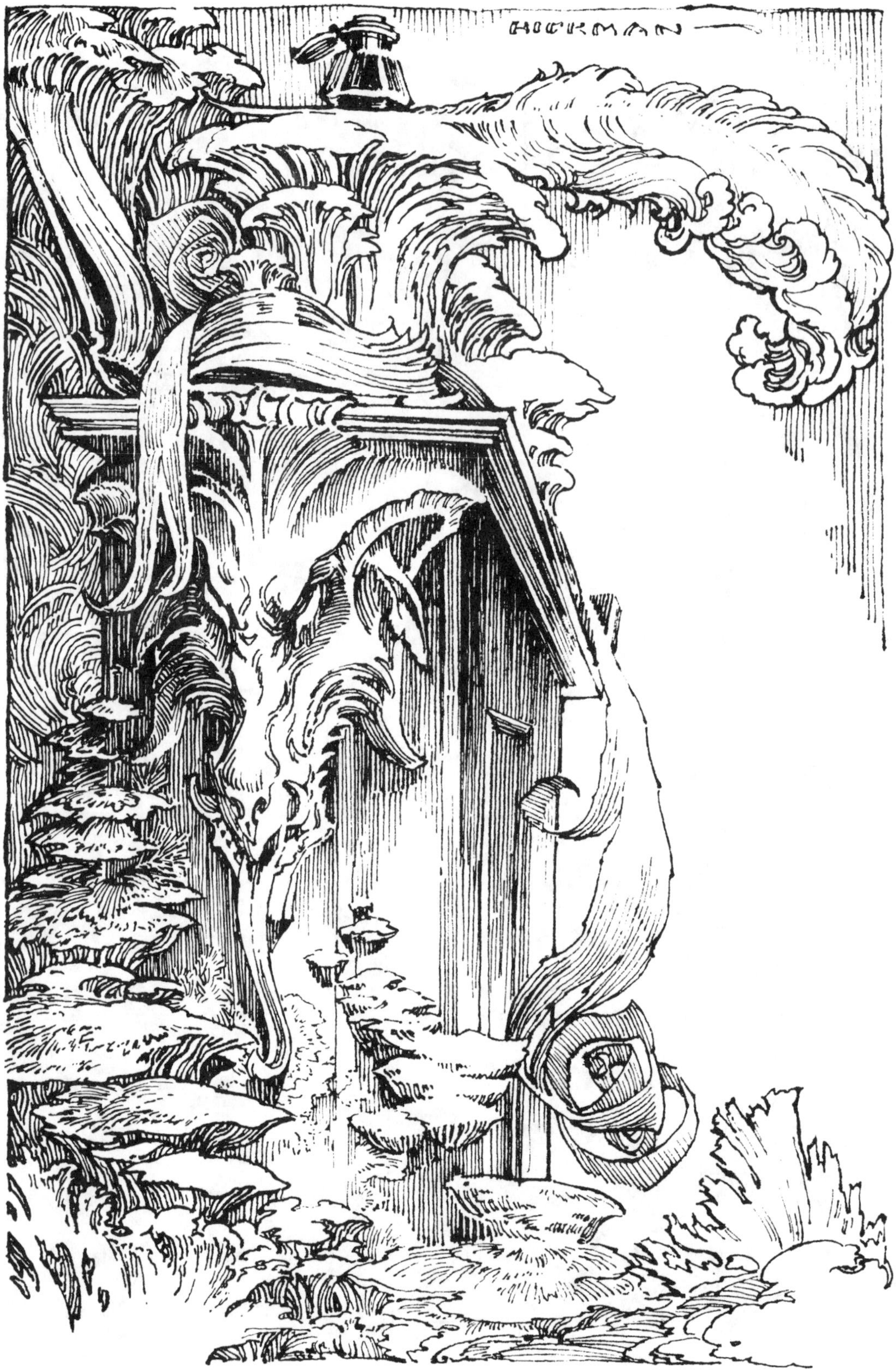
HICKMAN

Fungi From Yuggoth

The epic poem by H.P. Lovecraft
illustrated by

STEPHEN HICKMAN

JOHN COULTHART

MAXON CRUMB

KELLIE STRØM

ALLEN KOSZOWSKI

S. CLAY WILSON

SKOT OLSEN

JEFFREY JOHANNES

STEVEN CERIO

GERRY ALANGUILAN

PETER VON SHOLLY

ARNOLD ARRE

ANDY EWEN

RAFAEL AVILA

JEFF REMMER

TRINA ROBBINS

R.K. SLOANE

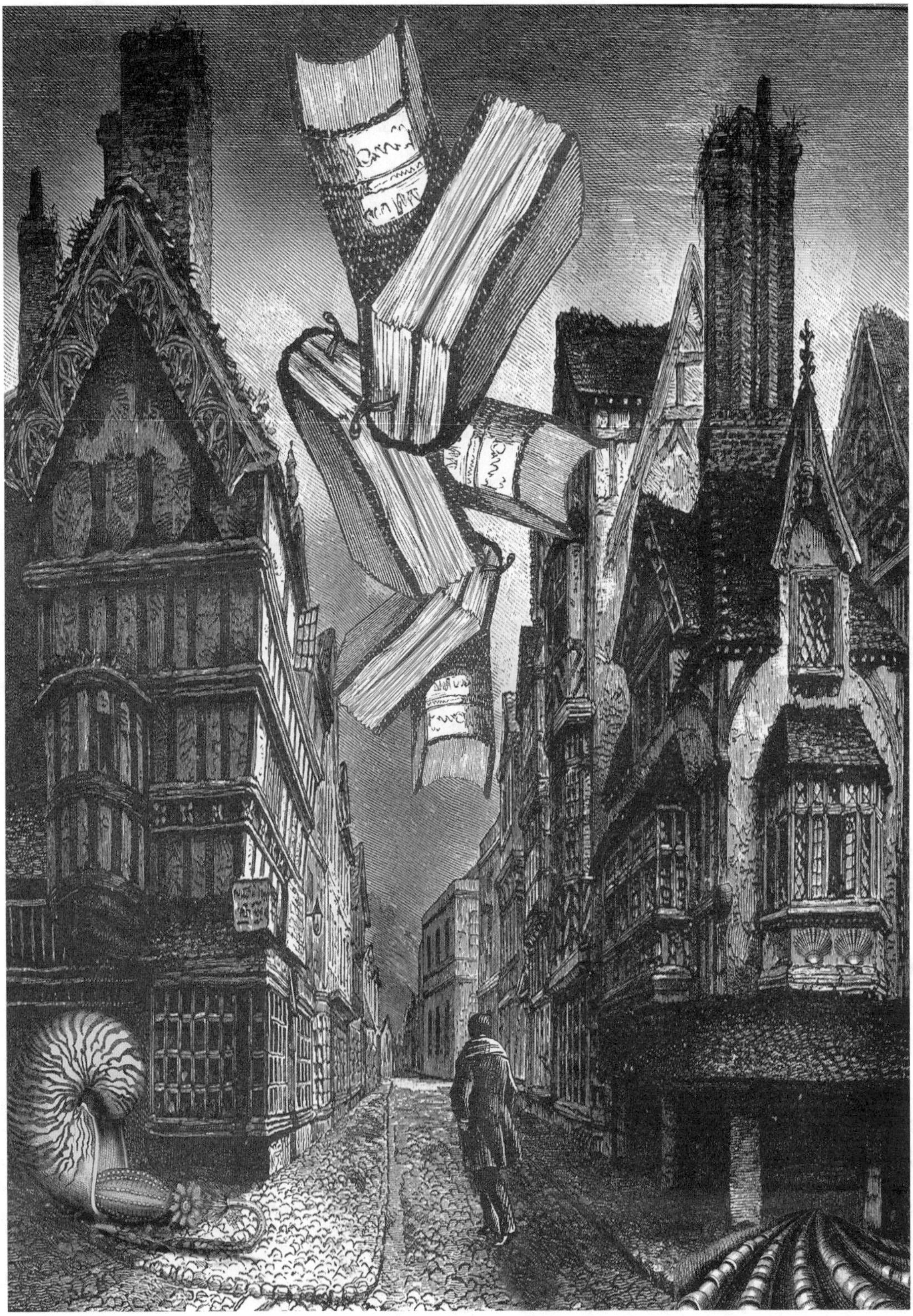

I. The Book

The place was dark and dusty and half-lost
In tangles of old alleys near the quays,
Reeking of strange things brought in from the seas,
And with queer curls of fog that west winds tossed.
Small lozenge panes, obscured by smoke and frost,
Just shewed the books, in piles like twisted trees,
Rotting from floor to roof — congeries
Of crumbling elder lore at little cost.

I entered, charmed, and from a cobwebbed heap
Took up the nearest tome and thumbed it through,
Trembling at curious words that seemed to keep
Some secret, monstrous if one only knew.
Then, looking for some seller old in craft,
I could find nothing but a voice that laughed.

II. Pursuit

I held the book beneath my coat, at pains
To hide the thing from sight in such a place;
Hurrying through the ancient harbor lanes
With often-turning head and nervous pace.
Dull, furtive windows in old tottering brick
Peered at me oddly as I hastened by,
And thinking what they sheltered, I grew sick
For a redeeming glimpse of clean blue sky.

No one had seen me take the thing — but still
A blank laugh echoed in my whirling head,
And I could guess what nighted worlds of ill
Lurked in that volume I had coveted.
The way grew strange — the walls alike and madding —
And far behind me, unseen feet were padding.

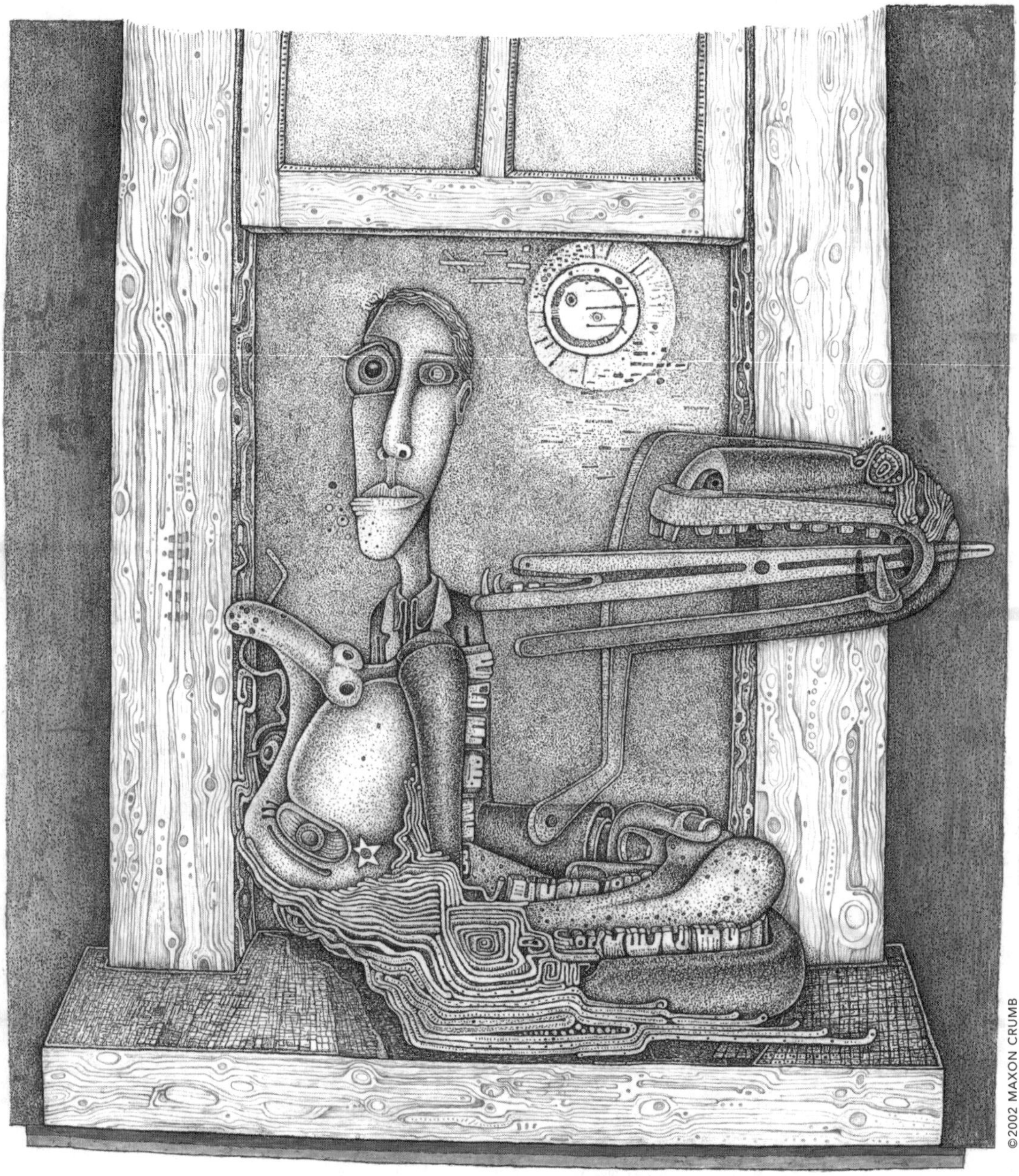

Maxon

III. The Key

I do not know what windings in the waste
Of those strange sea-lanes brought me home once more,
But on my porch I trembled, white with haste
To get inside and bolt the heavy door.
I had the book that told the hidden way
Across the void and through the space-hung screens
That hold the undimensioned worlds at bay,
And keep lost aeons to their own demesnes.

At last the key was mine to those vague visions
Of sunset spires and twilight woods that brood
Dim in the gulfs beyond this earth's precisions,
Lurking as memories of infinitude.
The key was mine, but as I sat there mumbling,
The attic window shook with a faint fumbling.

IV. Recognition

The day had come again, when as a child
I saw — just once — that hollow of old oaks,
Grey with a ground-mist that enfolds and chokes
The slinking shapes which madness has defiled.
It was the same — an herbage rank and wild
Clings round an altar whose carved sign invokes
That Nameless One to whom a thousand smokes
Rose, aeons gone, from unclean towers up-piled.

I saw the body spread on that dank stone,
And knew those things which feasted were not men;
I knew this strange, grey world was not my own,
But Yuggoth, past the starry voids — and then
The body shrieked at me with a dead cry,
And all too late I knew that it was I!

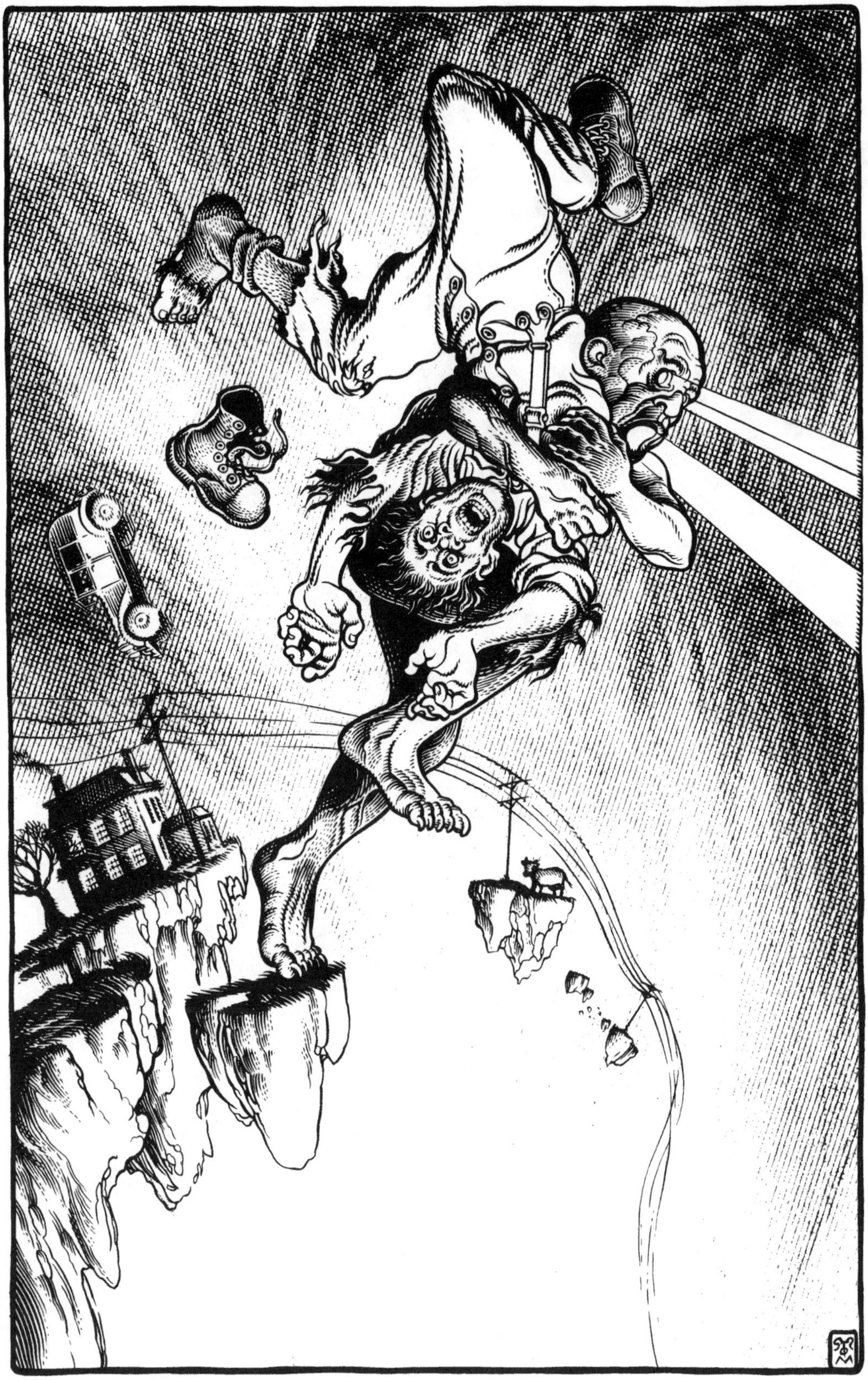

V. Homecoming

The daemon said that he would take me home
To the pale, shadowy land I half recalled
As a high place of stair and terrace, walled
With marble balustrades that sky-winds comb,
While miles below a maze of dome on dome
And tower on tower beside a sea lies sprawled.
Once more, he told me, I would stand enthralled
On those old heights, and hear the far-off foam.

All this he promised, and through sunset's gate
He swept me, past the lapping lakes of flame,
And red-gold thrones of gods without a name
Who shriek in fear at some impending fate.
Then a black gulf with sea-sounds in the night:
"Here was your home," he mocked, "when you had sight!"

VI. The Lamp

We found the lamp inside those hollow cliffs
Whose chiseled sign no priest in Thebes could read,
And from whose caverns frightened hieroglyphs
Warned every living creature of earth's breed.
No more was there — just that one brazen bowl
With traces of a curious oil within;
Fretted with some obscurely patterned scroll,
And symbols hinting vaguely of strange sin.

Little the fears of forty centuries meant
To us as we bore off our slender spoil,
And when we scanned it in our darkened tent
We struck a match to test the ancient oil.
It blazed — great God!... But the vast shapes we saw
In that mad flash have seared our lives with awe.

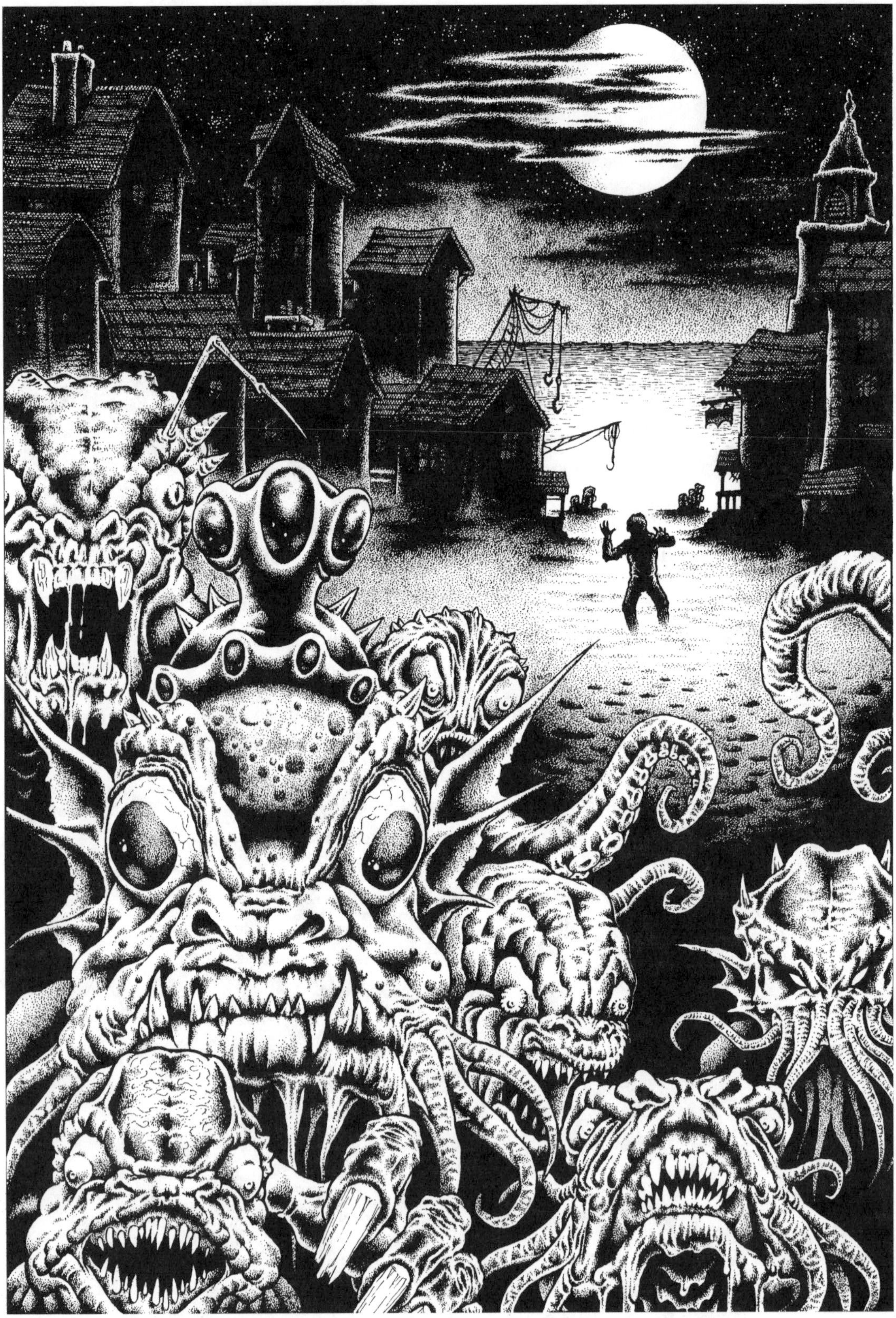

VII. Zaman's Hill

The great hill hung close over the old town,
A precipice against the main street's end;
Green, tall, and wooded, looking darkly down
Upon the steeple at the highway bend.
Two hundred years the whispers had been heard
About what happened on the man-shunned slope —
Tales of an oddly mangled deer or bird,
Or of lost boys whose kin had ceased to hope.

One day the mail-man found no village there,
Nor were its folk or houses seen again;
People came out from Aylesbury to stare —
Yet they all told the mail-man it was plain
That he was mad for saying he had spied
The great hill's gluttonous eyes, and jaws stretched wide.

VIII. The Port

Ten miles from Arkham I had struck the trail
That rides the cliff-edge over Boynton Beach,
And hoped that just at sunset I could reach
The crest that looks on Innsmouth in the vale.
Far out at sea was a retreating sail,
White as hard years of ancient winds could bleach,
But evil with some portent beyond speech,
So that I did not wave my hand or hail.

Sails out of Innsmouth! echoing old renown
Of long-dead times. But now a too-swift night
Is closing in, and I have reached the height
Whence I so often scan the distant town.
The spires and roofs are there — but look! The gloom
Sinks on dark lanes, as lightless as the tomb!

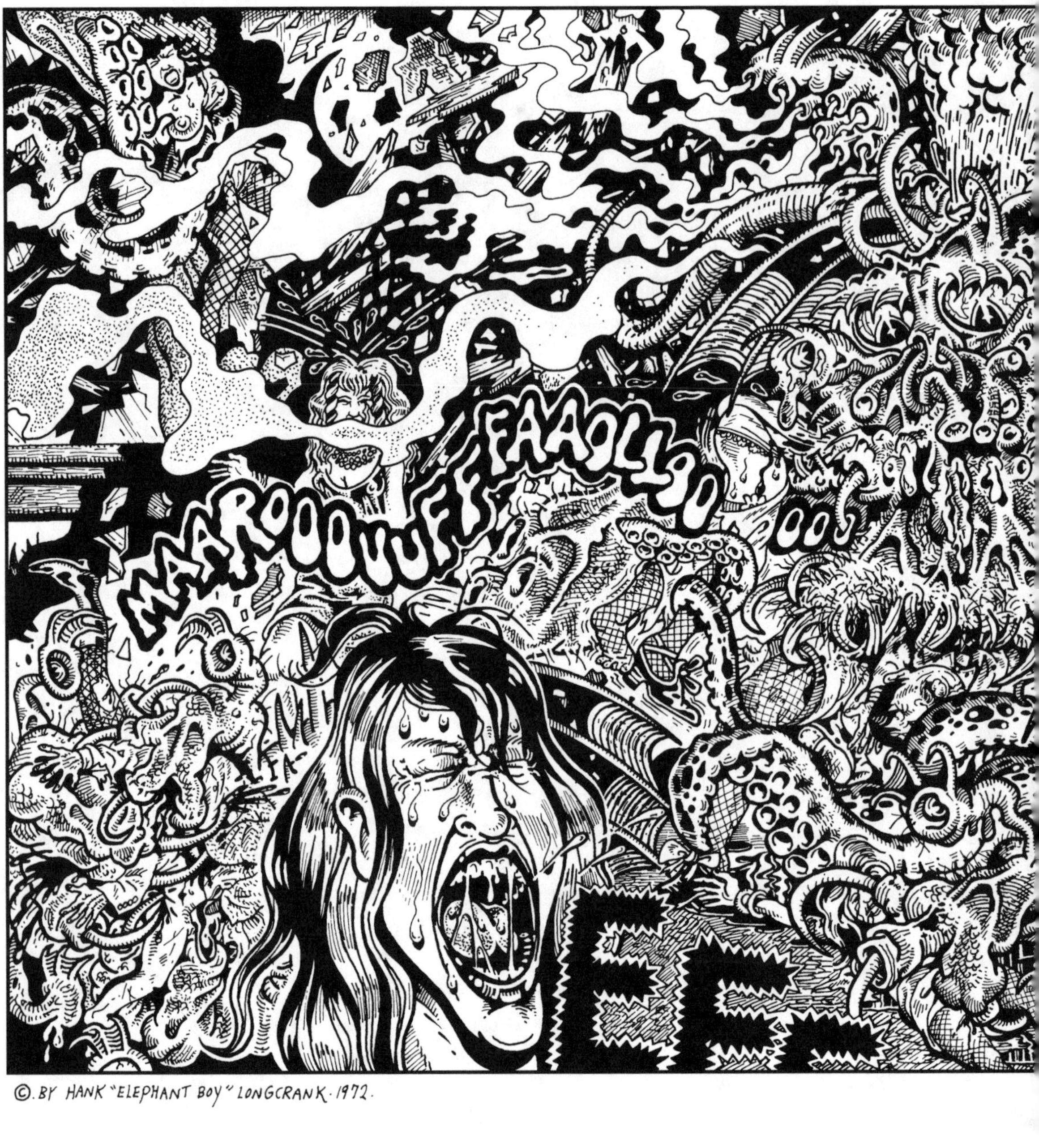
MAAROOOVUFF FAAOLLOO OOO

IX. The Courtyard

It was the city I had known before;
The ancient, leprous town where mongrel throngs
Chant to strange gods, and beat unhallowed gongs
In crypts beneath foul alleys near the shore.
The rotting, fish-eyed houses leered at me
From where they leaned, drunk and half-animate,
As edging through the filth I passed the gate
To the black courtyard where the man would be.

The dark walls closed me in, and loud I cursed
That ever I had come to such a den,
When suddenly a score of windows burst
Into wild light, and swarmed with dancing men:
Mad, soundless revels of the dragging dead —
And not a corpse had either hands or head!

X. The Pigeon-Flyers

They took me slumming, where gaunt walls of brick
Bulge outward with a viscous stored-up evil,
And twisted faces, thronging foul and thick,
Wink messages to alien god and devil.
A million fires were blazing in the streets,
And from flat roofs a furtive few would fly
Bedraggled birds into the yawning sky
While hidden drums droned on with measured beats.

I knew those fires were brewing monstrous things,
And that those birds of space had been Outside —
I guessed to what dark planet's crypts they plied,
And what they brought from Thog beneath their wings.
The others laughed — till struck too mute to speak
By what they glimpsed in one bird's evil beak.

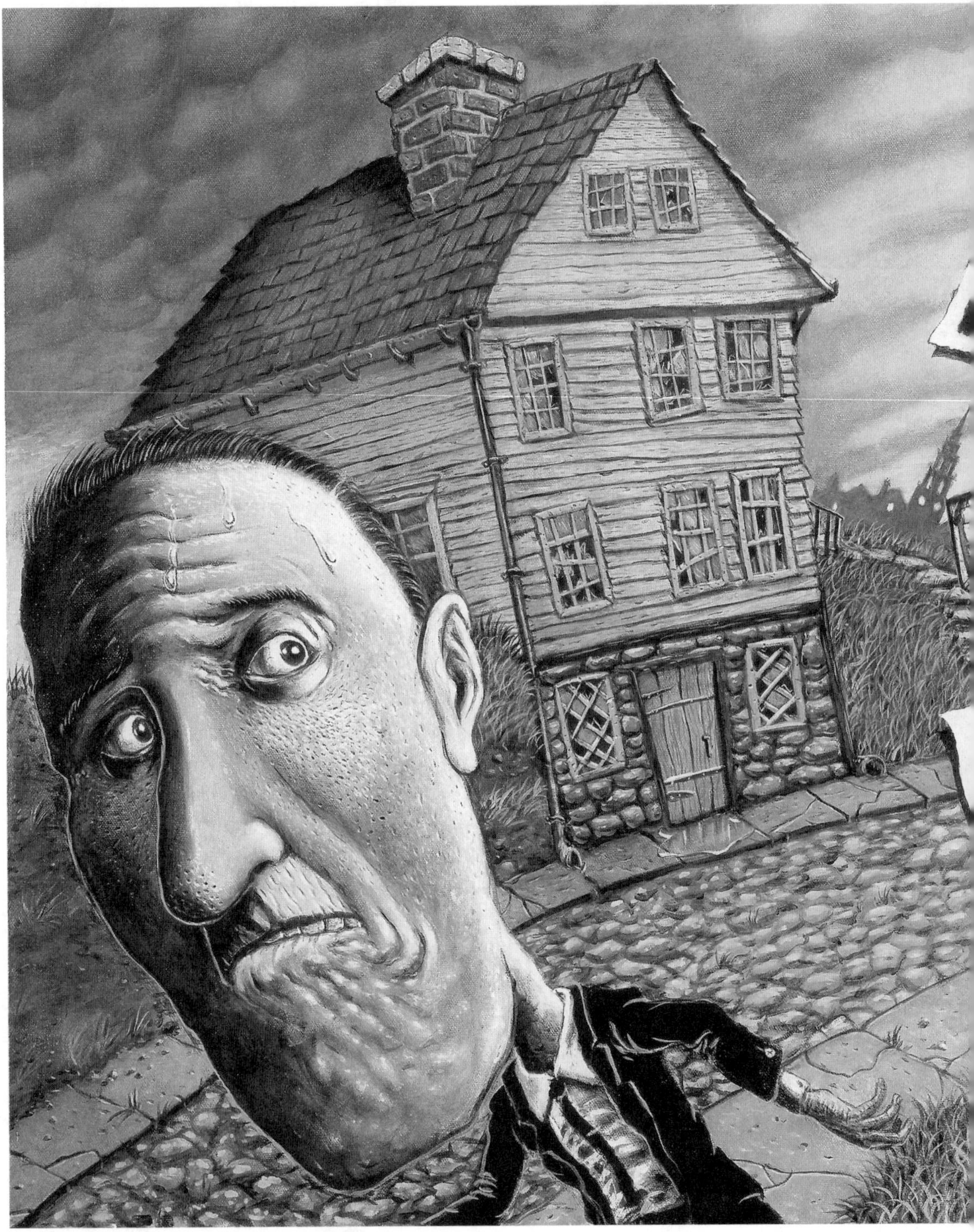

XI. The Well

Farmer Seth Atwood was past eighty when
He tried to sink that deep well by his door,
With only Eb to help him bore and bore.
We laughed, and hoped he'd soon be sane again.
And yet, instead, young Eb went crazy, too,
So that they shipped him to the county farm.
Seth bricked the well-mouth up as tight as glue —
Then hacked an artery in his gnarled left arm.

After the funeral we felt bound to get
Out to that well and rip the bricks away,
But all we saw were iron hand-holds set
Down a black hole deeper than we could say.
And yet we put the bricks back — for we found
The hole too deep for any line to sound.

XII. The Howler

They told me not to take the Briggs' Hill path
That used to be the highroad through to Zoar,
For Goody Watkins, hanged in seventeen-four,
Had left a certain monstrous aftermath.
Yet when I disobeyed, and had in view
The vine-hung cottage by the great rock slope,
I could not think of elms or hempen rope,
But wondered why the house still seemed so new.

Stopping a while to watch the fading day,
I heard faint howls, as from a room upstairs,
When through the ivied panes one sunset ray
Struck in, and caught the howler unawares.
I glimpsed — and ran in frenzy from the place,
And from a four-pawed thing with human face.

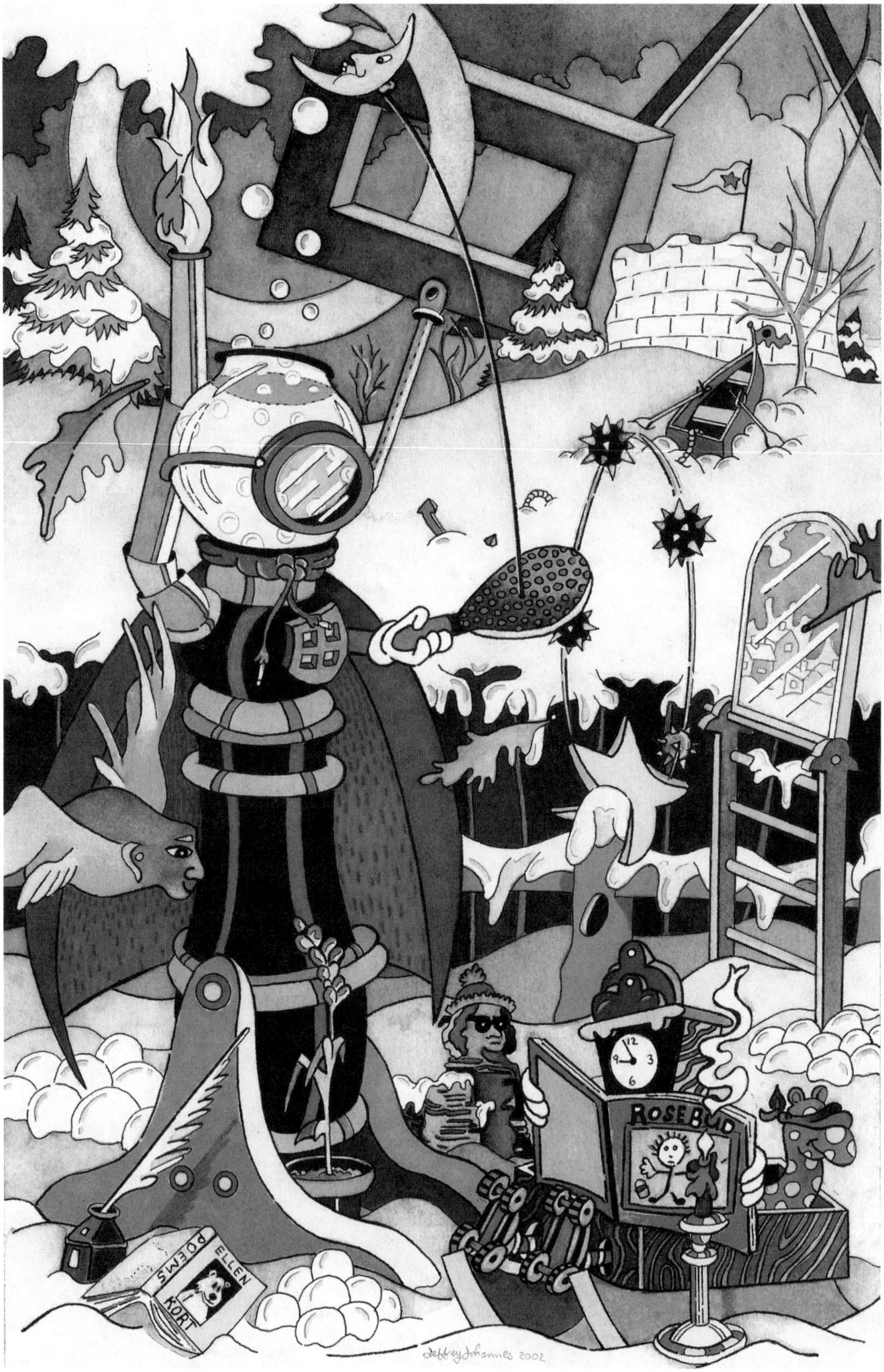
ROSEBUD
POEMS
ELLEN
KORT
Jeffrey Johannes 2002

XIII. Hesperia

The winter sunset, flaming beyond spires
And chimneys half-detached from this dull sphere,
Opens great gates to some forgotten year
Of elder splendours and divine desires.
Expectant wonders burn in those rich fires,
Adventure-fraught, and not untinged with fear;
A row of sphinxes where the way leads clear
Toward walls and turrets quivering to far lyres.

It is the land where beauty's meaning flowers;
Where every unplaced memory has a source;
Where the great river Time begins its course
Down the vast void in starlit streams of hours.
Dreams bring us close — but ancient lore repeats
That human tread has never soiled these streets.

XIV. Star-Winds

It is a certain hour of twilight glooms,
Mostly in autumn, when the star-wind pours
Down hilltop streets, deserted out-of-doors,
But shewing early lamplight from snug rooms.
The dead leaves rush in strange, fantastic twists,
And chimney-smoke whirls round with alien grace,
Heeding geometries of outer space,
While Fomalhaut peers in through southward mists.

This is the hour when moonstruck poets know
What fungi sprout in Yuggoth, and what scents
And tints of flowers fill Nithon's continents,
Such as in no poor earthly garden blow.
Yet for each dream these winds to us convey,
A dozen more of ours they sweep away!

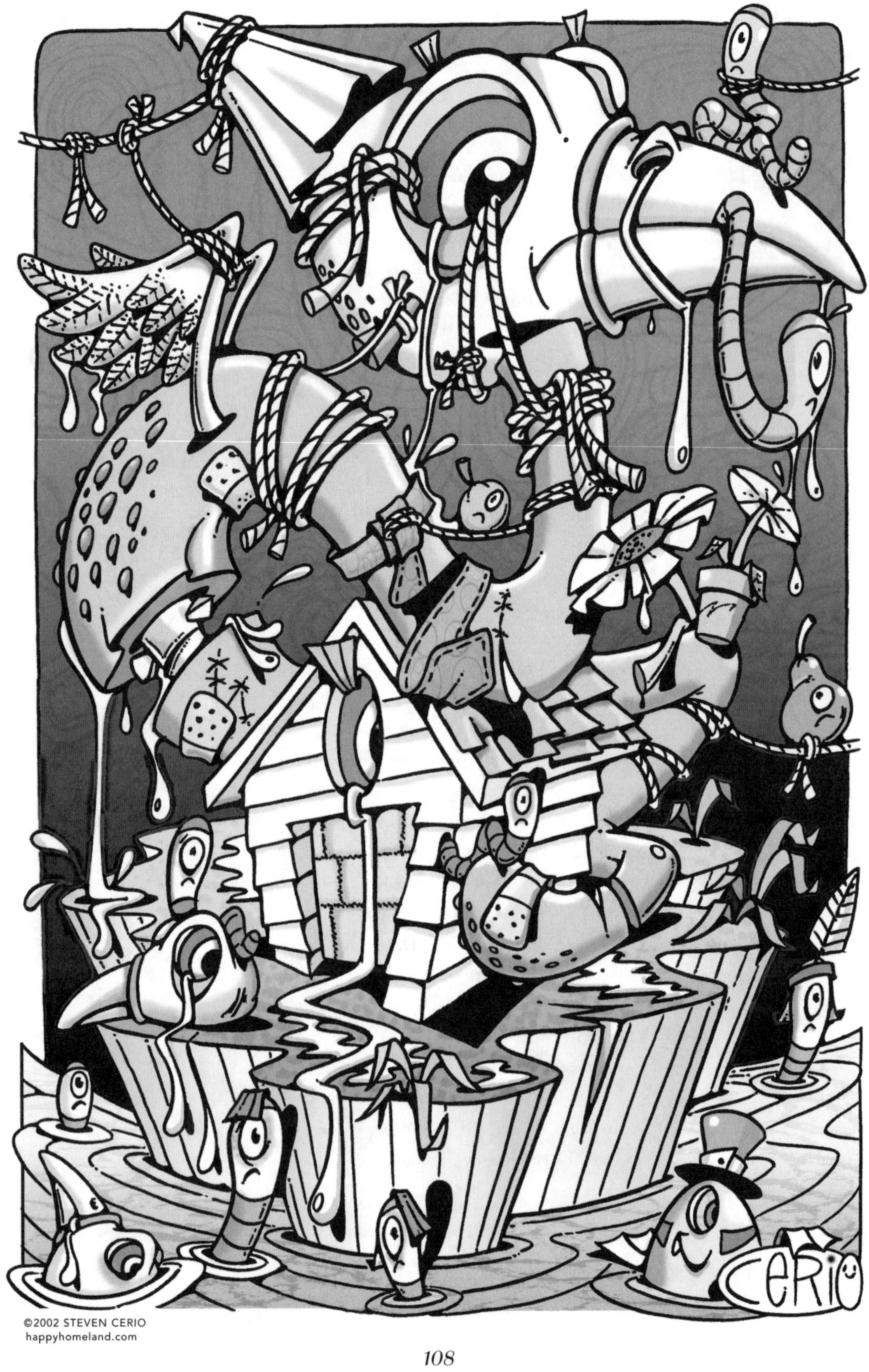
CERIO

XV. Antarktos

Deep in my dream the great bird whispered queerly
Of the black cone amid the polar waste;
Pushing above the ice-sheet lone and drearly,
By storm-crazed aeons battered and defaced.
Hither no living earth-shapes take their courses,
And only pale auroras and faint suns
Glow on that pitted rock, whose primal sources
Are guessed at dimly by the Elder Ones.

If men should glimpse it, they would merely wonder
What tricky mound of Nature's build they spied;
But the bird told of vaster parts, that under
The mile-deep ice-shroud crouch and brood and bide.
God help the dreamer whose mad visions shew
Those dead eyes set in crystal gulfs below!

XVI. The Window

The house was old, with tangled wings outthrown,
Of which no one could ever half keep track,
And in a small room somewhat near the back
Was an odd window sealed with ancient stone.
There, in a dream-plagued childhood, quite alone
I used to go, where night reigned vague and black;
Parting the cobwebs with a curious lack
Of fear, and with a wonder each time grown.

One later day I brought the masons there
To find what view my dim forbears had shunned,
But as they pierced the stone, a rush of air
Burst from the alien voids that yawned beyond.
They fled — but I peered through and found unrolled
All the wild worlds of which my dreams had told.

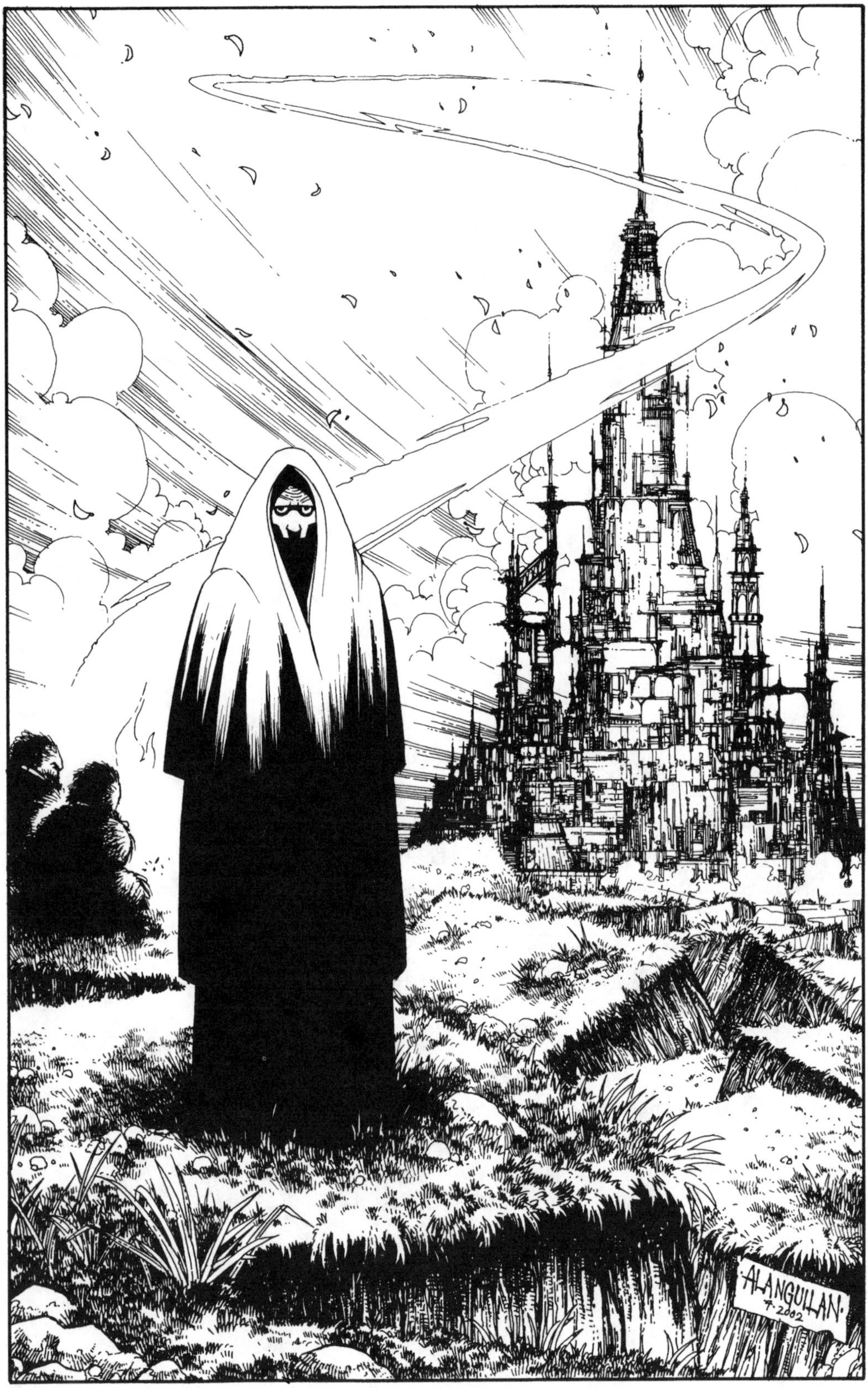
ALANGUILAN
7.2002

XVII. A Memory

There were great steppes, and rocky table-lands
Stretching half-limitless in starlit night,
With alien campfires shedding feeble light
On beasts with tinkling bells, in shaggy bands.
Far to the south the plain sloped low and wide
To a dark zigzag line of wall that lay
Like a huge python of some primal day
Which endless time had chilled and petrified.

I shivered oddly in the cold, thin air,
And wondered where I was and how I came,
When a cloaked form against a campfire's glare
Rose and approached, and called me by my name.
Staring at that dead face beneath the hood,
I ceased to hope — because I understood.

XVIII. The Gardens of Yin

Beyond that wall, whose ancient masonry
Reached almost to the sky in moss-thick towers,
There would be terraced gardens, rich with flowers,
And flutter of bird and butterfly and bee.
There would be walks, and bridges arching over
Warm lotos-pools reflecting temple eaves,
And cherry-trees with delicate boughs and leaves
Against a pink sky where the herons hover.

All would be there, for had not old dreams flung
Open the gate to that stone-lanterned maze
Where drowsy streams spin out their winding ways,
Trailed by green vines from bending branches hung?
I hurried — but when the wall rose, grim and great,
I found there was no longer any gate.

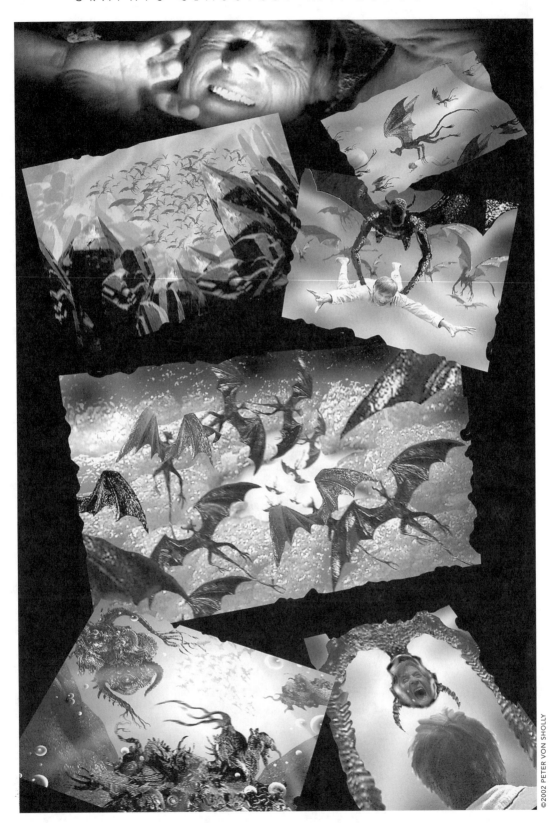

XIX. The Bells

Year after year I heard that faint, far ringing
Of deep-toned bells on the black midnight wind;
Peals from no steeple I could ever find,
But strange, as if across some great void winging.
I searched my dreams and memories for a clue,
And thought of all the chimes my visions carried;
Of quiet Innsmouth, where the white gulls tarried
Around an ancient spire that once I knew.

Always perplexed I heard those far notes falling,
Till one March night the bleak rain splashing cold
Beckoned me back through gateways of recalling
To elder towers where the mad clappers tolled.
They tolled — but from the sunless tides that pour
Through sunken valleys on the sea's dead floor.

XX. Night-Gaunts

Out of what crypt they crawl, I cannot tell,
But every night I see the rubbery things,
Black, horned, and slender, with membraneous wings,
And tails that bear the bifid barb of hell.
They come in legions on the north wind's swell,
With obscene clutch that titillates and stings,
Snatching me off on monstrous voyagings
To grey worlds hidden deep in nightmare's well.

Over the jagged peaks of Thok they sweep,
Heedless of all the cries I try to make,
And down the nether pits to that foul lake
Where the puffed shoggoths splash in doubtful sleep.
But oh! If only they would make some sound,
Or wear a face where faces should be found!

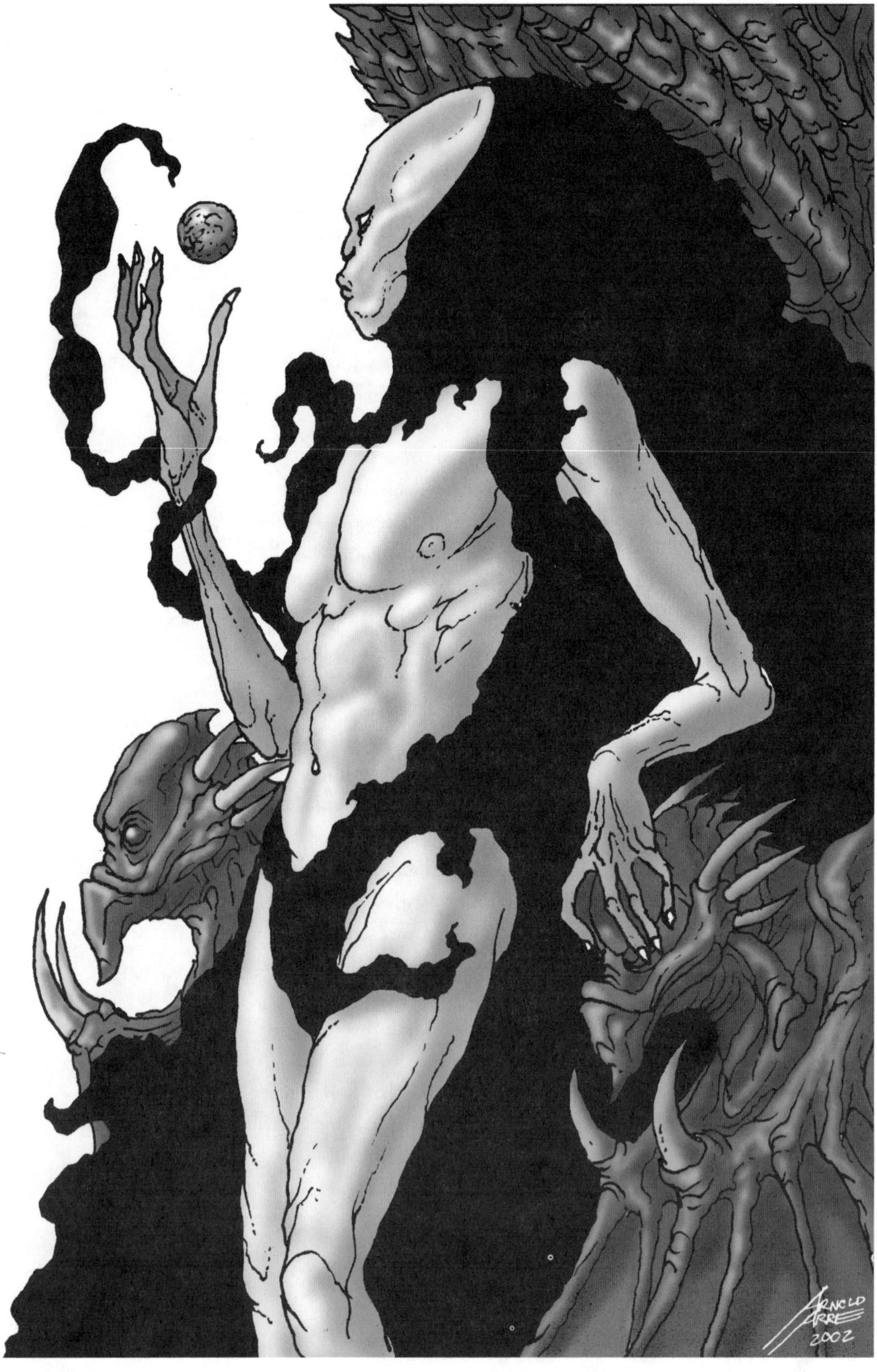
ARNOLD ARRE
2002

XXI. Nyarlathotep

And at the last from inner Egypt came
The strange dark One to whom the fellahs bowed;
Silent and lean and cryptically proud,
And wrapped in fabrics red as sunset flame.
Throngs pressed around, frantic for his commands,
But leaving, could not tell what they had heard;
While through the nations spread the awestruck word
That wild beasts followed him and licked his hands.

Soon from the sea a noxious birth began;
Forgotten lands with weedy spires of gold;
The ground was cleft, and mad auroras rolled
Down on the quaking citadels of man.
Then, crushing what he chanced to mould in play,
The idiot Chaos blew Earth's dust away.

XXII. Azathoth

Out in the mindless void the daemon bore me,
Past the bright clusters of dimensioned space,
Till neither time nor matter stretched before me,
But only Chaos, without form or place.
Here the vast Lord of All in darkness muttered
Things he had dreamed but could not understand,
While near him shapeless bat-things flopped and fluttered
In idiot vortices that ray-streams fanned. .

They danced insanely to the high, thin whining
Of a cracked flute clutched in a monstrous paw,
Whence flow the aimless waves whose chance combining
Gives each frail cosmos its eternal law.
"I am His Messenger," the daemon said,
As in contempt he struck his Master's head.

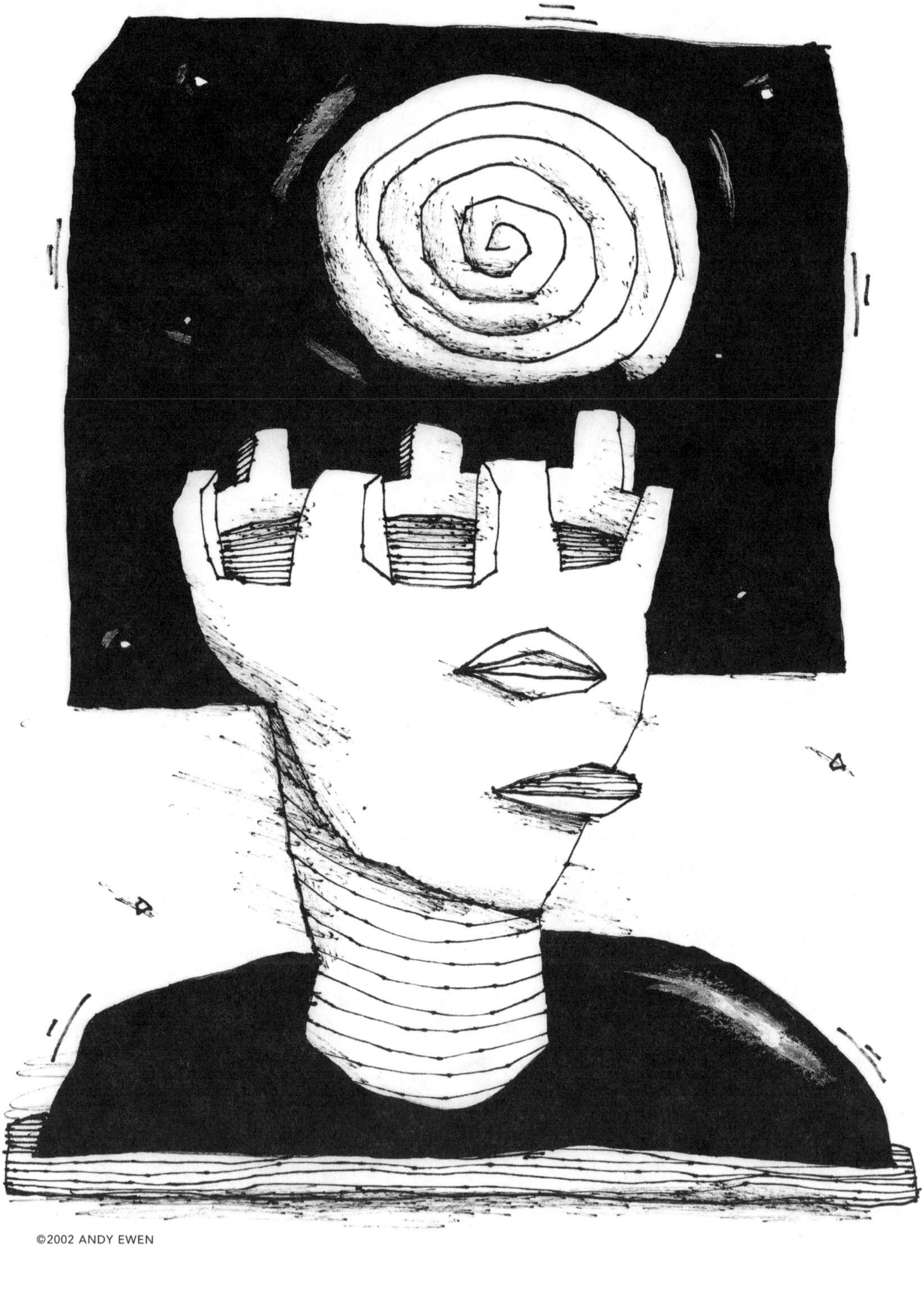

XXIII. Mirage

I do not know if ever it existed —
That lost world floating dimly on Time's stream -
And yet I see it often, violet-misted,
And shimmering at the back of some vague dream.
There were strange towers and curious lapping rivers,
Labyrinths of wonder, and low vaults of light,
And bough-crossed skies of flame, like that which quivers
Wistfully just before a winter's night.

Great moors led off to sedgy shores unpeopled,
Where vast birds wheeled, while on a windswept hill
There was a village, ancient and white-steepled,
With evening chimes for which I listen still.
I do not know what land it is — or dare
Ask when or why I was, or will be, there.

XXIV. The Canal

Somewhere in dream there is an evil place
Where tall, deserted buildings crowd along
A deep, black, narrow channel, reeking strong
Of frightful things whence oily currents race.
Lanes with old walls half meeting overhead
Wind off to streets one may or may not know,
And feeble moonlight sheds a spectral glow
Over long rows of windows, dark and dead.

There are no footfalls, and the one soft sound
Is of the oily water as it glides
Under stone bridges, and along the sides
Of its deep flume, to some vague ocean bound.
None lives to tell when that stream washed away
Its dream-lost region from the world of clay.

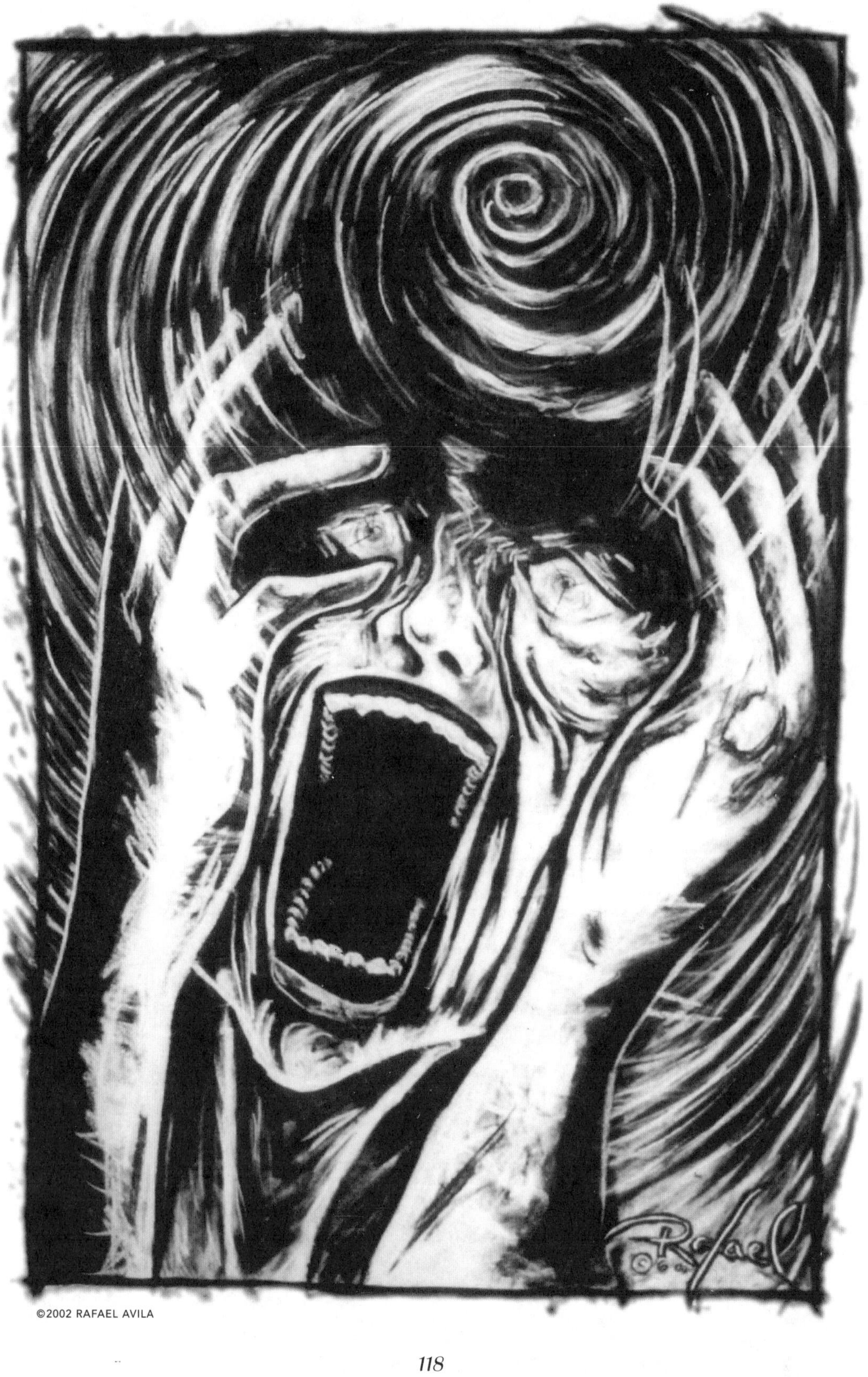
Rafael

XXV. St. Toad's

"Beware St. Toad's cracked chimes!" I heard him scream
As I plunged into those mad lanes that wind
In labyrinths obscure and undefined
South of the river where old centuries dream.
He was a furtive figure, bent and ragged,
And in a flash had staggered out of sight,
So still I burrowed onward in the night
Toward where more roof-lines rose, malign and jagged.

No guide-book told of what was lurking here —
But now I heard another old man shriek:
"Beware St.Toad's cracked chimes!" And growing weak,
I paused, when a third greybeard croaked in fear:
"Beware St. Toad's cracked chimes!" Aghast, I fled —
Till suddenly that black spire loomed ahead.

XXVI. The Familiars

John Whateley lived about a mile from town,
Up where the hills begin to huddle thick;
We never thought his wits were very quick,
Seeing the way he let his farm run down.
He used to waste his time on some queer books
He'd found around the attic of his place,
Till funny lines got creased into his face,
And folks all said they didn't like his looks.

When he began those night-howls we declared
He'd better be locked up away from harm,
So three men from the Aylesbury town farm
Went for him — but came back alone and scared.
They'd found him talking to two crouching things
That at their step flew off on great black wings.

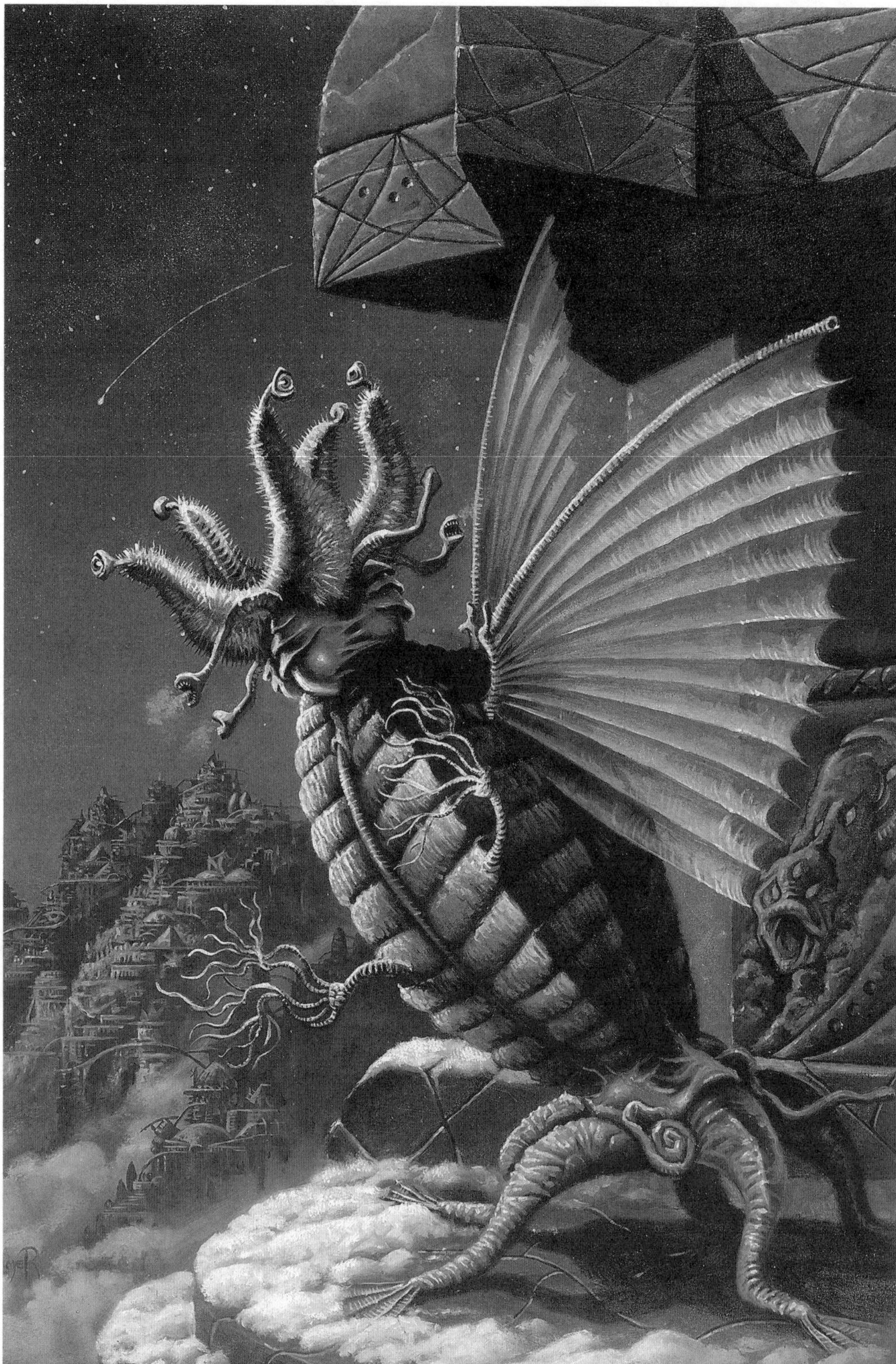

XXVII. The Elder Pharos

From Leng, where rocky peaks climb bleak and bare
Under cold stars obscure to human sight,
There shoots at dusk a single beam of light
Whose far blue rays make shepherds whine in prayer.
They say (though none has been there) that it comes
Out of a pharos in a tower of stone,
Where the last Elder One lives on alone,
Talking to Chaos with the beat of drums.

The Thing, they whisper, wears a silken mask
Of yellow, whose queer folds appear to hide
A face not of this earth, though none dares ask
Just what those features are, which bulge inside.
Many, in man's first youth, sought out that glow,
But what they found, no one will ever know.

XXVIII. Expectancy

I cannot tell why some things hold for me
A sense of unplumbed marvels to befall,
Or of a rift in the horizon's wall
Opening to worlds where only gods can be.
There is a breathless, vague expectancy,
As of vast ancient pomps I half recall,
Or wild adventures, uncorporeal,
Ecstasy-fraught, and as a day-dream free.

It is in sunsets and strange city spires,
Old villages and woods and misty downs,
South winds, the sea, low hills, and lighted towns,
Old gardens, half-heard songs, and the moon's fires.
But though its lure alone makes life worth living,
None gains or guesses what it hints at giving.

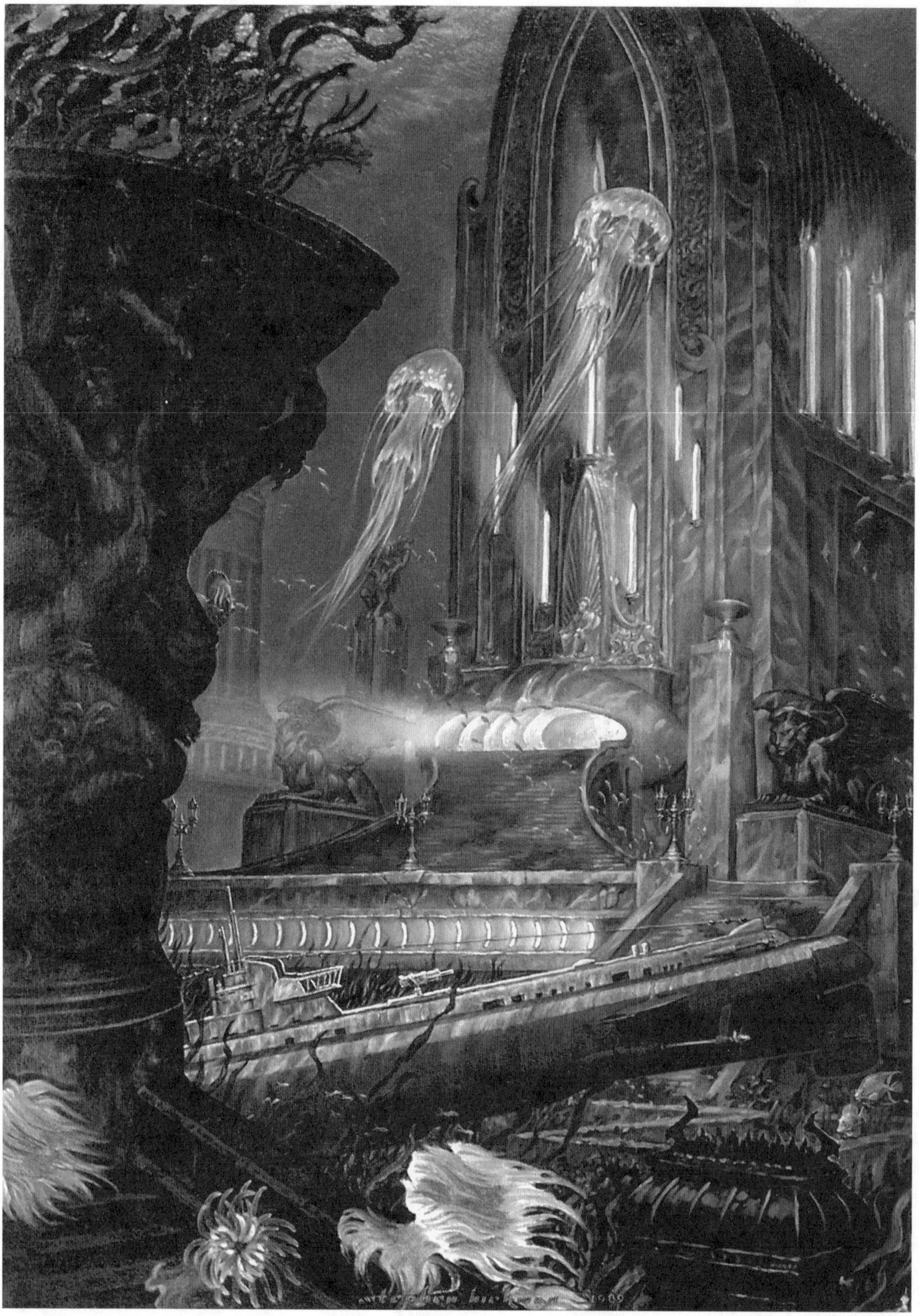

XXIX. Nostalgia

Once every year, in autumn's wistful glow,
The birds fly out over an ocean waste,
Calling and chattering in a joyous haste
To reach some land their inner memories know.
Great terraced gardens where bright blossoms blow,
And lines of mangoes luscious to the taste,
And temple-groves with branches interlaced
Over cool paths — all these their vague dreams shew.

They search the sea for marks of their old shore —
For the tall city, white and turreted —
But only empty waters stretch ahead,
So that at last they turn away once more.
Yet sunken deep where alien polyps throng,
The old towers miss their lost, remembered song.

XXX. Background

I never can be tied to raw, new things,
For I first saw the light in an old town,
Where from my window huddled roofs sloped down
To a quaint harbour rich with visionings.
Streets with carved doorways where the sunset beams
Flooded old fanlights and small window-panes,
And Georgian steeples topped with gilded vanes —
These were the sights that shaped my childhood dreams.

Such treasures, left from times of cautious leaven,
Cannot but loose the hold of flimsier wraiths
That flit with shifting ways and muddled faiths
Across the changeless walls of earth and heaven.
They cut the moment's thongs and leave me free
To stand alone before eternity.

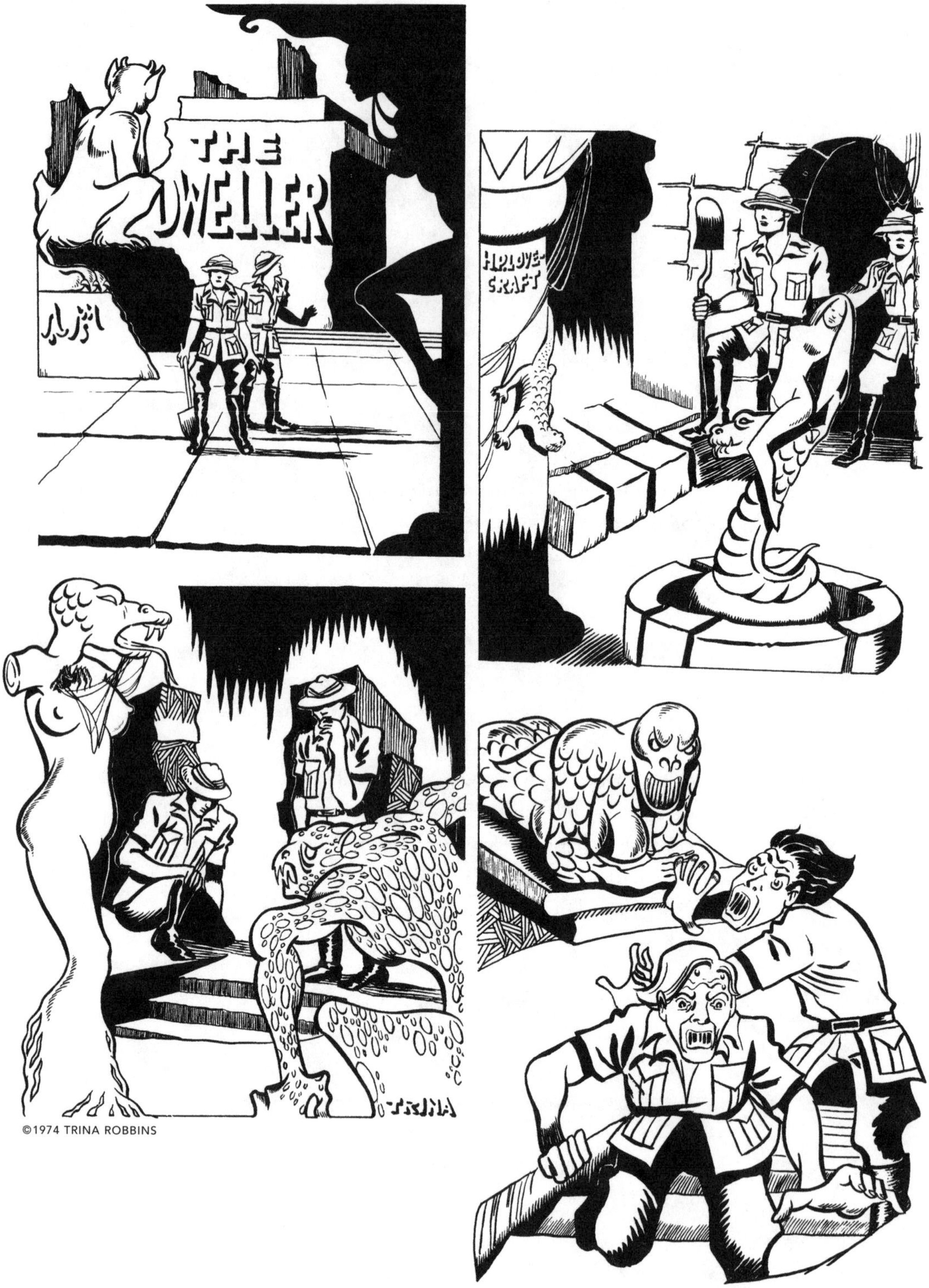
THE
DWELLER
H.P. LOVE-
CRAFT
TRINA

XXXI. The Dweller

It had been old when Babylon was new;
None knows how long it slept beneath that mound,
Where in the end our questing shovels found
Its granite blocks and brought it back to view.
There were vast pavements and foundation-walls,
And crumbling slabs and statues, carved to shew
Fantastic beings of some long ago
Past anything the world of man recalls.

And then we saw those stone steps leading down
Through a choked gate of graven dolomite
To some black haven of eternal night
Where elder signs and primal secrets frown.
We cleared a path — but raced in mad retreat
When from below we heard those clumping feet.

XXXII. Alienation

His solid flesh had never been away,
For each dawn found him in his usual place,
But every night his spirit loved to race
Through gulfs and worlds remote from common day.
He had seen Yaddith, yet retained his mind,
And come back safely from the Ghooric zone,
When one still night across curved space was thrown
That beckoning piping from the voids behind.

He waked that morning as an older man,
And nothing since has looked the same to him.
Objects around float nebulous and dim —
False, phantom trifles of some vaster plan.
His folk and friends are now an alien throng
To which he struggles vainly to belong.

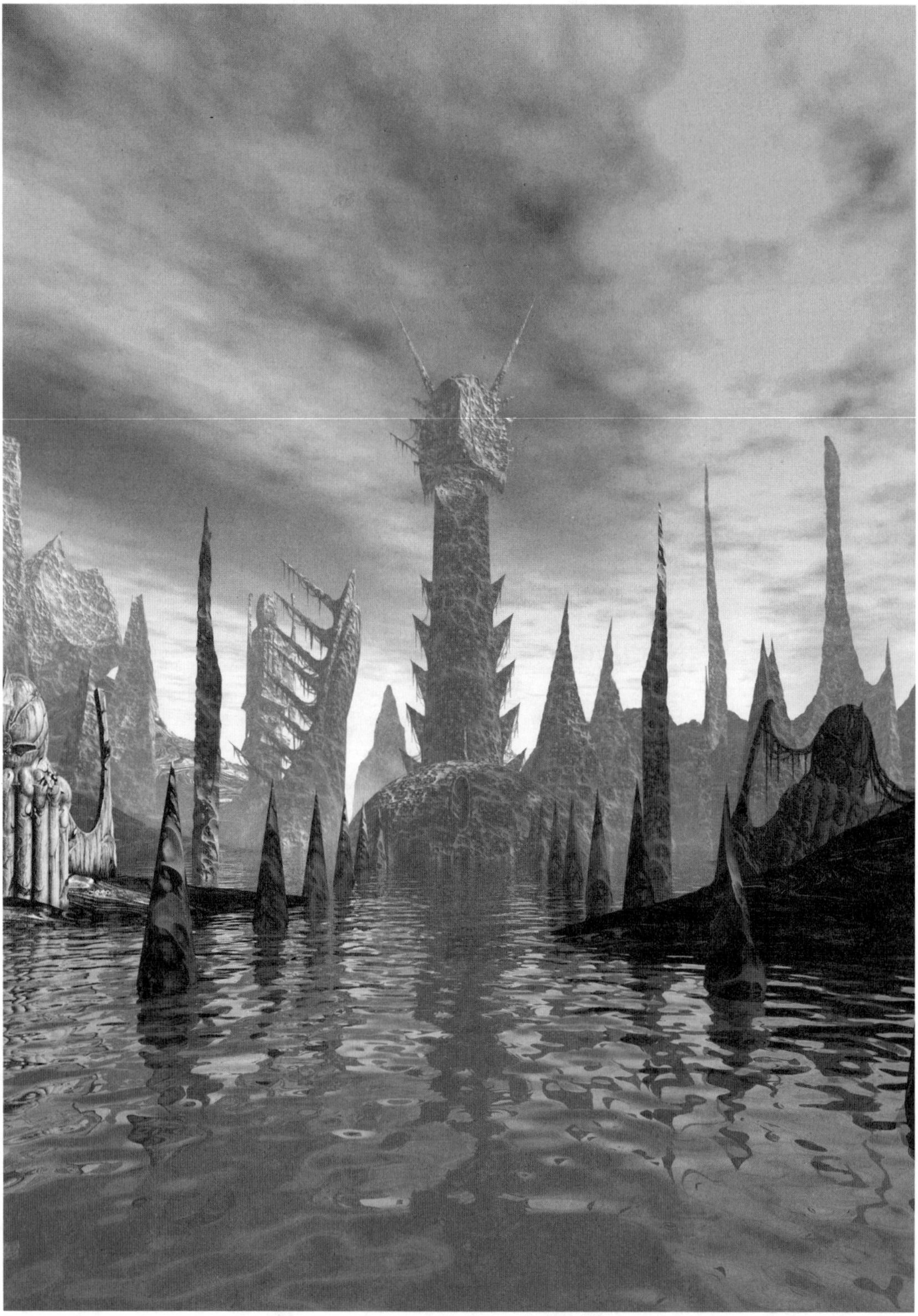

XXXIII. Harbour Whistles

Over old roofs and past decaying spires
The harbour whistles chant all through the night;
Throats from strange ports, and beaches far and white,
And fabulous oceans, ranged in motley choirs.
Each to the other alien and unknown,
Yet all, by some obscurely focussed force
From brooding gulfs beyond the Zodiac's course,
Fused into one mysterious cosmic drone.

Through shadowy dreams they send a marching line
Of still more shadowy shapes and hints and views;
Echoes from outer voids, and subtle clues
To things which they themselves cannot define.
And always in that chorus, faintly blent,
We catch some notes no earth-ship ever sent.

XXXIV. Recapture

The way led down a dark, half-wooded heath
Where moss-grey boulders humped above the mould,
And curious drops, disquieting and cold,
Sprayed up from unseen streams in gulfs beneath.
There was no wind, nor any trace of sound
In puzzling shrub, or alien-featured tree,
Nor any view before — till suddenly,
Straight in my path, I saw a monstrous mound.

Half to the sky those steep sides loomed upspread,
Rank-grassed, and cluttered by a crumbling flight
Of lava stairs that scaled the fear-topped height
In steps too vast for any human tread.
I shrieked — and knew what primal star and year
Had sucked me back from man's dream-transient sphere!

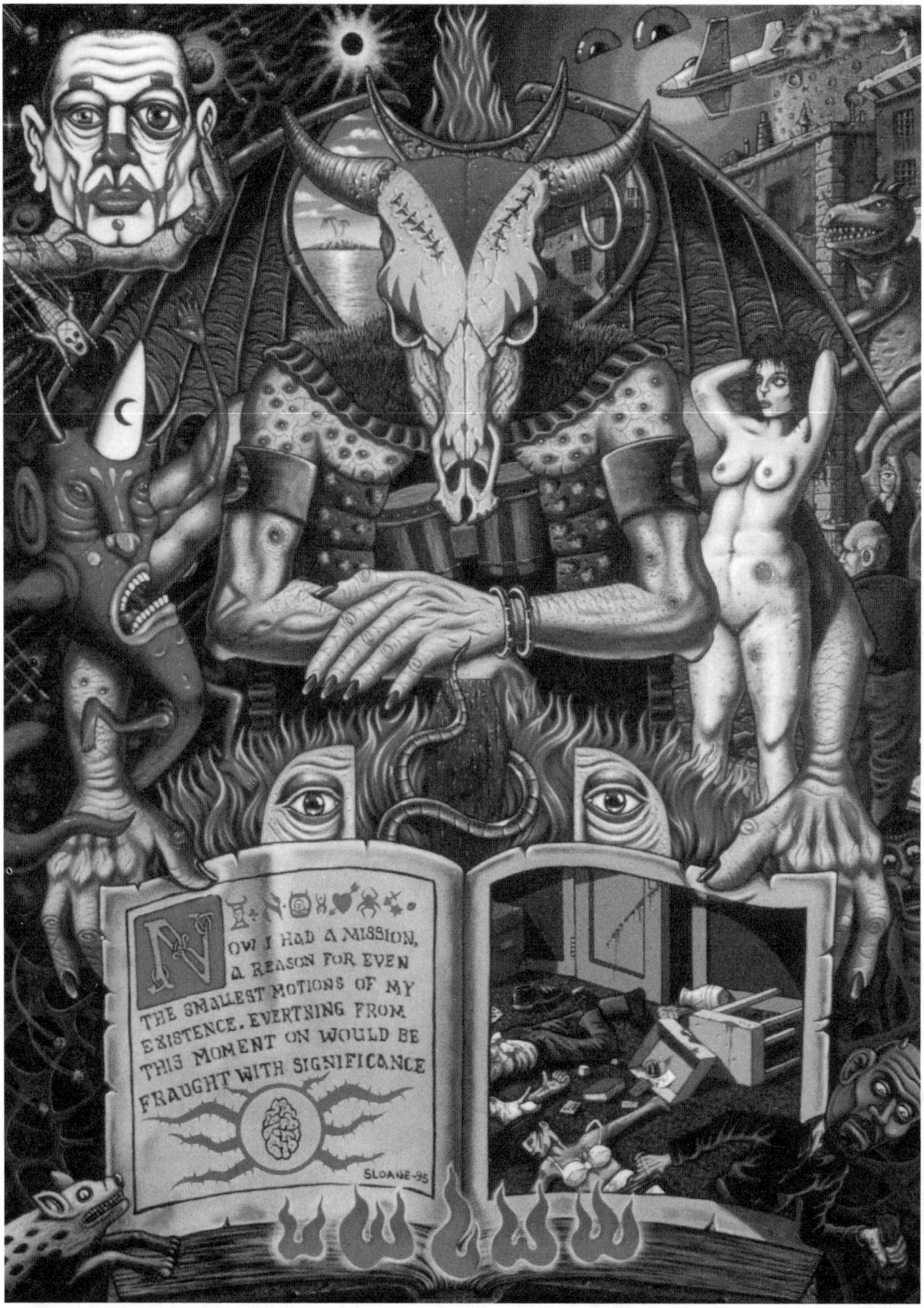
NOW I HAD A MISSION,
A REASON FOR EVEN
THE SMALLEST MOTIONS OF MY
EXISTENCE. EVERTNING FROM
THIS MOMENT ON WOULD BE
FRAUGHT WITH SIGNIFICANCE
SLOANE-95

XXXV. Evening Star

I saw it from that hidden, silent place
Where the old wood half shuts the meadow in.
It shone through all the sunset's glories — thin
At first, but with a slowly brightening face.
Night came, and that lone beacon, amber-hued,
Beat on my sight as never it did of old;
The evening star — but grown a thousandfold
More haunting in this hush and solitude.

It traced strange pictures on the quivering air —
Half-memories that had always filled my eyes —
Vast towers and gardens; curious seas and skies
Of some dim life — I never could tell where.
But now I knew that through the cosmic dome
Those rays were calling from my far, lost home.

XXXVI. Continuity

There is in certain ancient things a trace
Of some dim essence — more than form or weight;
A tenuous aether, indeterminate,
Yet linked with all the laws of time and space.
A faint, veiled sign of continuities
That outward eyes can never quite descry;
Of locked dimensions harbouring years gone by,
And out of reach except for hidden keys.

It moves me most when slanting sunbeams glow
On old farm buildings set against a hill,
And paint with life the shapes which linger still
From centuries less a dream than this we know.
In that strange light I feel I am not far
From the fixt mass whose sides the ages are.

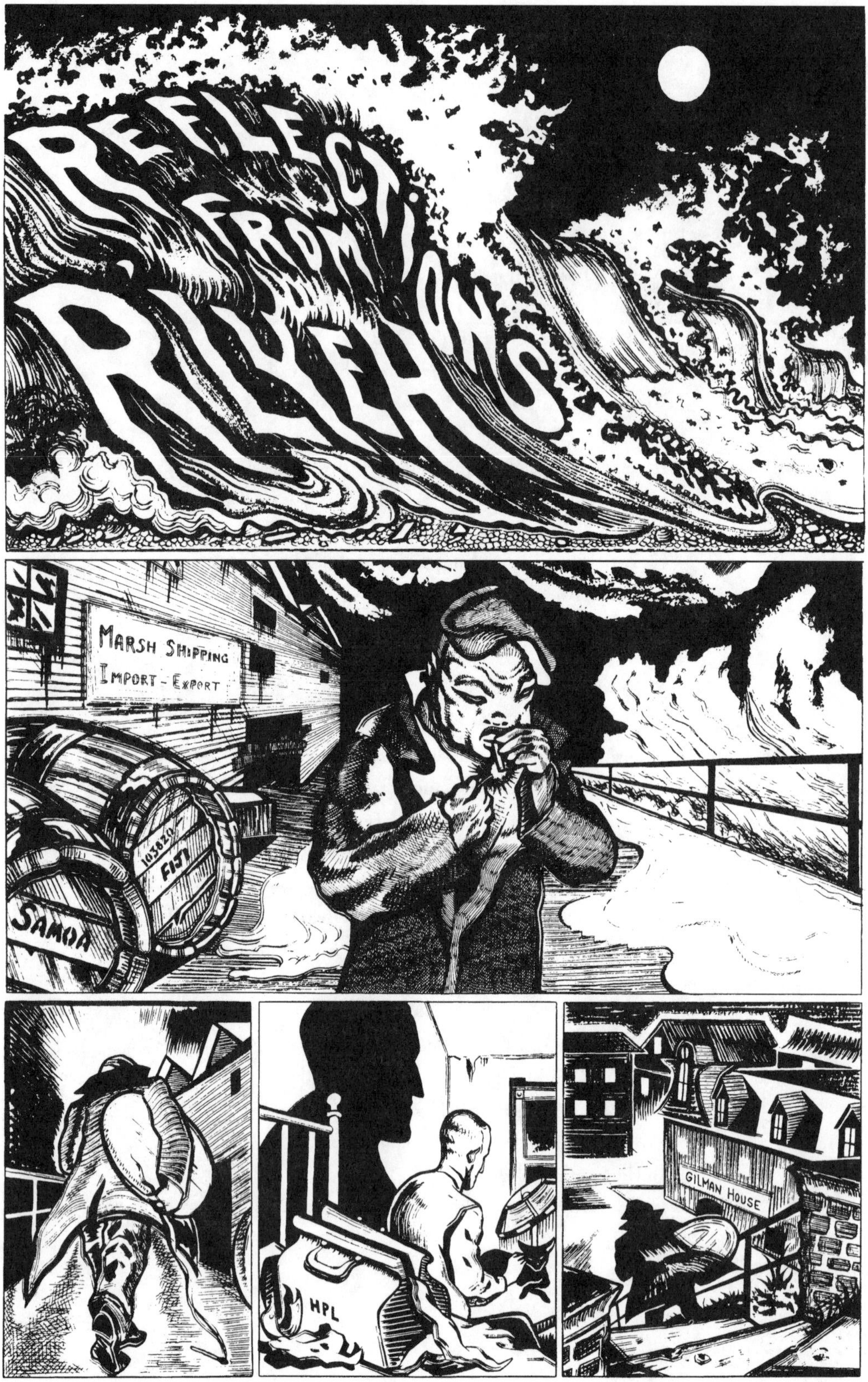
REFLECTIONS FROM RLYEH
MARSH SHIPPING
IMPORT - EXPORT
103820
FIJI
SAMOA
HPL
GILMAN HOUSE

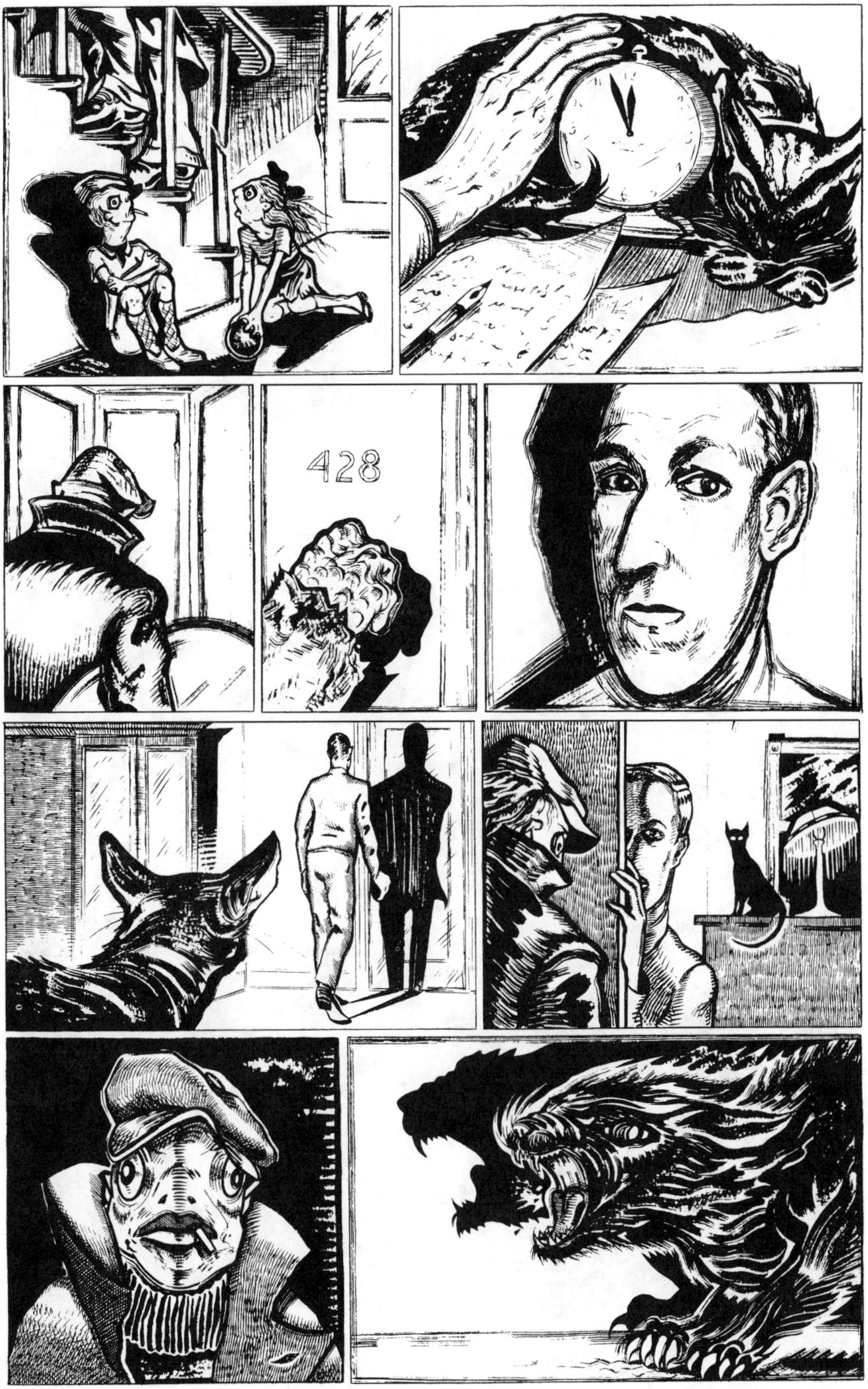
428

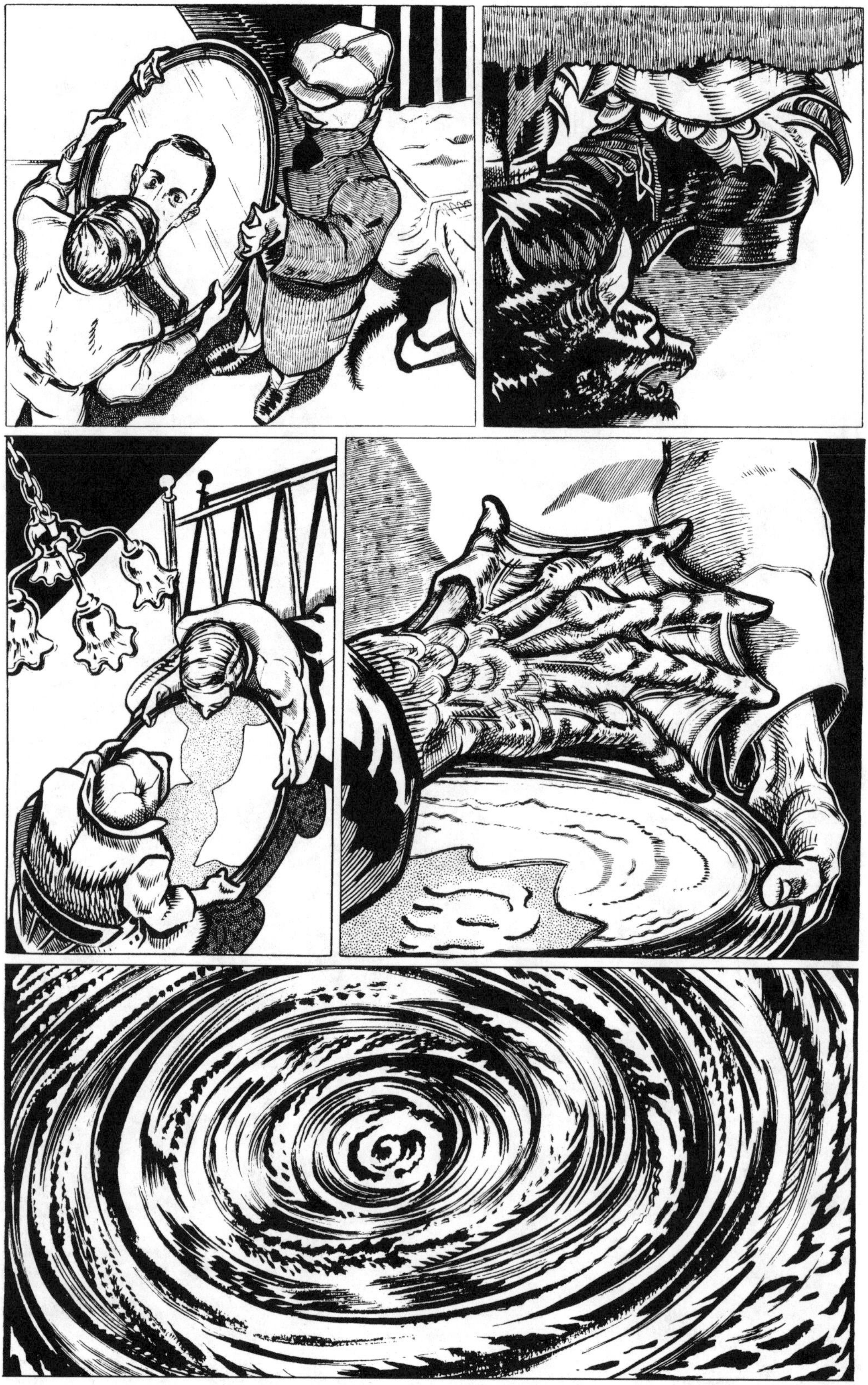

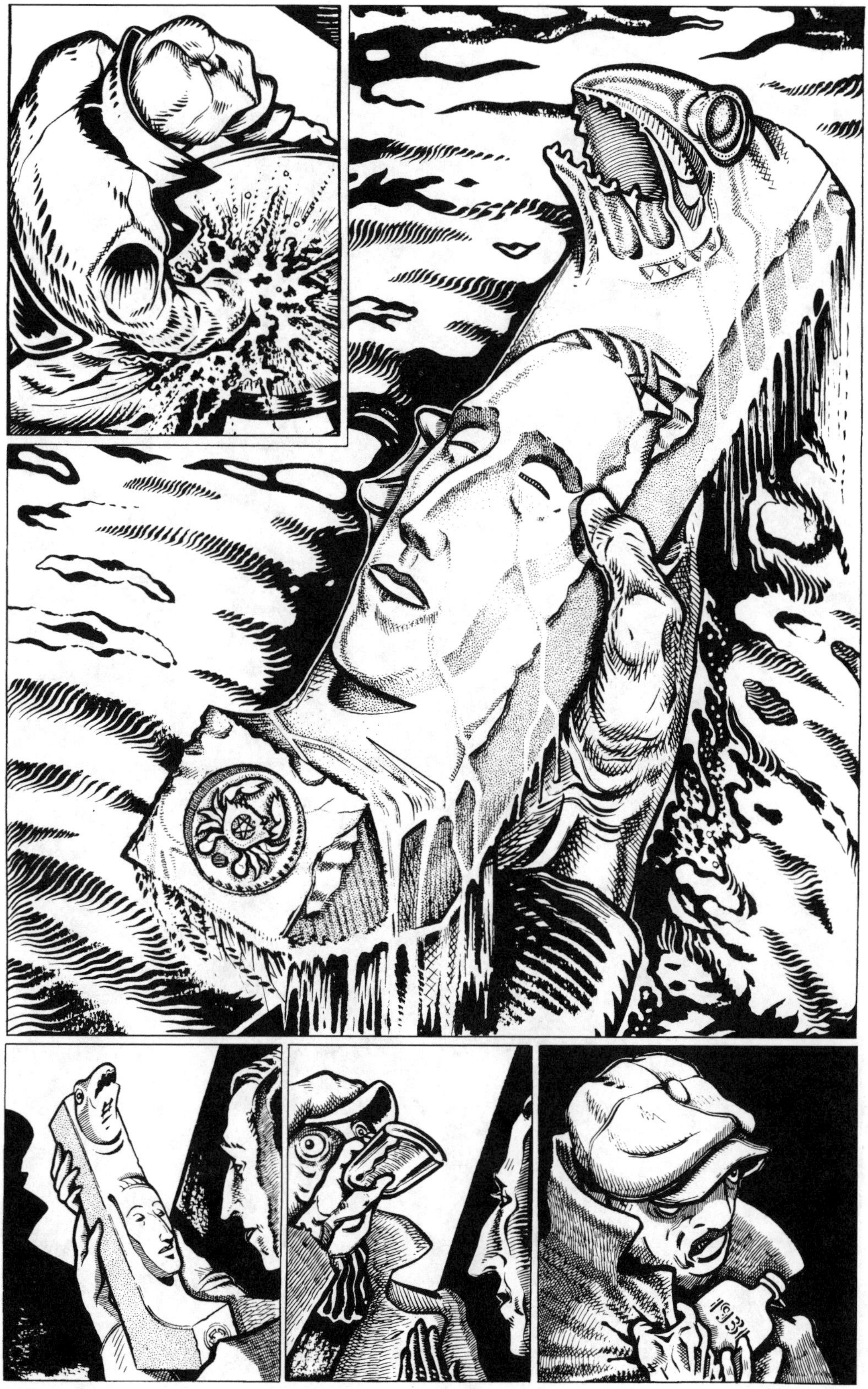
1931

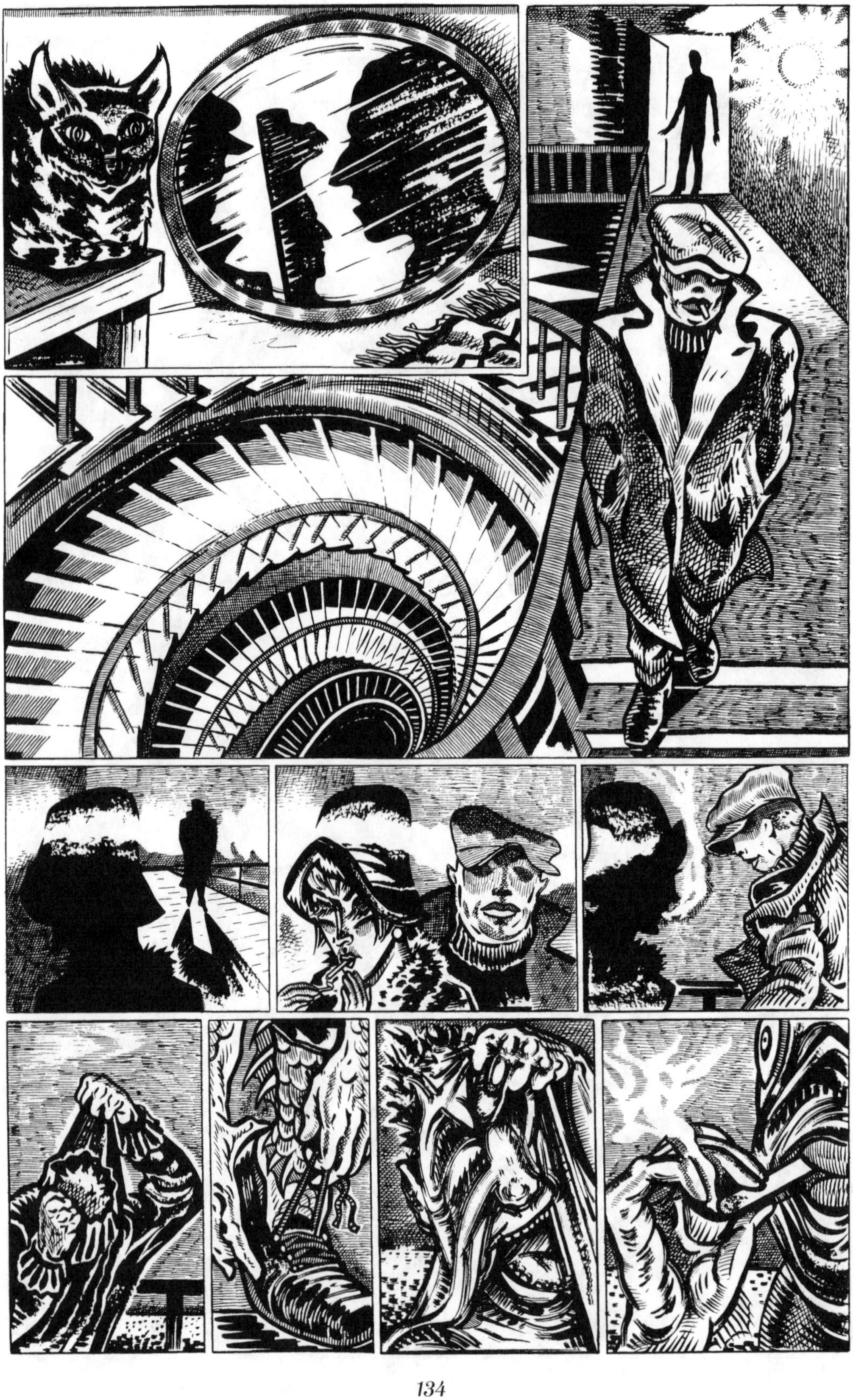

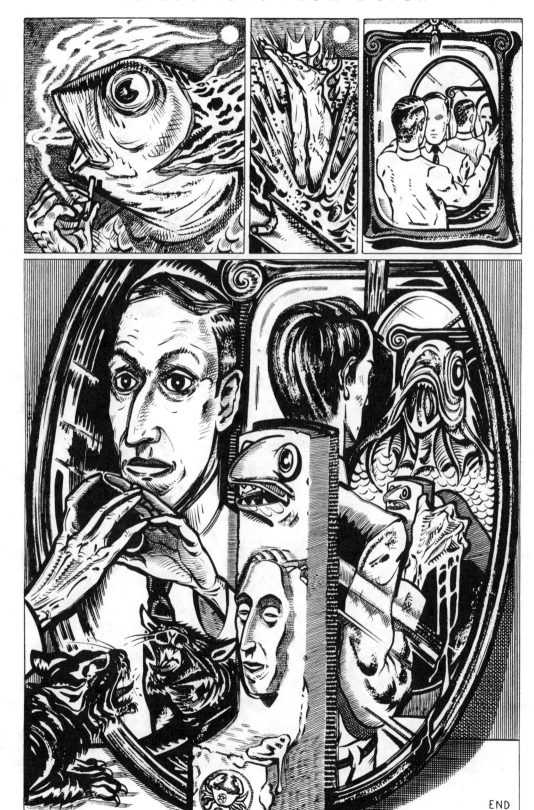

END

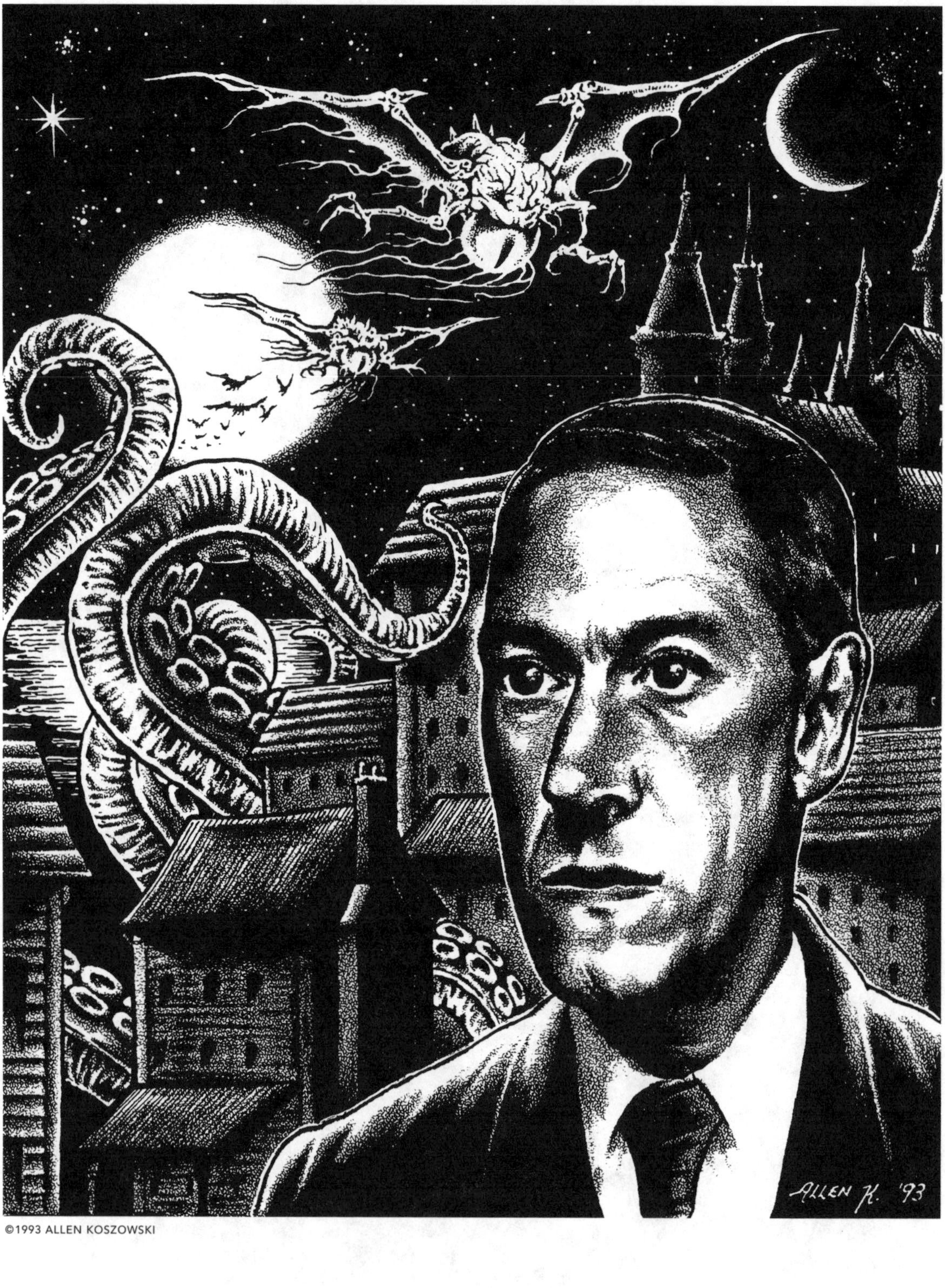
ALLEN K. '93

H.P. LOVECRAFT

Howard Phillips Lovecraft was born in Providence, Rhode Island in 1890. His father died in 1898, and his mother suffered from mental instability until her death in 1921. Poor health and his neurotic, overprotective mother combined to make something of a recluse of Lovecraft. Growing up, he had little contact with other children, and as an adult maintained his many long-distance relationships through voluminous correspondence. He was obsessed with dreams, and wrote most of his stories and poems around a central theme of ancient gods who once ruled the earth and are merely awaiting a return to power. His writings appeared mostly in the "pulp" magazines of his time and received little critical attention outside of the horror genre. Since Lovecraft's death in 1937, his stories have grown in popularity and have spawned a huge cult of both fans and professional writers who continue to expand Lovecraft's themes through stories set in the "Cthulhu Mythos."

TODD SCHORR *(cover)*

Todd Schorr calls his painting style "cartoon realism." He draws on the images of popular culture and is influenced by artists from Vermeer and Picasso to Robert Williams and Tex Avery. He began a successful professional career as a commercial illustrator, but soon left illustration behind to give vent to his personal obsessions in large-scale canvasses. Since moving from Connecticut to Los Angeles, he has become one of the leading practitioners of a broad movement commonly called "lowbrow art." Todd's art was collected in 1998 for *Secret Mystic Rites* (Last Gasp Publishing). He says he first became aware of HPL in high school and became "totally consumed in his writings." "When read now," continues Todd, "Lovecraft's work still retains the same spine-shivering thrills I first experienced." You can view more of Todd's art at www.toddschorr.com.

SAVERIO TENUTA *(title page)*

Born in Rome in 1969, Saverio Tenuta graduated from the Rome Academy of Fine Arts and began working as an advertising designer and art engraver. But drawing comics has always been Tenuta's dream, so he eventually left his former occupations to enlist in the International School of Comics in Rome. He started teaching comic book, sci-fi and fantasy courses at the same school in 1992. His first professional comics work was in Italy, and he has recently worked for publishers in the U.S., including *Heavy Metal* and DC Comics. See Tenuta's art at www.saveriotenuta.com.

JIM NELSON *(page 2)*

Jim Nelson's work has appeared in fantasy role-playing games, books and magazines. He has been represented in the juried annual *Spectrum: The Best in Contemporary Fantastic Art* as both an artist and art director. Jim lives and works in Chicago, where he is currently working on Wizards of the Coast's popular *Magic: The Gathering* card game and is also involved in projects for White Wolf, *Weekly Reader* and *Riotminds*. His artwork was also featured in *Graphic Classics: H.G. Wells*. Jim drew inspiration from a recent trip to Cambodia for his Lovecraft illustration.

GAHAN WILSON *(page 4)*

Gahan Wilson's instantly-recognizable macabre drawings have appeared in numerous magazines including *Playboy* and *The New Yorker*. He has published fifteen collections of his cartoons, the most recent being *Gahan Wilson's Even Weirder* (Forge Books, 1996). He has written and illustrated several children's books, and his work has recently been adapted to animation for TV. Wilson is also an accomplished writer. His *The Manuscript of Dr. Arness* appeared in *Rosebud 23*, and his illustrated version of *The Conqueror Worm* appeared in *Graphic Classics: Edgar Allan Poe*. A longtime Lovecraft aficionado, Gahan designed the "Howard" award of the World Fantasy Convention as a bust of HPL.

PAUL CARRICK *(page 8)*

The son of a children's book writer/illustrator team, Paul Carrick studied art at the Rhode Island School of Design, where he says it took him four full years to win the respect of some teachers for his fantasy art, which they looked down on as "white trash van art." But, says Paul, "Isn't the ceiling of the Sistine Chapel a form of fantasy art?" Since graduating in 1994, he has illustrated children's books and has concentrated on illustrating role-playing games for all the major publishers in the field, including Wizards of the Coast, Chaosium, and Five Rings Publishing. Visit www.nightserpent.com for samples of Paul's work.

GEORGE KUCHAR *(page 9)*

George Kuchar and his twin brother, Mike, were born in Manhattan in 1942. George was trained as a commercial artist in a vocational high school and upon graduation drew weather maps for a local news show. All during this dark period he and his brother were making 8mm movies which were showcased in the then-burgeoning underground scene alongside films by Andy Warhol, Kenneth Anger and Stan Brakhage. When laid off from the commercial art job he never returned to what he calls "that nightmare world." Kuchar was offered a teaching job in the film department of the San Francisco Art Institute, where he has taught since the early 1970s. It was in San Francisco that he became involved with underground comics via his neighbor, Art Spiegelman, and Bill Griffith. They both wound up in his movies and George wound up in their publications. His comics biography of HPL was first printed in *Arcade #3* in 1975, where it garnered a flood of complaints from offended Lovecraft loyalists.

R.K. SLOANE *(pages 12, 128)*

Ric Sloane claims that as a child he passed the time preparing for his dream of having his own carnival sideshow act, which included biting the heads off live, defenseless critters while riding a unicycle standing on his head. After a short but successful career in the carnival, he moved on to digging graves at the local cemetery, and finally to a life as a painter of his strange, personal and somewhat disturbing visions. You can view more of his work at www.rksloane.com.

RICHARD CORBEN *(page 14)*

One of the most enduring cult favorites in comics, Richard Corben is also an "artist's artist," widely respected by his peers, which made him the perfect choice for the lead spot in our unique four-artist adaptation of *Reanimator*. Richard's first underground comic, *Fantagor*, was self-published in 1970. He has since worked for all the major comics publishers including Warren, Métal Hurlant, Dark Horse, Marvel and DC. He has a lifelong interest in film and animation and his "Den" character was adapted in the first *Heavy Metal* movie. Corben's interests in making movies and drawing comics have always complemented each other. He calls his comic work "a detailed storyboard for a movie." Corben resides in Kansas City, where he continues to work on animation, illustration, and comics.

RICK GEARY *(page 19)*

Rick is best known for his thirteen years as a contributor to *The National Lampoon*. His work has also appeared in Marvel, DC, and Dark Horse comics, *Rolling Stone*, *MAD*, *Heavy Metal*, *Disney Adventures*, *The Los Angeles Times* and *The New York Times Book Review*. He has written and illustrated five children's books and published a collection of his comics, *Housebound with Rick Geary*. He has most recently completed the fourth in his continuing book series *A Treasury of Victorian Murder*. *The Mystery of Mary Rogers* (NBM Publishing, 2001) examines the famous 1841 murder which inspired Poe's *The Mystery of Marie Roget*. Rick is the only artist to have appeared in all four volumes of *Graphic Classics*, and he will be represented by *The Leopard Man's Story* in *Graphic Classics: Jack London*. He joined *Rosebud* as its regular feature cartoonist with Issue 22. You can view more of Rick's art on the web at www.rickgeary.com.

J.B. BONIVERT *(page 24)*

Jeffrey Bonivert is a Bay Area native with a varied background in independent comics as both artist and writer, contributing to such books as *Mister Monster*, *Turtle Soup* and *The Funboys*. His unique adaptation of Poe's *The Raven* appeared in *Graphic Classics: Edgar Allan Poe*, and he contributed *The Los Amigos Fiasco* to *Graphic Classics: Arthur Conan Doyle*. Jeff's Casey Jones/Teenage Mutant Ninja Turtles epic, *Muscle and Faith*, is online at www.flyingcolorscomics.com, and his comic book bio of artist Murphy Anderson appears in *Spark Generators* (SLG Publishing).

MARK A. NELSON *(page 29)*

Mark was a professor of art at Northern Illinois University for twenty years, and has taught courses in illustration, printmaking, and drawing. He is currently working at Raven Software as a staff artist doing conceptual work, painting digital skins and creating textures for their computer games. His comics credits include *Blood and Shadows* for DC; *Aliens* for Dark Horse Comics; and

Feud for the Marvel Epic line. He has worked for numerous publishers, and his art is represented in *Spectrum #4, #5, #6* and *#8*. Mark illustrated a memorable version of an Ambrose Bierce tale in *Rosebud 18*, and with his wife Anita, co-illustrated the *Best of Rosebud* anthology. His stunning images for Clive Barker's *New Murders in the Rue Morgue* appeared in *Graphic Classics: Edgar Allan Poe*, and he created a color painting of *The Lost World* for the back cover of *Graphic Classics: Arthur Conan Doyle*.

TOM SUTTON *(page 34)*

Tom Sutton was born in 1937, and grew up on a diet of the adventure strips of Caniff, Raymond and Foster, and later the great EC comic books. After graduation from high school, he enlisted in the Air Force, where he was eventually assigned to *Stars and Stripes* and there created his first comic strips. After leaving the service, Sutton attended The School of the Museum of Fine Arts in Boston and worked as a freelance commercial artist. His first mainstream comics work was for Warren publications, and he went on from there to produce comics for nearly every company in the business including Marvel, DC and Charlton. Much of his later work was x-rated stories for Eros Comix under the pseudonym "Dementia." But his best work was in the horror and fantasy genres. *The Dream-Quest of Unknown Kadath* was originally produced as a limited-edition portfolio published by Another World, Ltd. in 1978. Tom Sutton died in May 2002, during production of this book, and it is respectfully dedicated to his memory.

DEVON DEVEREAUX *(page 41)*

Painter and illustrator Devon Devereaux lives in Portland, Oregon. He has self-published a comics adaptation of Poe's *The Oblong Box* and also *the children*, which he describes as "kind of like Lovecraft meets *Saved by the Bell*." Devon is currently involved in illustrating a book written by David Quinn, titled *The Littlest Bitch*. He would like to thank Patty Hendricks for introducing him to Lovecraft and *The Outsider*. You can see more of Devon's work at www.devondevereaux.com.

MATT HOWARTH *(page 47)*

Matt Howarth has spent his career mixing the genres of science fiction, comic books, and alternative music. Probably best known for his *Those Annoying Post Bros.* comic book series, he has recently done comics adaptations of George Bear's *Petra* and Vernor Vinge's *Original Sin* for the 2001 and 2002 World Science Fiction Convention programmes. He adapted *How It Happened* in *Graphic Classics: Arthur Conan Doyle*, and now H.P. Lovecraft. "I was exposed to Lovecraft's material at a very early age," says Matt, "and it affected me deeply, almost on a genetic level. There are HPL elements running through much of my work, both on an intentional and subconscious basis. The opportunity to do an actual HPL adaptation was a thoroughly enjoyable challenge." Currently, Matt is exploring the digital genre with a variety of online comics and is reviving his *Keif Llama: Xenotech* series, as well as working on an adaptation of *The Shadow and the Flash* for *Graphic Classics: Jack London*. You are invited to visit www.matthowarth.com for more entertainment.

DIERDRE LUZWICK *(page 70)*

Dierdre Luzwick lives in Cambridge, a small town in Wisconsin, where she is a social and environmental activist as well as an artist. She has published two collections of her art, *The Surrealist's Bible* (1976, Jonathan David Publishing), and *Endangered Species* (1992, HarperCollins). Her dramatic, large-scale drawings are done in charcoal on canvas. Dierdre was the featured artist in the first issue of *Rosebud*, and returned in the fifth anniversary issue, *Rosebud 16*.

ONSMITH JEREMI *(page 72)*

Jeremy Smith (aka "Onsmith Jeremi") grew up in a couple of small towns in central Oklahoma, putting in his factory and fast food time while nurturing his interest in small press comics, cartoons and "zines." He then moved to Chicago, where he started a small press anthology, *Bomb Time for Bonzo* with fellow artists Ben Chandler and Henry Ng (of the *Non* comics anthology). With no formal art education and only two years of making comic stories under his belt, he's managed to appear in *Proper Gander, Flotation Device* (#8 & #9), *Studygroup 12* (#2) and the *EXPO 2002*

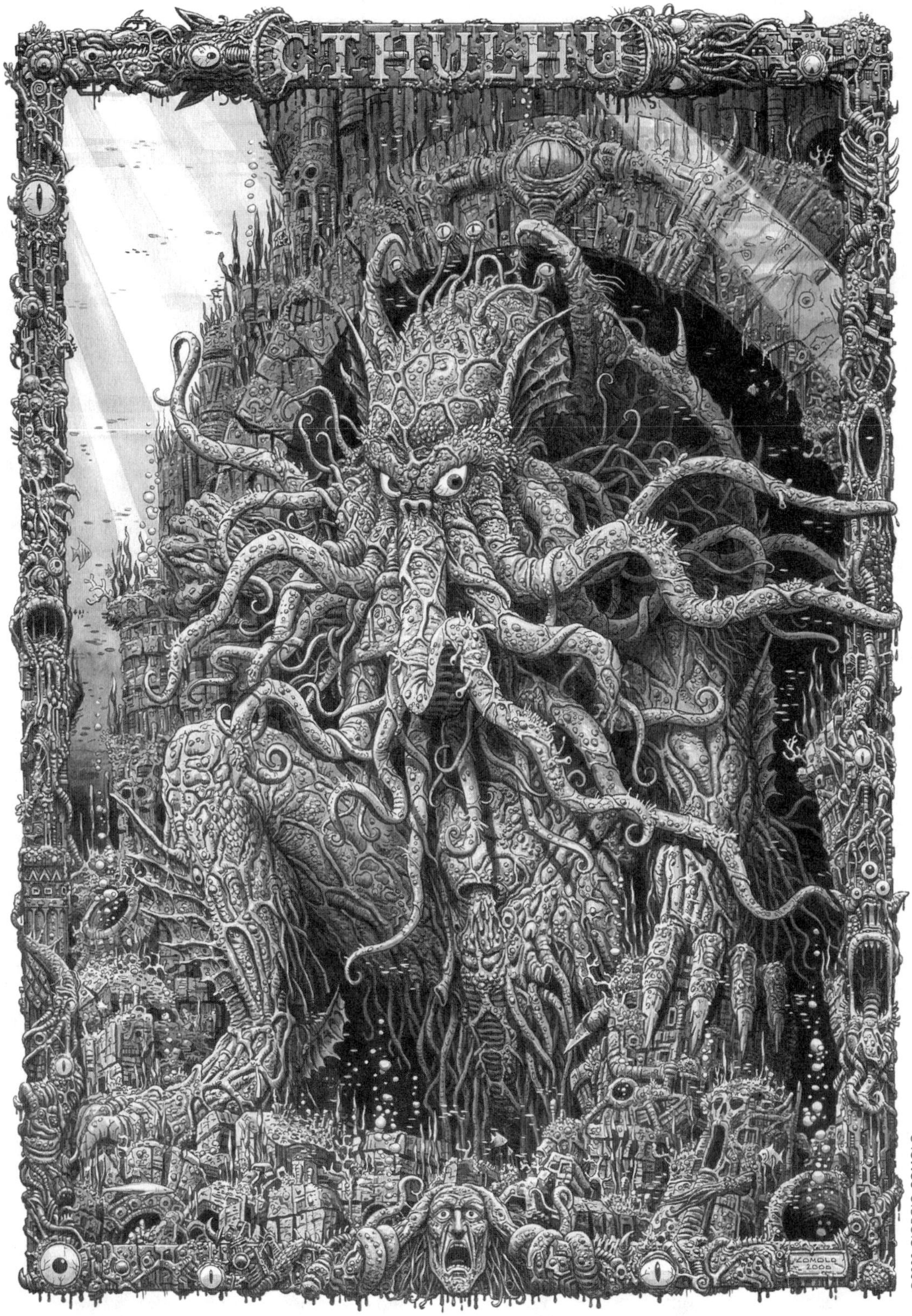
CTHULHU
COMOLO 2000

anthology as well as all five issues of *Bomb Time for Bonzo*. Onsmith is now working on an adaptation of *Just Meat* for *Graphic Classics: Jack London*. To see more of his work go to www.comixwerks.com.

LISA K. WEBER *(page 77)*

Lisa is a graduate of Parsons School of Design in New York City, where she is currently employed in the fashion industry, designing prints and characters for teenage girls' jammies, while free-lancing work on children's books and character design for animation. Other projects include her "creaturized" opera posters and playing cards. She says that she fears her preoccupation with macabre creatures and freaks has "had a severe effect on her social life, but remains optimistic and hell-bent on world domination." Lisa provided the cover and illustrations for *Hop-Frog* in *Graphic Classics: Edgar Allan Poe*. Illustrations from her in-progress book *The Shakespearean ABCs* are currently appearing in *Rosebud 25*. More of her art can be seen online at www.creatureco.com.

DOMINIQUE SIGNORET *(page 90)*

French artist Dominique Signoret was born in Paris in 1964 and studied Fine Arts in Orleans. He works in illustration, computer art and sculpture, including the design of cast miniatures for role-playing games. Dominique's first exposure to Lovecraft came by way of the role-playing game *The Call of Cthulhu*, and in 1999 he illustrated the cover of *Guide du Mythe de Cthulhu* for Encrage Editions. *Cthulhu's Dreams* is a series of parodic comics set in the Lovecraft universe which originally appeared in the French fanzine *Sens Fiction*. *Le Chaos Rapant* was created in 1999, but was revised by Dominique in English for *Graphic Classics*. It features Lovecraft's Nyarlathotep, known as "The Crawling Chaos," which tranlates to French as "Le Chaos Rampant." Dominique dropped the "m", and Nyarlathotep became a hip-hop artist.

STEPHEN HICKMAN *(pages 92, 122)*

Stephen Hickman has been illustrating science fiction and fantasy for over two decades. His paintings have been used as covers for many contemporary writers, including Gordon Dickson, Harlan Ellison, Robert Heinlein, Anne McCaffrey, Larry Niven, and Steve Stirling. Hickman has illustrated approximately 350 covers for Ace, Baen, Ballantine, Bantam, Berkeley, Dell, Del Rey, Doubleday, Phage Press, Tor, and Warren Publications. In 1994 he was awarded a Hugo Award for the U.S. Postal Service's Space Fantasy Commemorative Booklet of stamps. Stephen illustrated the cover of Lovecraft's *The Call of Cthulhu* from Baen Books and in 1966 he created a Cthulhu statuette based on the cover, and later a bust of the author. Both are produced and distributed by Bowen Designs, www.bowendesigns.com.

JOHN COULTHART *(pages 7, 94, 126)*

John Coulthart lives in Manchester, England and divides his time as as an illustrator, comic artist, CD and book designer. Since 1989 he has worked with Savoy Books on David Britton's controversial *Lord Horror* comic series and more recently has been responsible for the packaging of their new line of prestigious book reprints. His adaptations of H.P. Lovecraft stories were collected as *The Haunter of the Dark and other Grotesque Visions* by Oneiros Books in 1999. Future projects include Savoy's illustrated edition of *The House on the Borderland* by William Hope Hodgson, *Luvkraft vs Kthulhu*, an illustrated novella by Grant Morrison and *The Soul*, a comic series with Alan Moore.

MAXON CRUMB *(page 96)*

Maxon will be familiar to many readers from his appearance in Terry Zwigoff's 1994 award-winning film, *Crumb*. While his older brother Robert's work may be more well-known, Maxon is equally talented as both a writer and artist. His gritty fantasy story, *Stigmata*, appears in *Crumb Family Comics*, and his illustrated novel of sex, violence and incest, *Hard Core Mother*, was published in 2000 by CityZen Books. Illustrations from his first book, *Maxon's Poe* (1997, Cottage Classics) appeared in *Graphic Classics: Edgar Allan Poe*. He calls his new illustration for this volume a "payback" for the enjoyment he has received from reading Lovecraft, whom he describes as "a stark, independent mind, beyond fear, and possibly the best 20th-century American writer. Lovecraft let himself enter the higher consciousness and retain the full composition of the human being. He was not afraid. He desired it."

KELLIE STRØM (page 98)

Kellie Strøm was born in Copenhagen, grew up in Ireland, and now lives and works in London. Since 1985 he has done cartoons and illustrations for various papers and magazines in Dublin, London and Copenhagen. In 1992 he illustrated *The Acid Bath Case* for Kitchen Sink Press, and he has just completed a set of painted illustrations for the *Star Wars Tales* comic. His *Airforce Amazons* short strips have appeared in various small press publications in Europe. He is now working on a children's picture book called *Sadie the Air Mail Pilot*. Besides comics and general illustration work, Kellie has done film and theatre design for Jim Henson's Creature Shop, and is currently developing an animated film for Balsko Film in association with the Irish Film Board. You can see more of his work at www.balsko.com.

ALLEN KOSZOWSKI (pages 100, 136)

A former U.S. Marine infantryman and a decorated Vietnam war veteran with a Purple Heart, Allen is one of the most prolific artists in the horror and SF field. Since his first professional sale to *Asimov's SF Magazine* in 1982, he has published more than 2,700 illustrations for hundreds of genre publications such as *Asimov's*, *The Magazine of Fantasy & SF*, *Cemetery Dance*, *Whispers*, *Fantasy Tales*, *Weird Tales*, *The Horror Show* and *The Robert Bloch Companion*. He has won numerous awards, including Best Artist and other categories for the Small Press Writers and Artists Organization, for eight years in a row. *Travelers by Twilight*, a collection of his drawings, is available from Magic Pen Press.

S. CLAY WILSON (page 102)

One of the original infamous *Zap* cartoonists of the 1960s, S. Clay Wilson creates shocking, violent strips inhabited by pirates, dykes and demons. Robert Crumb cites him as a liberating influence on his own work. Wilson has illustrated the books of William S. Burroughs and recently created a volume of children's fairy tales, *Wilson's Grimm* (1999, Cottage Classics). "I always wanted to be a children's book illustrator," he says, "but I took some LSD and took a left turn graphically." Wilson refers to his dense style as "graphic agoraphobia," a fear of open space. The illustration reproduced here was created in 1972 and originally appeared in *Zap #7*. Wilson says it represents "the monster of domestic strife entering my life in the guise of H.P. Lovecraft."

SKOT OLSEN (page 104)

Skot received his diploma from the Joe Kubert School of Cartoon and Graphic art in 1991. This art training is evident in his paintings, which are cartoonish in style, but realistically rendered. He delights in playing with texture, as each painting is full of woodgrain, stonework, veins and various skin blemishes. His paintings deal with the human condition, blending pain and suffering with humor via a story that unravels within the picture before the viewer. Skot now lives on the edge of the Florida Everglades with his wife and their dog. His "lowbrow" art has been featured in numerous national and international publications, and is collected by a diverse group ranging from tattoo artists and hipsters to business people and retirees. You can see more at www.skotolsen.com.

JEFFREY JOHANNES (page 106)

Jeffrey began copying the Sunday funnies at an early age, and in junior high school he received a "D+" in algebra because he spent more time drawing cartoons than paying attention in class. He started teaching high school art in 1974 and claims he "has the gray hairs to prove that he has been working hard at it for nearly thirty years." His award-winning artwork has been displayed in shows throughout the Midwest. In addition to painting, he is now writing poetry and playing Native American flute, and is expecting to see these creative journeys merge. His love of Walt Disney and surrealism is evident in his Lovecraft piece, and he considers this work "a new beginning toward illustrative art." Jeffrey's paintings will be featured in *Rosebud 26*.

STEVEN CERIO *(page 108)*

"Artists try to create their surroundings to make the universe fit what they think it should be," Steven Cerio says. Cerio studied art in his hometown at Syracuse University, then moved to New York City in 1988. His first job was at Psychedelic Solution, a gallery at the center of Greenwich Village. There he encountered Robert Crumb, whose comment on Steven's work was "Hey Cerio, you think you're going to make a fucking living drawing like this?" Steven responded by pursuing illustration work. His first job was "a woman with six tits and fangs" for *Screw* magazine. He soon worked for other publications including the *Village Voice*, *Guitar World* and *Entertainment Weekly*, and his art is now shown in galleries nationwide. Steven's first full-length comic book, *PIE*, came out in 1996. *Steven Cerio's ABC Book – A Drug Primer* was published in 1998, and he continues to do commercial work for clients including Nickelodeon. Steven is also a drummer for his musical project, Lettuce Little, and he has long been involved artistically with legendary San Francisco group The Residents.

GERRY ALANGUILAN *(page 110)*

Gerry Alanguilan is a licensed architect who chooses to write and draw comic books. In his native Philippines he has created comics including *Timawa*, *Crest Hut Butt Shop*, *Dead Heart* and *Wasted*. In America, he has contributed inks on titles such as *X-Men*, *Fantastic Four*, *Wolverine*, *X-Force*, *Darkness* and *Stone*, working with pencillers Leinil Francis Yu and Whilce Portacio. Gerry has written the screenplay and is starring in an independent motion picture adaptation of his book *Wasted*, currently being shot in the Philippines. His work can be seen at www.alanguilan.com/sanpablo.

PETER VON SHOLLY *(page 112)*

Pete Von Sholly was born in NYC in 1950, and has storyboarded over one hundred feature films including *The Shawshank Redemption*, *The Mask*, *Mars Attacks!*, *The Green Mile*, *James and the Giant Peach* and *Darkman*. His comics work has appeared in *Dark Horse Presents*, *Timothy Leary's Neurocomics*, Last Gasp's *Forbidden Knowledge*, and Semic's *Zembla*. He can, he believes, play the guitar better than Jack Kirby and draw better dinosaurs than Jimi Hendrix. Lovecraft has always been a favorite. His series of fake *Classics Illustrated* Lovecraft covers can be seen at www.hplovecraft.com/popcult/art. He lives on a plateau in Sunland, California with his wife, son and several animals.

ARNOLD ARRE *(page 114)*

Filipino artist Arnold Arre worked in several ad agencies before deciding on a career as a free-lancer, saying, "I guess I'm more of a storyteller than an advertiser." He tells his stories through illustration, comics and gallery paintings, as can be seen on his website at www.arnold-arre.com. Arnold has won awards for his graphic novels *The Mythology Class* (2000) and *Trip to Tagaytay* (2001) released under his own graphic design/publishing company Tala Studios, and he recently illustrated the introduction to *Graphic Classics: Arthur Conan Doyle*. He says comics are "a powerful medium that can reach out to audiences unlike any other. It is nothing like reading a book or watching a movie. It is somewhere in between." Arnold is now working on the cover art for *Graphic Classics: Jack London*.

ANDY EWEN *(page 116)*

Andy's illustrations have appeared in *The Progessive*, *Isthmus*, and *The New York Times Book Review*. He was the featured artist in *Rosebud 10* in 1997 and has contributed many illustrations to the magazine since, including a series in *Rosebud 22*. His personal, dreamlike drawings added a new dimension to *Spirits of the Dead* in *Graphic Classics: Edgar Allan Poe*. In addition to his ability as a graphic artist, Ewen is also a talented musician. For nearly twenty years he has been the lead singer, guitarist and songwriter for Honor Among Thieves, one of the Madison, Wisconsin area's most respected bands. His CDs are available through The Rosebud Store, www.rsbd.net.

RAFAEL AVILA *(page 118)*

Rafael Avila was born in São Paulo, Brazil in 1975. He studied at the Pennsylvania School of Art and Design and the Maryland Institute. He now teaches drawing at School 33 in Baltimore. His illustrations have appeared in *Prairie Journal Trust*, *The Mystery Review* and *Potpourri Magazine*. He has also done work for local rock bands, storyboard illustrations for Eisner Communications and is currently engrossed in *Naked Soul*, a graphic novel of his own creation. Rafael cites comic books, melancholy song lyrics and German Expressionist art as his greatest influences. Samples of his work can be viewed at www.portfolio.com/rafaelavila.

JEFF REMMER *(page 120, back cover)*

Jeff grew up on a steady diet of horror, fantasy and science fiction thanks in part to his mom's love of movies and his own infatuation with the Warren magazines. "My mom kept a crayon drawing of mine from when I was five of a fire-breathing dragon destroying a hill full of houses." From there he would draw his own scenarios of favorite movies and TV shows. After discovering Frazetta, Corben and Whelan, he knew he wanted to be an illustrator, and furthered his education at the University of New Mexico. He has contributed to Malibu Comics, Wizards of the Coast, Image Comics and various fantasy magazines. Jeff has been a full time video game artist since 1993, working for Sega and now Sony Computer Entertainment in San Diego. For the last two years he has been concentrating on painting characters and scenes from the writings of Lovecraft and is writing and illustrating his own Lovecraftian story.

TRINA ROBBINS *(page 124)*

Trina has been called "the first female underground cartoonist." Finding the 1970 San Francisco underground comix scene a "closed boy's club," she founded *It Ain't Me, Babe*, a comic created solely by women artists. In addition to her thirty years of comics work she has written several books. The latest, *The Great Women Cartoonists* (2001), was listed among *Time Magazine's* top ten comics of the year. She is currently scripting *Go Girl!* (Image Comics), a superheroine series illustrated by Anne Timmons. Trina and Anne are also collaborating on a story for *Graphic Classics: Jack London*.

CHRIS PELLETIERE *(page 130)*

Chris Pelletiere is a painter, illustrator, and cartoonist who cites his early influences as the pre-code crime and horror comics. His cartoons and illustrations have appeared in small horror and fantasy magazines from Fantico Press, and he was also a political cartoonist for *The Soho Weekly News*. Published work includes *The A to Z Encyclopedia of Serial Killers*, *Song* by Brigit Pegeen Kelly, *Art and the Law*, *Dagon* and *The Grabinski Reader* (vols. 4 & 5). His work is in many public and private collections including The Museum of Modern Art, The Metropolitan Museum, The Brooklyn Museum, The New York Public Library, Stephen King, Zak Norman, Robert Bloch, Roald Dahl, John Collier, Ramsey Campbell, and Albert Boime. His paintings can be seen online at www.newyorkartworld.com.

GIORGIO COMOLO *(page 140)*

Giorgio Comolo is a professional advertising illustrator born in Varallo Sesia, Italy in 1961. American super-heroes were his steady diet as a child. As he grew, his appreciation for those larger-than-life stories became a love for the men behind them: John Romita, Gil Kane, Gene Colan, Steve Ditko and above all, Jack Kirby. Later, Comolo discovered European comics by the likes of Moebius, Caza and Jimenez and those too made a strong impression on his style. Now, as a side to his advertising work, Giorgio draws the characters that filled his life (and those of countless other fans), paying homage to the comics greats. You can see his portraits of super-heroes as well as his Lovecraftian art at www.redsectorart.com.

TOM POMPLUN

Tom is a longtime Lovecraft devotee with a background in both fine and commercial arts. He has designed and produced *Rosebud*, a journal of fiction, poetry and illustration since 1993, and in 2001 began publishing as well as designing *Graphic Classics*. Tom is currently working on *Graphic Classics: Jack London*, scheduled for release in March 2003.